War
Crimes

War Crimes

Brutality, Genocide, Terror, and the Struggle for Justice

Aryeh Neier

TIMES BOOKS

RANDOM HOUSE

Library of Congress Cataloging-in-Publication Data
Neier, Aryeh.
    War crimes: brutality, genocide, terror, and the struggle for justice
        p.   cm.
    ISBN 0-8129-2381-2 (acid-free paper)
    1. War crimes.   2. War crime trials.   3. World politics—1945–
    I. Title.
    K5301.N45   1998
    341.6′9—dc21   98-5783

Maps: Paul J. Pugliese

Text design: Meryl Sussman Levavi/digitext, inc.

For Alex and Sara

Acknowledgments

It would require much space to name all those who contributed to my knowledge and understanding of the issues explored in this book, and inevitably there would be embarrassing omissions. Accordingly, I mention only a few to whom I owe debts that are greater than they probably realize.

Much of my thinking about the book's themes evolved in conversation with my longtime colleague at Human Rights Watch, Juan E. Méndez, now executive director of the Inter-American Institute for Human Rights, based in San José, Costa Rica. The fieldwork in the former Yugoslavia by another of my associates at Human Rights Watch, Ivana Nizich, now of the International Criminal Tribunal for the Former Yugoslavia, educated me in the early months of the war there about that conflict and how it differed from others I had known. I owe thanks in more ways than I can list to Lionel Rosenblatt, president of Refugees International, my resourceful traveling companion to Croatia and Bosnia during the war. And I am grateful beyond measure to two men I looked forward to seeing on my visits to Sarajevo: a Bosnian, Zdravko Grebo—law professor, radio broadcaster, and foundation colleague—who epitomizes for me the cosmopolitan and humane values that were under siege; and an American, the late Fred Cuny, the most politically astute of humanitarian relief specialists, whose heroic efforts helped many Sarajevans survive the siege. Professor Theodor Meron, of New York University Law School, has been my guide on the questions of international law raised by the crimes committed in the conflicts in the former Yugoslavia and in Rwanda, as he has been for many others who have sought ways to hold those responsible accountable.

For similar reasons, I mention only a handful of those who actually made it possible for this book to be published: a fine editor, Mike Ruby; my dedicated agent, Patricia van der Leun; an extraordinary photographer, Gilles Peress, for the use of some of his powerful images; and my three wonderful assistants at the Open Society Institute, Claudia E. Hernández, Maria Ribar, and Elise van Oss. I am not able adequately to express my thanks to them.

As is obvious, I am solely responsible for the assertions of fact and the opinions expressed in the book, and I apologize to those who informed me and shaped my thinking for anything that I got wrong.

Contents

PART TWO

Bosnia, Rwanda, and the Search for Justice

Introduction

The memorial is at the site of the old Levetzowstrasse Synagogue, where Berlin's Jews were required to assemble for deportation to the east. The synagogue itself is long gone, though a representation of it appears in a group of iron plaques set into the pavement depicting the principal buildings of Berlin's organized Jewish community. Nearby, a large blocklike marble sculpture suggests a mass of bodies bound by ropes being dragged toward a hideous, rusting train. Towering over this scene is a sheet of rusted iron, perhaps thirty feet tall and eight feet wide, pierced so that the sunlight shines through with the dates of more than sixty mass deportations from that site, the number of people deported on each occasion, and their destination, most often Auschwitz.

It is a powerful memorial, startling to anyone who chances upon it in what is otherwise a bland, middle-class neighborhood. And especially so to me. On this first visit to Berlin, I had set out in search of 13 Levetzowstrasse, a modest apartment house where I had lived as an infant before my family fled to England in 1939 and which, it turns out, was one of the few on the street to have survived the war. But until that moment, I had not known that the gathering place for deportations from Berlin was on the street where I was born, just a stone's throw from my first home.

The memorial on Levetzowstrasse is a permanent reminder—of where the crimes it commemorates were plotted and directed, of those who were once saluted by all Berliners, and of the political responsibility subsequent generations share to familiarize themselves with their city's shameful past. Writing in the immediate aftermath of World War II, when the full extent of Nazi barbarity was being revealed, the German philosopher Karl Jaspers explored the question of guilt. Jaspers rejected the concept of collective *criminal* guilt, but he argued that Germans shared *political* responsibility for the Holocaust. Only by accepting that responsibility, he contended, could they make the transition to political liberty. Nuremberg, the trial of Adolf Eichmann in Jerusalem, and the many trials of accused Nazi war criminals before German courts were central in fostering that political responsibility. These judicial proceedings help to explain why so many Germans take to the streets in protest when hoodlums attack a Turkish family and why, in 1988, more than four decades after the war, Germans put up the memorial on Levetzowstrasse.

The Holocaust, of course, was a singular event in world history, and efforts to suggest contemporary comparisons have always seemed odious. Yet they are difficult to resist when it comes to the former Yugoslavia and Rwanda. Traditional objectives of war—to conquer territory or to subjugate others—were secondary, if present at all. Instead, in both cases, the central purpose of those behind these crimes was to eliminate entire populations: through a combination of "ethnic purification" and murder in the former Yugoslavia; through breathtaking slaughter—800,000 killed in three months—in Rwanda.

These great crimes had become my preoccupation by the time I found the memorial at Levetzowstrasse. I had spent my entire career on efforts to defend rights, and I firmly believe in naming names of those who have committed grave abuses and, if possible, holding them accountable. Actual judicial punishment of those who committed even the most heinous violations of rights has been infrequent since the war crimes trials after World War II. Yet the struggle to secure a reckoning—central to the international human rights movement in recent years—has seemed worthwhile. It has kept the focus on atrocities and stigmatized those behind them. It has reaffirmed the laws that prohibit war crimes and, above all, demonstrated respect for victims by not countenancing political accommodation with their persecutors.

Now I looked to the past for guidance to the present. If the character and magnitude of the crimes in the former Yugoslavia and in Rwanda seemed to have historical analogues in Germany and Japan, then wouldn't justice be served in an attempt to replicate what took place at Nuremberg and Tokyo after World War II? International criminal tribunals, the focus of my efforts, seemed entirely appropriate given the circumstances.

There is a tragic irony in this. An international system of rights protection grew out of World War II in direct reaction to the crimes of the Nazis. Its main provisions included the United Nations Charter, the statutes for the Nuremberg and Tokyo tribunals, the Genocide Convention of December 9, 1948, and the following day, the Universal Declaration of Human Rights. Next came the four Geneva Conventions of August 12, 1949, with their provisions spelling out war crimes. That it should nevertheless be possible for Nazi-like crimes to be repeated a half century later in full view of the whole world points up the weakness of that system—and the need for fresh approaches.

In fact, the two ad hoc tribunals established to deal with the former Yugoslavia and Rwanda are already leading the way in what may prove to be the most dramatic innovations in international law to protect human rights in a half century. For the first time, serious violations of the laws of war that apply to internal armed conflicts are subject to international criminal sanctions as well. The concept of universal jurisdiction—that is, the right of a state to prosecute and punish those who commit certain crimes outside its territory and not involving its nationals—also has been greatly strengthened and broadened. Meanwhile, efforts to establish a permanent international criminal court are gaining more and more adherents.

Further, the lasting legal consequences will reflect how today's tribunals deal with the way "ethnic cleansing" was carried out in the former Yugoslavia and the way genocide was committed in Rwanda, in much the same way that international law has built on the work of the prosecutors and judges at Nuremberg in responding to specific crimes such as medical experiments on concentration camp inmates. The Yugoslavia tribunal, for instance, must focus on the indiscriminate bombardment of civilian populations and mass rape, because Bosnia was notorious for both crimes. The Rwanda tribunal will try to discover the line that divides freedom of expression from incitement to mass murder, because appeals to carry out the genocide were broadcast by local radio.

This book tells the story behind the establishment of the tribunals, places them in historical context, and discusses some of the key questions raised by all such efforts to determine accountability. It is also a story of political paralysis and sometimes craven behavior. The war in the Balkans began in Slovenia and Croatia in 1991. In a small Croatian city called Vukovar the pernicious character of the conflict became manifest early on. But it was the fighting in Bosnia the following year that administered a particular shock to the international system, demonstrating that Europeans were still thoroughly capable of inflicting on one another the kind of vile abuses Westerners with short memories had come to expect only in distant, Third World lands. Bosnia also stripped the veneer of relevance from postwar institutions designed to promote prosperity and peace, among them the European Union and the United Nations. Indeed, the international tribunal for Bosnia was the UN's only successful assertion of moral authority—and even the implementation of that decision was woefully tardy.

Ultimately the United States, acting through NATO, summoned the will to put an end to the war in Bosnia. Had it not done so, NATO would have joined the list of international institutions with self-inflicted wounds from the war. Moreover, if NATO troops leave Bosnia without apprehending the principal indicted war criminals and turning them over to the proper authorities for prosecution, its mission may yet be judged a failure.

Of course, NATO is no substitute for the civilian institutions needed to prevent future Bosnias. It remains unclear whether new international peacemaking or peacekeeping institutions will emerge, or whether significant efforts will be made to reform those that failed to stop the war. So far, the only bodies to emerge are the two tribunals, and they are still being tested. The heart says civilized men and women with respect for the rule of law cannot permit these kinds of crimes to happen again. The mind, sadly, sends a different message.

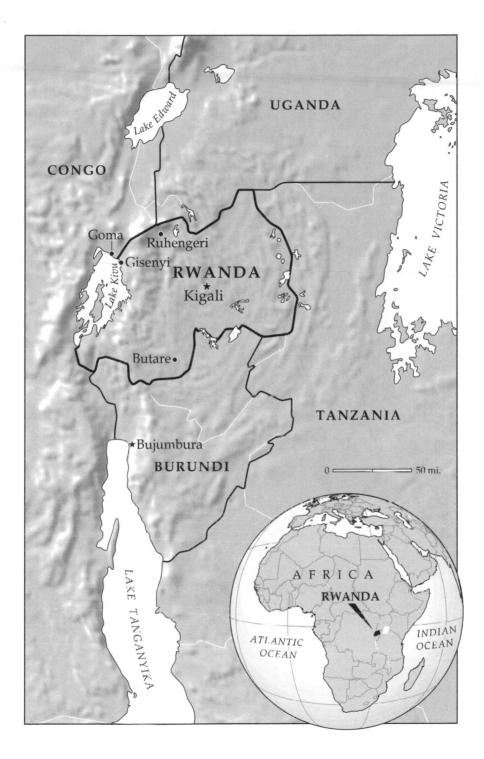

CONGO

UGANDA

Lake Edward

Lake Victoria

Goma

Ruhengeri

Gisenyi

RWANDA

★ Kigali

Lake Kivu

Butare

TANZANIA

★ Bujumbura

BURUNDI

0 ⸻ 50 mi.

LAKE TANGANYIKA

AFRICA

RWANDA

ATLANTIC OCEAN

INDIAN OCEAN

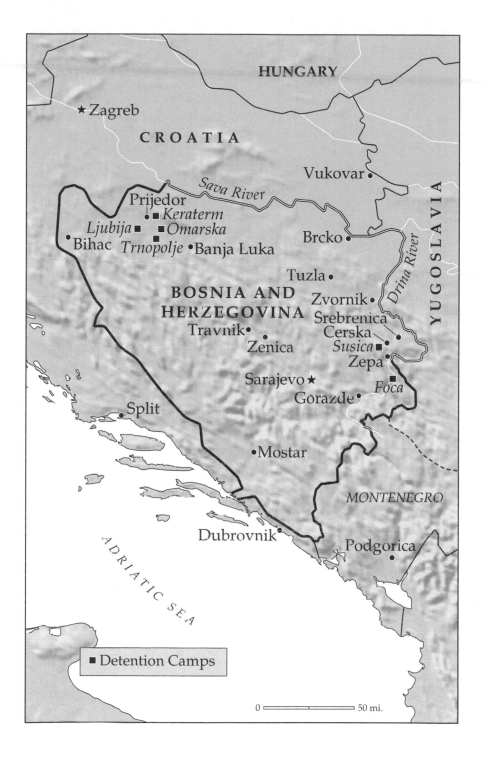

HUNGARY

★ Zagreb

C R O A T I A

Sava River

Vukovar •

Prijedor
• ■ *Keraterm*
Ljubija ■ ■ *Omarska*
• Bihac *Trnopolje* • Banja Luka

Brcko •

Drina River

Tuzla •

BOSNIA AND
HERZEGOVINA

Zvornik •
Srebrenica
Cerska •
Susica ■
Zepa

Travnik• •
Zenica

Sarajevo ★

Foca ■

Gorazde •

Split •

• Mostar

MONTENEGRO

Dubrovnik •

Podgorica •

A D R I A T I C   S E A

YUGOSLAVIA

■ Detention Camps

0 ⸻ 50 mi.

PART ONE

Dealing with War Crimes Before Bosnia

1

Vukovar: Where It Began

O N A MAP, Croatia resembles a horseshoe, or an inverted and tilted U. The prong that extends northeast is somewhat distended in that direction and cuts a broader swath than the southwestern prong, which is dotted with the resort towns of the Dalmatian Coast along the Adriatic Sea. The territory that is surrounded on three sides by the horseshoe is Bosnia-Herzegovina, and at the end of each of the prongs are the two republics that have remained parts of Yugoslavia following that country's dissolution: Montenegro in the west and Serbia, divided from Croatia by the Danube, at the end of the broader eastern prong. Those two republics also form the southern border of Bosnia-Herzegovina, where the Drina River separates Serbia from such previously obscure towns as Gorazde, Srebrenica, Cerska, and Zepa.

Vukovar is the largest town on the Croatian side of the Danube. Until June 1991, when the war began there, 44 percent of its residents were Croats and 37 percent were Serbs. Many of the remainder were Yugoslavs—that is, persons of mixed descent; others were Hungarians, Ruthenians, Slovaks, Ukrainians, Albanians, Jews, and Gypsies.

The villages around Vukovar on both sides of the Danube were populated mainly by Serbs.

In Yugoslavia before the breakup, in 1991, the Serbs were the largest and most politically powerful ethnic group, though the country's longtime dictator, Josip Broz Tito, was half Slovene and half Croat. Of Yugoslavia's 23.5 million people, 36 percent were Serbs; Croats, the next largest ethnic group, were 20 percent of the population. The Serbs dominated the armed forces, both officers and enlisted men, which reinforced their sense of security. In the newly independent Croatia, however, Serbs suddenly became a minority of 11 percent—550,000 in an overall population of 4.5 million. If the former Yugoslavia was determinedly multiethnic, the new Croatia was the opposite. The ethnicity of its overwhelming majority was precisely its reason for becoming a state.

The Serbs in Croatia had lived in harmony with their Croatian neighbors since the end of World War II and spoke the same language—Serbo-Croatian—though the Serbs use the Cyrillic alphabet, named for St. Cyril, who converted the South Slavs to Christianity, while the Croatians employ the Latin alphabet. They worked together, attended school together (where the children learned both alphabets), played together, drank together, and frequently intermarried. Yet old enmities had not been forgotten. Of common Slavic heritage and indistinguishable from each other in physical characteristics, they were separated along religious lines during the eleventh century. The Serbs follow the rites of the Eastern Orthodox Church; the Croats are Roman Catholics.

In the 1990s, neither people has demonstrated great religious devotion, though remembered persecution played a role in the Serb reaction to its sudden minority status in independent Croatia. More important was racial heritage, or fantasies about racial heritage. Reflecting the nasty work of its masters, the Ustasha regime that ruled Croatia as a Nazi puppet state during World War II had enacted blood laws of its own, thereby helping to establish the importance of race, or ethnicity.

The Ustasha not only killed Jews, as the Nazis did in the countries of Europe that they occupied, but they also massacred Serbs. Serb nationalists tend to put the figure at 700,000. Croatian nationalists claim that is greatly exaggerated; a figure some of them have used is 60,000. The truth probably lies close to the midpoint of these two extremes. The only country in Europe where a greater portion of the population died during the war than in Yugoslavia was Poland, where there had been the largest Jewish population and where nearly all the death camps—other than those in Croatia—were located. Most of the killing in Poland was done by Germans, and virtually all of it was carried out under their direction. In Yugoslavia the carnage was largely a domestic affair.

Though the Ustasha did much of the killing in Yugoslavia during World War II, they did not enjoy a monopoly on mass murder. Chetniks—Serbian irregular forces seeking to restore the monarchy in Serbia—also engaged in slaughter, frequently attacking Croatian villages and murdering the residents because they were Croats. Tito's Partisans, the Communist forces that seized power at the end of the war, also got into the slaughter business; they took revenge on many of their enemies by summarily executing them, thereby largely dispensing with war crimes trials like those the Allies convened at Nuremberg. So many people died in Yugoslavia—more than 1.7 million, according to a government commission that conducted an inquiry after the war—that there can have been few families that did not lose a parent, a child, or some other relative to the Ustasha, the Chetniks, or the Partisans.

Against that history, it was not difficult for Serbian nationalists to whip up intense fears in the Serbian minority of the newly independent Croatian state and equally intense feeling among Serbs in Serbia that it was their duty to protect their ethnic brethren. Their task was made easier by the emergence as leaders of the new state of such Croatian nationalists as Franjo Tudjman, a former general who had served a long prison sentence after he broke with the Tito regime. Tudjman, who became president of Croatia, and his associates promulgated a constitution that provided in its preamble that "the Republic of Croatia is comprised as the national state of the Croatian people" and identified the Serbs as one among many minorities—along with "Muslims, Slovenes, Czechs, Slovaks, Italians, Hungarians, Jews, and others"—that would be protected. The Serbs had sought the same constitutional status as Croats in Croatia and had demanded such manifestations of political autonomy as their own police force. Serb fears about their new minority status were exacerbated by the Tudjman government's dismissal of Communist bureaucrats, many of them Serbs, from a large number of government posts and their replacement by Croats—members of the president's party, the Croatian Democratic Union (Hrvatska Demokratska Zajednica, or HDZ).

Moreover, the insistence by Tudjman and company on using such traditional symbols of Croatian nationalism as the *sahovnica,* a red-and-white checkerboard flag, and the national anthem—both associated a few decades earlier with the Ustasha—provoked apprehension among Serbs in Croatia that they might become victims of the kind of bloodbath their parents or grandparents had suffered during World War II. These concerns were intensified by reunified Germany's behavior: It was Germany, wartime patron of the Ustasha, that had taken the lead internationally in recognizing President Tudjman's government in Zagreb. All these developments doubtless influenced the thinking of the Yugoslav armed forces and of the Serbian militias—quickly labeled by others and by themselves as Chetniks, after their World War II counterparts—who started the war immediately after Croatia's declaration of independence on June 25, 1991.

The attack on Vukovar began two months later, on August 25, 1991. For eighty-eight days, the city was under siege, bombarded by mortars, howitzers, and tanks belonging to the Yugoslav Army. An ancient and graceful city, its streets once lined with fine baroque buildings, was reduced to rubble and, with the flight of most of its residents, became a ghost town.

Those who could not leave included many of the patients at Vukovar's hospital, among them soldiers and militia members injured in the nearby villages or in the bombardment of the city itself, and others in the hospital who were too sick or too old to flee. In addition, most of the staff of three hundred doctors, nurses, and other hospital personnel stayed at their posts to maintain care. It wasn't easy. Not only were essential supplies, such as running water, cut off during the siege, but the hospital itself was shelled constantly. Patients and staff were casualties of the shelling, but the hospital continued to function by shielding patients in the basement until the Croatian forces defending the city capitulated on November 18, 1991.

The fall of the city did not end the suffering of its residents. By this time, several thousand had been killed and most of the rest had fled. A city of 84,000 now had been reduced to 15,000—civilians who had hidden in basements for months, soldiers and militiamen who had been wounded in the fighting, patients and staff from the hospital, and a few others.

During the next three days, survivors of the siege were rounded up by the conquering forces of the Yugoslav People's Army (JNA) and by the Serbian paramilitaries who had joined the regular troops in the siege. A Serbian journalist who had spent months with the troops and had entered Vukovar with the victors, and was apparently trusted by them as a fellow Serb, subsequently told Human Rights Watch what he saw: "After Vukovar fell, people were lined up and made to walk to detention areas. As the prisoners walked by, local Serbian paramilitaries pulled people out of the lines at random, claiming that they had to be executed because they were 'war criminals.' " The Serb journalist identified the JNA officer who supervised this selection: a Major Veselin Sljivancanin, who was in charge of security in Vukovar after the city's fall.[1]*

According to the Serb journalist, hundreds of prisoners picked out in this fashion, many of whom had been patients at Vukovar's hospital, were taken to the Ovcara farm, near Petrova Gora in the Vukovar municipality. The journalist said he had not been permitted to go to this site with the prisoners, who were led away by drunken reservists with the Yugoslav Army. The following morning, however, the journalist joined the reservists as they sat around a fire drinking coffee and brandy and boasting that they had executed hundreds of Ustasha and dumped their bodies in a pit. The journalist identified some of the reservists and their commanders.[2]

The more than two hundred hospital patients who were led off to the Ovcara farm were not the only victims of such reprisals when Vukovar fell. As the city's residents were rounded up, many were beaten, and although the majority of those captured were civilians, they were sent to detention camps. One of those detained for several weeks was the hospital director, Dr. Vesna Bosanac, who subsequently told me that her captors interrogated her extensively about the patients, accusing her of favoring those of Croatian origin and neglecting Serbs. Dr. Bosanac, who had obtained part of her medical education in the Serbian capital at the University of Belgrade, insisted to me that not only was such discrimination unthinkable at the hospital, but in many cases she did not know whether patients were of Serb or Croatian origin, and the hospital did not maintain information on the ethnicity of its patients. When we spoke, she had with her a printout listing the patients. Pointing to the names, she told me that though it was clear from some whether they were Serb or Croat, in many cases it was impossible to tell.

Of some 15,000 persons believed to be in Vukovar on November

18, 1991, close to 3,000 are missing. There have been claims by the Croatian government and others that mass executions took place at several sites. Since Vukovar remained under Serb control for several years, it was not possible to obtain access to all these sites to verify these claims. But considerable evidence supports the Serbian journalist's account of the execution of the patients from the Vukovar hospital. As a result, JNA major Veselin Sljivancanin, subsequently lieutenant colonel, who was shown on Belgrade television on the night of November 20, 1991, blocking officials of the International Committee of the Red Cross from access to the hospital grounds, and two of his fellow officers who were named by witnesses as those in charge of the executions became the first Serbs and Montenegrins from the Federal Republic of Yugoslavia itself to be indicted by the tribunal.

The steps leading to their indictment began in March 1992, when representatives of Human Rights Watch traveled to Vukovar and attempted to go to the killing field at the Ovcara farm. Their way was blocked by Yugoslav Army troops. Several months later, however, with the assistance of civilian police from the United Nations Protection Forces (UNPROFOR), another human rights group reached the site.

Physicians for Human Rights is a Boston-based organization that has specialized in conducting forensic exhumations at sites of mass killings. The organization's director at the time, Eric Stover, and the anthropologist on whom much of its work was centered, Dr. Clyde Snow, had pioneered in unearthing skeletal remains to identify the victims of human rights abuses and determine how and when they died. Testimony by Snow, a shambling, slow-talking Oklahoman with a keen mind and several decades of experience in examining bones to assist in homicide prosecutions and to solve historical mysteries— ranging from the deaths of Butch Cassidy and the Sundance Kid in Bolivia to that of Josef Mengele in Brazil—had played a crucial part in the criminal convictions of two former presidents and other military leaders responsible for more than 9,000 abductions and murders during the "dirty war" in Argentina in the late 1970s. Snow also conducted exhumations to assist in human rights investigations in several other Latin American countries and in Iraqi Kurdistan, as well as in the former Yugoslavia, and he trained many of the other forensic anthropologists who have taken part in such investigations worldwide.[3]

With the help of directions and maps provided by witnesses to the executions, Snow and his team found the grave site on October 18, 1992, nearly a year after the killings, in an isolated wooded area of the Ovcara farm. On their first visit to the site, the investigators found three skeletons of young adult males protruding from the earth. Perimortem trauma was evident on two of the skeletons, indicating that the men were beaten near the time they had died. One skeleton had a gunshot wound in the left temple. Though the International Criminal Tribunal for the Former Yugoslavia did not yet exist, and was only established by the UN Security Council half a year later, this discovery persuaded UNPROFOR to provide round-the-clock guards at the site to safeguard the evidence.

In mid-December, Snow and his colleagues returned for three days of work at the site. Despite the cold, which made efforts to excavate the bodies difficult, they dug a trench seven meters long and one meter wide until human remains were exposed. They found nine skeletons with clothing still in place and, to their surprise, given the passage of time, with some tissue, hair, and skin still present. The trench covered just a portion of a larger site that evidently had been dug out at about the same time; it allowed Snow's team to make a number of preliminary findings. A mass execution had taken place there; the grave had been dug by a bulldozer; the isolated location indicated that an attempt had been made to bury the bodies secretly; the location of spent cartridges and bullet marks on trees showed that the executioners faced their victims from the northern boundary of the grave and fired to the south and southeast; the bodies were then covered over by the bulldozer; the number of bodies uncovered in the trench suggested that the entire grave held more than two hundred bodies; one man was shot trying to escape, and his body was left lying in the woods; two of the bodies of the nine exhumed from the trench had necklaces with Roman Catholic crosses, one of which had a small metal plaque inscribed "God and Croatians," suggesting that the victims were Croats; and the evidence collected at the grave was consistent with the testimony previously collected about what happened to the men taken from the Vukovar hospital.

Additional testimony that Physicians for Human Rights obtained from witnesses fleshed out the story. Before they were killed, the patients from the Vukovar hospital were taken to a large garage at the Ovcara farm used to store farm equipment. Yugoslav Army soldiers and Serbian paramilitary troops beat the injured men with blunt instruments as they were moved from buses to the garage and continued to beat them for several hours inside the garage. At least two men died of these beatings. At about 6:00 P.M. on November 20, 1991, about twenty men in the garage were separated from the others and taken away in a group by truck, apparently to the site where the mass grave was found. Fifteen or twenty minutes later, the truck returned to the garage to pick up another load, the process continuing until more than two hundred men had been taken away for execution. Not all those in the garage were beaten to death or executed by the firing squad. Some survived.

More than a dozen survivors were subsequently identified. Apparently, some were spared because they were recognized as members of the hospital staff by the Serbian soldiers or militiamen. Some of the Serb militiamen were from Vukovar and had grown up with the men they took from the hospital. The survivors spent months in detention camps before eventual release, generally in prisoner exchanges arranged by the International Committee of the Red Cross. As they were identified, more testimony became available and more details became known about what happened to the patients taken from the Vukovar hospital. In this way, additional officers and men involved in the killings were identified.

Following the excavation conducted in December 1992, Physicians for Human Rights, which conducted its investigation under the sponsorship of a UN War Crimes Commission, established by the Security Council the previous October, appealed to the United Nations for logistical assistance to unearth the remainder of the bodies at the site. In turn, the UN asked its member states for such support. Most Western governments, including Britain and the United States, said no. Eventually, the Netherlands provided a company of thirty-five combat engineers, and in November 1993, two years after the killings, PHR and the Dutch troops went back to complete the work. Though Serb authorities who controlled the area had indicated they would be allowed to proceed, the Yugoslav Army troops in the region blocked their access.

No progress was made before the War Crimes Commission wound up its work on April 30, 1994. Yet substantial evidence was available to the tribunal's prosecutors from the preliminary excavation and from testimony from survivors and witnesses. The tribunal charged Sljivancanin and two fellow officers in the Yugoslav Army with the murder of 261 men, who are named in the indictment. At this writing, none of the indicted men has been turned over for trial. For a period, Sljivancanin commanded a brigade of the Yugoslav Army (successor to the Yugoslav People's Army) in Podgorica, the capital of Montenegro; more recently he was moved to Belgrade, perhaps out of concern that the Montenegrin authorities might decide to cooperate with the tribunal. One of the other defendants, Mile Mrksic, who led the attack on Vukovar, was promoted from colonel to general in the Yugoslav Army after that city fell. Though President Slobodan Milosevic signed the Dayton agreement, pledging to cooperate with the tribunal, and these men are directly under his control, thus far he has defied the tribunal's warrants ordering their arrest and delivery to The Hague. When I met in Belgrade with Milan Milutinovic, the Yugoslav foreign minister,[4] in June 1997, he insisted that these defendants would never stand trial. Two weeks later, however, one of those charged with responsibility for the massacre of the hospital patients, Slavko Dokmanovic, was apprehended and taken to The Hague. He had been indicted secretly, and therefore unsuspectingly went to a meeting with UN officials, who made it possible for tribunal personnel to arrest him. A civilian, Dokmanovic had become mayor of Vukovar when the city was overrun by Serb military and paramilitary forces.

2

The Laws
of War

By all accounts, the first instance of an international trial for war crimes took place in Breisach, Germany, in 1474, when twenty-seven judges of the Holy Roman Empire sat in judgment of Peter van Hagenback for violating the "laws of God and man" by allowing his troops to rape, murder, and pillage. He was convicted, sentenced to death, and executed. More commonly, those brought to trial for such crimes committed in connection with armed conflict appeared before national courts, such as the courts of chivalry of the later Middle Ages.

The laws of war are of antique origin. In essence, they rest on two broad principles: the principle of necessity and the principle of humanity. Under the first, that which is necessary militarily to vanquish the enemy may be done. Under the second, which may be considered one of the defining ideas of civilized society even though it has often been disregarded in practice, that which causes unnecessary suffering is forbidden. As they have been elaborated in our own era, the laws of war have become highly detailed, resolving seeming conflicts between these two fundamental principles. They protect combatants by requiring that they enjoy certain rights as prisoners of war once they have been captured and disarmed; that they are to be safeguarded against execution or deliberate injury when they are hors de combat because they have been wounded or they have surrendered; and that certain weapons, such as poisonous gases, may not be used against them. They also protect noncombatants against deliberate or indiscriminate attacks, reprisal killings, seizure as hostages, starvation or deportation, and destruction of their cultural objects and places of worship. Combatants and noncombatants alike are protected against criminal sanctions unless they are accorded due process of law.

Herodotus tells us that such rules were recognized by the ancient Persians and Greeks, as in his account of the killing of the Persian heralds in Sparta. Sparta (also known as Lacedaemon) subsequently sent to the Persians envoys who were supposed to pay for the crime with their own lives. However, King Xerxes demurred, saying "he would not be like the Lacedaemonians, for they," he said, "have broken what is customary usage among all mankind by killing the heralds; but I will not myself do what I rebuke them for, nor by counterkilling will I release the Lacedaemonians' guilt."[1] Xerxes thereby not only acknowledged a prohibition on reprisal killings of noncombatants, he also recognized that if he engaged in the same practices as the Spartans, the effect would be to mitigate the opprobrium that attached to them. Similar values were expressed in the codes of other ancient peoples and later in the writings of Christian theologians such as St. Augustine and St. Thomas Aquinas and in the rules of chivalry that prohibited attacks on the sick and the wounded or on women or children. They were comprehensively codified as early as 1625 by a Dutch scholar, Hugo Grotius, who is regarded as the father of international law.

It was not until the nineteenth century, however, that formal international agreements embodying these principles were accepted and ratified by governments. And perhaps the key ingredient was not some artfully argued legal theory but the emergence of a wholly unanticipated factor: the war correspondent.

Phillip Knightley, a British journalist who has written a history of war correspondents,[2] has pointed out that they were first employed during the Crimean War, of 1854–56, when Samuel F. B. Morse's new invention, the telegraph, had just come into general use. The epitaph in St. Paul's Cathedral of William Howard Russell, of *The Times* (London), who reported the charge of the Light Brigade, claims that he was "the first and greatest" war correspondent. Military officers used to fighting wars without being subjected to public scrutiny were not thrilled by the advent of war correspondents. Previously, what was known about the conduct of war derived mainly from the often self-serving accounts of military commanders long after the events. Typically, the emphasis was on deeds of bravery, not on the pain and suffering of noncombatants in harm's way or of combatants captured or injured. A British commander, a General Pennefeather, is said to have remarked, "By God, Sir, I'd as soon see the devil" when he encountered Russell in the Crimea.[3] One consequence of Russell's reporting was that the British public became aware of the dismal state of the army's medical services, prompting Florence Nightingale to sail to the Crimea with thirty-eight nurses to provide the needed care. Nightingale's efforts aroused international public concern for care of the wounded, which became the focus of the first Red Cross Convention, adopted just a decade after her arrival in Crimea.

If the Crimea was the first war reported by journalists on the scene, the first covered by a large number of correspondents was the American Civil War, 1861–65. According to Knightley, "some 500 went off to report the war for the North alone."[4] Their telegraphed accounts spurred the development of many local newspapers and gave the American public a window on the battlefields. Technological progress had not yet reached the point that the press could print Matthew Brady's photographs of the war, but dispatches filed by journalists from countless battles depicting great suffering aroused strong reactions. Responding to these accounts, President Abraham Lincoln authorized the War Department to promulgate a code, consisting of 159 articles, to govern the conduct of the United States Army during the Civil War. Drafted in 1863 by Francis Lieber, a German immigrant who became a professor of law at Columbia University, the code helped to advance efforts to make such rules binding on all military forces worldwide. The very first international agreement, a "Convention for the Amelioration of the Condition of the Wounded in Armies in the Field," was signed by twelve European governments in Geneva the following year. (It contained several provisions that were violated by the Serbian forces at Vukovar.) Thirty-five years later, in 1899, a "Convention with Respect to the Laws and Customs of War on Land" was adopted at The Hague that codified generally accepted principles of customary international law prohibiting the mistreatment of combatants who are hors de combat and protecting civilians and civilian objects. (Again, the events at Vukovar would have been covered.) By the outbreak of World War II, additional international agreements on the laws of war had been adopted at conferences that met at The Hague and at Geneva, and these helped to form the legal backdrop for the international war crimes trials that took place at Nuremberg and at Tokyo.

The decision to bring German and Japanese war criminals before international tribunals was not a foregone conclusion. At the end of World War I, the British had favored the establishment of a tribunal to try the Kaiser and other German leaders. But Woodrow Wilson, who shared a widespread antagonism in the United States to the idea that international law should take precedence over the domestic laws of nations, opposed a tribunal. Though the Versailles Treaty provided for international prosecution of those charged with "acts in violation of the laws and customs of war," American opposition and a concern for a fragile postwar German state killed the idea. Instead, the World War I Allies left it to Germany to prosecute its own war criminals, and a small number were tried and convicted before the Supreme Court in Leipzig.

As World War II drew to a close, the positions were reversed. Winston Churchill favored the summary execution of top Nazis— though he was repulsed by Stalin's proposal at one of the meetings of Allied leaders that as many as 50,000 German officers should be shot—but this time the Americans favored trials. After Franklin Delano Roosevelt died, on April 12, 1945, Harry Truman maintained American support. A month later, the British dropped their opposition and the die was cast.

One of the arguments against the trials at Nuremberg and Tokyo at the time they were held, and ever since, is that they represented "victor's justice." That is, the Allies won the war and then appointed prosecutors and judges from their own side to try leaders of the losing side. To critics, this made the trials inherently unfair, both because those on the winning side who committed crimes were not also being prosecuted and because the judges were aligned with the victors.

The complaints cannot simply be dismissed. General principles of the laws of armed conflict protecting noncombatants from military operations, though not as well defined in treaties that preceded the war as in the revised Geneva Conventions adopted four years after it and in the Additional Protocols adopted a generation later, were strik-

ingly violated by the Allies. There was the bombing of Dresden in
February 1945 by the British, when the war in Europe was all but
over, creating a firestorm that incinerated tens of thousands of its
civilian residents. There was the firebombing of Tokyo by American
planes in March 1945 at a cost of 80,000 to 100,000 civilian lives, up
to then the largest number ever killed in any aerial attack. And, of
course, there were the atomic bombs dropped on Hiroshima and Nagasaki.

An innovation at Nuremberg that inspired strong criticism at the
time and has ever since was that the top Nazis were charged with a
crime for which there was little foundation in international law: waging aggressive war. To a lesser extent, there was also opposition to
the designation of certain offenses as "crimes against humanity."
These included crimes committed against nationals of the perpetrator state not covered by the concept of war crimes—a term that applied only to acts against combatants and noncombatants on the
opposing side. The Nuremberg Charter specified murder, extermination, enslavement, deportation, and other inhuman acts against the
civilian population as part of a campaign of persecution on political,
racial, or religious grounds. Some labeled this retroactive justice. Adherents of positive law—that is, those who reject the application of
natural law or higher law principles and who believe that only laws
actually enacted by appropriate authorities are valid—argued that trying Germans and Japanese for crimes against humanity violated the
fundamental principles of legality: *nullum crimen sine lege* (no crime
without law) and *nulla poena sine crimine* (no penalty without
crime).

Proponents of the tribunals contended that the concept of crimes
against humanity was established in customary international law,
which has the same binding effect as conventional law (that is, positive law). Indeed, the Hague Convention on Laws and Customs of
War on Land of 1899 provides in its preamble: "Until a more complete code of laws is issued, the High Contracting Parties think it is
right to declare that in cases not included in the Regulations adopted
by them, populations and belligerents remain under the protection
and empire of the principles of international law as they result from
the usages established between civilized nations, from the laws of
humanity, and the requirements of public conscience."

Subsequent to Nuremberg, international jurisdiction to bring to
justice those responsible for crimes against humanity, especially

when committed in connection with international armed conflict, has been a widely accepted principle of international law. Crimes against humanity is simultaneously a broader and a narrower concept than war crimes. It is broader in that the latter encompasses only crimes against belligerents or nationals of a hostile power or an occupied territory. This leaves out, for example, the crimes the Nazis committed against German Jews and Gypsies or those of countries such as Hungary and Romania that made common cause with the Axis Powers. Also, war crimes may only take place in times of armed conflict or occupation. Crimes against humanity, it is now accepted, can also take place in times of peace (although at Nuremberg and Tokyo, the post–World War II tribunals considered that their own jurisdiction was limited to acts committed during wartime).

In a different sense, however, the concept of war crimes is broader in that it applies to even a single crime committed in violation of the laws of war, regardless of whether that crime was part of a widespread practice. Therefore, for example, the Canadian soldiers who were accused of torturing to death a man in Somalia during the UN occupation of that country could properly be prosecuted for committing a war crime though no pattern of such abuse was demonstrated. In contrast, the concept of crimes against humanity applies only to crimes committed on a large scale. A defendant charged with crimes against humanity may be convicted only if the prosecution establishes the connection between the particular crime and a broad pattern and practice of the commission of such crimes for reasons of political, ethnic, or religious persecution. Accordingly, the evidentiary burden on prosecutors is far greater when they prosecute a defendant for crimes against humanity than when they must demonstrate to a court the commission of a war crime.

Despite significant shortcomings, the post–World War II war crimes trials were a great achievement. They produced overwhelming evidence of the atrocities for which the defendants were responsible and enhanced the credibility and power of that evidence by demonstrating that it could withstand the best efforts by the defendants and their attorneys to discredit it. They reaffirmed the principle that military and civilian leaders holding positions of command and power are responsible for the crimes committed under their direction and authority. They helped to individualize guilt by connecting great crimes to the prisoners in the dock, men who had formerly exercised virtually unconstrained power, rather than allow it to be attributed collectively to entire races or nations. By the care with which the judges, particularly at Nuremberg, weighed the evidence, differentiated between the defendants, and acquitted some, the trials demonstrated that it is possible to respond conscientiously, fairly, and humanely, but nevertheless firmly and justly, even to such appalling crimes as those committed under German and Japanese occupation. The tribunals advanced the idea that law generally, and international law in particular, can deal with great matters and that legal process may be relied upon to deal appropriately with the most grievous offenses by human beings against other human beings.

Unfortunately, the aftermath of the trials at Nuremberg and Tokyo was not so salutary; in Japan especially, there was a quick end to all efforts to hold accountable those responsible for war crimes. Many trials were held in both countries, and thousands of Germans and Japanese were convicted, but the number of Germans tried was far greater than the number of Japanese, because while Germany held its own trials after international prosecutions were completed, Japan never did so. (Even so, the number of Japanese executed for war crimes—more than nine hundred, reflecting the fact that many Japanese defendants were convicted of crimes against Allied prisoners of war—was far larger than the number of Germans who paid the ultimate price.) Some in both countries who were responsible for crimes against humanity were prosecuted, convicted, and sentenced severely; others escaped entirely. Purges of officials from various public posts also took place in both countries, but these were poorly carried out. In Germany, many who had willingly administered the policies that characterized the Nazi state were certified as "denazified" after they paid small fines, and most lawyers and judges who had participated in the travesties that constituted Nazi justice simply remained in their posts. These shortcomings did not prevent Germans from absorbing the lessons of Nuremberg, however, because what was established at the first trials there was reinforced from time to time by additional trials before German courts and before the courts of other countries that apprehended Nazi war criminals over a period of several decades and brought them to trial.

In the period immediately following the trials at Nuremberg and Tokyo, proposals were made at the United Nations for the establishment of a permanent international criminal court, but they were doomed by the onset of the Cold War. A proposal for such a court has continued to obtain support from proponents of an expanded role for international law, but prior to the establishment of the ad hoc tribunals for ex-Yugoslavia and Rwanda, it never had sufficient political backing. Too many governments have feared that they, or their allies, might one day find themselves in the dock.

Still, what happened at Nuremberg and Tokyo had a profound impact on the body of international law that emerged after World War II and helped to guide the drafting of the four Geneva Conventions of 1949. For the first time, explicit language designated certain acts as war crimes. The Third Convention, for example, deals with treatment of prisoners of war and proscribes "willful killing, torture or inhuman treatment, including biological experiments, willfully causing great suffering or serious injury to body or health . . . or willfully depriving a prisoner of war of the rights of fair and regular trial." When the Serbs killed military men taken from the Vukovar hospital, they violated the Third Convention.

The Fourth Convention uses much the same language but applies it to civilians and adds "unlawful deportation or transfer or unlawful confinement of a protected person . . . taking of hostages and extensive destruction and appropriation of property not justified by military necessity and carried out unlawfully and wantonly." When the Serbs killed civilian patients taken from the Vukovar hospital, they violated the Fourth Convention.

These provisions are binding international law—applicable everywhere in the world, since virtually every government has accepted their tenets by formally ratifying them. And they bind even new states born of geopolitical change—the former republics of the Soviet Union, for example. Or Bosnia and Croatia. More important, the war crimes provisions of the Geneva Conventions are so fundamental and so widely accepted that they have the force of "customary international law"—that is, they bind a government regardless of whether it has formally ratified a treaty accepting their obligations.

In 1977, two additional protocols were promulgated to expand the protection of the Geneva Conventions in armed conflicts. One adds to the list of offenses considered war crimes; the other applies to internal armed conflicts. The year had special significance for another reason: The Nobel Peace Prize for 1977 went to a group, little known then, called Amnesty International, and that, in turn, helped to galvanize a nascent, disparate human rights movement into a global force.

That it took so long for an *international* human rights movement to develop has much to do with the inertial power of history, the idea—effectively embodied in English, French, and American charters of rights—that rights derive principally or even solely from citizenship in a state, which has the duty to protect them. In contrast, the movement believes that rights are attributes of humanity, therefore universal, and that all are deserving of protection regardless of the state in which they live. Those in the human rights movement also believe in accountability, manifest in the disclosure and acknowledgment of abuses, the purging of those responsible from public office, and the prosecution and punishment of those who commit crimes against humanity.

Between judgment at Nuremberg and the Balkans tribunal at The Hague is a half-century struggle for accountability—imperfect, passionate, yet rooted in law and universal principles. Understanding how that struggle played out is critical to understanding what happened in the Balkans and Rwanda, what led to the war crimes tribunals for them, and whether they will prove successful.

3

The
United Nations

Tʜᴇ ᴅᴇᴄɪsɪᴏɴ ʙʏ the United Nations Security Council in 1993 to establish a war crimes tribunal for ex-Yugoslavia set a precedent for the world body: It was the first time in its forty-eight-year history that it tried to bring anyone to justice for committing human rights abuses. This fact probably comes as no surprise even to casual observers of the UN, which is widely derided for its inability to put its muscle and moral authority where its mouth is. But if the UN hasn't lived up to the expectations for it a half century ago, it is not the utter failure its harshest critics contend. The declarations and treaties it has promulgated over the years are the standard against which the conduct of governments is measured—an indirect yet still important contribution to human rights. The charter for the ex-Yugoslavia war crimes tribunal, for example, uses language from the UN's 1948 Genocide Convention, even though the convention itself was never invoked before Bosnia.

The UN's good words begin with the very first article in its charter, which states that "promoting and encouraging respect for human rights" is one of the purposes of the world body. Other articles stress "fundamental freedoms for all without distinction as to race, sex, language or religion," and require member states "to take joint and separate action in cooperation with the Organization" to achieve these purposes.

This was something new. Before World War II, it was generally accepted that what a government did to its own nationals was not a legitimate concern in international relations. The slave trade was prohibited by the Treaty of Vienna of 1815; the pre–World War II Geneva Conventions and Hague Conventions regulated treatment of combatants and civilians of the opposing side, and the Covenant of the League of Nations required that states administering trust territories should respect the dignity of the inhabitants. Yet these precedents fell far short of an acknowledgment that there should be any limits on a government's treatment of its own people. The revelations of Nazi war crimes, the most grotesque abuses in human history, changed that forever. Adoption of the United Nations Charter represented an enormous advance because it legitimized international efforts to protect human rights everywhere.

At the same time, the vague wording of the charter reflected the wishes of its powerful constituencies. The Soviet Union, for example, would have balked had the charter explicitly condemned the repression routinely practiced by its leaders. At the other end of the human rights spectrum, even the Americans had reasons to be sensitive. Jim Crow was alive and well in the American South, so Washington preferred a provision that limited the United Nations to efforts "to promote" observance of human rights without distinction as to race instead of a clear prohibition of racial discrimination. As a leading scholar of international law has pointed out, "the principal powers [in 1945] were not prepared to derogate from the established character of the international system by establishing law and legal obligation that would penetrate Statehood in that radical way: clearly they themselves were not ready to submit to such law."[1]

By 1948, however, Harry Truman had ordered the desegregation of the federal government, including the military, and signaled the administration's intention to attack segregation more broadly. America thus led the way in drafting the UN's Universal Declaration of Human Rights, which included clear-cut protection for the rights systematically denied in the Soviet Union as well as an explicit ban on race discrimination. The declaration was adopted by the UN General Assembly without dissent, the entire Soviet bloc abstaining.

In practice, of course, the gap between the Universal Declaration's language and UN efforts to uphold its provisions was enormous. A human rights commission had been set up in 1946, but its members protected themselves from denunciation.[2] The superpowers, meanwhile, protected their client states. Over time, as membership in the world body grew, an Islamic bloc and an African bloc emerged, with lessons well learned: They, too, protected their members against opprobrium. A UN treaty, the International Covenant on Civil and Political Rights, followed the Universal Declaration in 1966, binding on all governments that are parties to it (132 at this writing). But the UN bodies charged with promoting compliance with the terms of such treaties did precious little. The African bloc saw to it that the UN Human Rights Commission did not speak out against Idi Amin while Ugandans suffered under his rule. Competition between the Soviet Union and the United States for strategic influence in China—readmitted to the UN in 1971 in place of Taiwan—effectively silenced the UN about the terrible crimes during Mao's Great Leap Forward and the decade-long Cultural Revolution. The UN's response to the slaughter by the Khmer Rouge, whose interests were protected by China, was barely discernible.[3] Over the years, the United Nations Human Rights Commission focused much of its attention on genuine human rights abuses by Israel and South Africa, not because these were worse than those of many other countries but because these states were the targets of denunciations by large blocs and had few defenders.

In early 1994, pushed by the Clinton administration, the United Nations created a new office, High Commissioner for Human Rights. If the world body's top human rights official were given such status, Amnesty International and others argued, UN efforts would gain more visibility and clout. Instead, governments concerned that the high commissioner might point the finger at them took care that the office would have a tiny budget, $700,000 a year—a pittance if serious investigations of abuses are to be conducted.[4] More important, they made it clear that they did not want anyone appointed to the post who would give them grief. In deference to such concerns, Secretary General Boutros Boutros-Ghali designated an Ecuadorian diplomat, José Ayala Lasso, to serve as high commissioner, though he had no background in human rights. With denunciation of those responsible for abuses the only means available for carrying out his mission, Ayala Lasso managed to go through his first year in his post without publicly criticizing a single government anywhere in the world.[5] In 1997, Boutros-Ghali's successor, Kofi Annan, named former Irish president Mary Robinson to the post. The appointment was widely hailed both because Robinson had been a leading human rights lawyer before becoming president of Ireland and because her international prominence ensured that her office would acquire the visibility that it lacked under Ayala Lasso. At this writing, she has recently taken up her new duties and, though far more vigorous than her predecessor, has yet to prove that she can be effective operating from a base at the United Nations.

The Cold War ended in 1989 with the revolutions in Eastern and Central Europe that overthrew Communism. For many people long disappointed by the performance of the United Nations on human rights matters, the stirring events of that year meant the dawn of a new day. And suddenly, the UN seemed ready to deliver on its promise with assertive action in such trouble spots as Cambodia, Nicaragua, and El Salvador.

In Paris, eighteen governments, which included all five permanent members of the Security Council, met with the four factions at war in Cambodia, launching talks that led to the signing of a peace accord two years later, on October 23, 1991. Its terms required that the observance of human rights be monitored and enforced by an agency to be established by the UN during a transition period when Cambodian refugees would be repatriated, the various military forces would be largely disarmed and demobilized, and elections would be held. The United Nations had never been so deeply involved in any country's affairs.

Still, even though the United Nations Transitional Authority in Cambodia (UNTAC) was given the responsibility by the peace settlement to promote human rights, there was a conspicuous omission from its mandate: nothing was said about bringing the Khmer Rouge to justice for its crimes against humanity more than a decade earlier. It was a bitter pill to swallow, but many dedicated advocates of accountability did not dispute the political judgment that a peace settlement would have been impossible without Khmer Rouge participation. What made that pill easier to digest was the absence of any provision for an amnesty, preserving the possibility that Khmer Rouge's leaders one day might be brought to book for the slaughter of hundreds of thousands of Cambodians.

UNTAC performed only moderately well in promoting human rights in Cambodia while it governed the country, but it succeeded in repatriating nearly 400,000 refugees and in holding an election, in May 1993, that was widely considered a great success. Roughly 90 percent of those eligible to vote took part. By the time of the election, however, the Khmer Rouge had pulled out of the peace process and resumed its armed struggle. Since then, Cambodia has gone through several turns and is still a country in near-constant turmoil, but for a while, at least, the UN showed that it could have a positive impact in a troubled land.

Nicaragua was a bigger success. Here was a nation in violent and bitter conflict in the decade since the Sandinista revolution of 1979, and yet the UN helped to bring about a peaceful transfer of power. Hundreds of United Nations observers helped to ensure that the elections went smoothly, and they played an essential role in persuading the Sandinistas to accept their defeat. But there was a price: accountability. In the period between their election loss in February 1990 and their departure from office two months later, the left-wing Sandinistas emulated right-wing dictatorships elsewhere in the hemisphere by promulgating an amnesty law intended to forgive themselves for politically motivated crimes. In the nature of such amnesties, the law also prohibited prosecution of crimes committed by the American-backed contra forces that had tried to overthrow them. If prosecutions had been permitted, much of the contra leadership could have been indicted, but the Sandinistas were willing to forgo this satisfaction to save their own skins. The United Nations said nothing about the amnesty law, and it was quietly accepted by the incoming government of Violeta Chamorro.

It was in El Salvador that the UN put down a significant human rights marker, demonstrating a new range of the possible. Its role began in October 1989 as a witness to talks between the government and the Marxist FMLN guerrillas, and several months later, as the mediator between the two sides. By July 1991, six months before the Salvadoran war ended as a result of the UN-sponsored negotiations, the mediators had put in place, with the agreement of both parties, a human rights monitoring program under UN auspices. That monitoring proved crucial in ending the war, because it persuaded the guerrillas that attacks they might suffer after laying down their weapons would gain international attention—and an international response.

The peace agreement had two other features unprecedented in the history of UN efforts to promote human rights: establishment of a UN Truth Commission and of a Salvadoran body known as the Ad Hoc Commission. The Truth Commission consisted of three members chosen by the United Nations: Belisario Betancur, former president of Colombia; Reinaldo Figuerido, former foreign minister of Venezuela; and Thomas Buergenthal, an American law professor who had served as president of the Inter-American Court of Human Rights of the Organization of American States. They were assisted by a talented staff of young Latin American human rights professionals led by Patricia Valdez, an Argentine who had directed a human rights office in Peru sponsored by the Roman Catholic Church. Their charge was to examine the abuses by both sides during twelve years of war in El Salvador—tens of thousands of killings of noncombatants that included a series of episodes, from the murder of the country's archbishop while he was saying mass to several massacres in which hundreds of peasants were killed at a time, that had aroused worldwide outrage—and to assess responsibility for these crimes.

A UN Truth Commission was a particularly appropriate means to secure accountability for El Salvador. Throughout the war, those engaged in abuses had sought either to deny that such abuses had occurred or to deny their own responsibility. The hallmark of human rights abuse in El Salvador was the "death squad" killing—typically, six or eight men wearing civilian clothes riding in unmarked vehicles who sought out their victims at their homes or places of work and gunned them down. Abundant circumstantial evidence indicated that these murders were committed by the armed forces. In the early 1980s, for example, when the largest number of such killings took place, a curfew had been in effect, and anyone on the street at night could expect to be shot. The death squads were nevertheless able to carry out their business unhampered during curfew hours. (The U.S. ambassador to El Salvador at the time, Deane W. Hinton, told me a "joke" making the rounds in those days: Two soldiers spotted a drunk on the street at 10:45 P.M. One raised his rifle and shot the drunk. When the second soldier pointed out that there were fifteen minutes to go until curfew, the first soldier responded: "I knew that guy. He lived a long way from here and never would have made it home in time anyway.")

The Salvadoran government always claimed that the killings were the work of mysterious extremist elements, a denial of responsibility backed by the Reagan and Bush administrations, which were intent on maintaining U.S. support in the face of criticism from human rights groups, the press, and Congress. In the struggle within the United States over military and financial support for the Salvadoran government, one of the most hotly debated foreign policy issues of the early 1980s, most arguments turned on the facts: Was the human rights situation improving, as the Reagan Administration insisted? Were the death squads connected to the armed forces, as human rights groups alleged? Truth was the battleground.

The United Nations Truth Commission was given less than nine months to do its job, and it released its report on March 15, 1993.[6] Among its most widely publicized findings was its account of a massacre at El Mozote in December 1981. It was carried out by an American-trained battalion, the Atlacatl, and involved the murder of close to a thousand people in a group of small hamlets where many of the villagers belonged to evangelical churches and had made determined efforts to stay out of the conflict. The massacre had been reported soon after it happened in front-page stories in *The New York Times* by Raymond Bonner and in *The Washington Post* by Alma Guillermoprieto.[7]

A few days after those accounts appeared, Assistant Secretary of State Thomas Enders, representing the Reagan administration, denied before the Senate Foreign Relations Committee that the massacre had taken place. A decade later, the United Nations Truth Commission enlisted a team of forensic scientists from Argentina (trained by Clyde Snow, who conducted the exhumation at Vukovar) to unearth the bodies of those who died at El Mozote. Most of the skeletal remains they uncovered were of very young children. The scientific investigators proved that the truth matched the reporting of Bonner and Guillermoprieto.[8]

Another of the Truth Commission's findings involved the murder of six Jesuit priests, along with their housekeeper and her daughter, in San Salvador on November 16, 1989, a crime that reverberated worldwide. The American ambassador to El Salvador, William Walker, had speculated publicly that this was the work of the FMLN guerrillas, whose purpose was to discredit the Salvadoran government. But circumstantial evidence collected at the scene of the crime by journalists and human rights investigators suggested otherwise, and in due course, a Salvadoran colonel, Oscar Benavides, and a junior officer were arrested and convicted. Even that was a cover-up, the Truth Commission determined, and it identified the higher-ups who had ordered the crime: Salvadoran defense minister General René Emilio Ponce, deputy defense minister General Juan Orlando Zepeda, Air Force chief General Juan Rafael Bustillo, and other members of the military high command.

The naming of names was important, a way to make the guilty pay a price, since it was the commission's political judgment that they could not be prosecuted. Were their rights violated in turn, as critics of the commission claimed? After all, they were not provided hearings to defend themselves and subject their accusers to cross-examination. (General Ponce wrote a letter to the commission making the point four months before it named him.) Even to dedicated defenders of civil liberties, however, this was not persuasive. Those named were spared the penalties that may be imposed after criminal due process is observed. Moreover, the reason that criminal trials could not be held in El Salvador is that those named had made them impossible. During the twelve years of the war in El Salvador, high-ranking military officers were prosecuted only once—in a case involving the kidnappings of wealthy Salvadorans for profit—and that resulted in dismissed charges after one judge was intimidated and another was murdered.

The Truth Commission also documented crimes by the FMLN, including abductions and assassinations, and identified its leaders who committed abuses, among them Joaquín Villalobos, the FMLN's top military commander. But it did not recommend prosecutions of any in the armed forces or among the guerrillas, because, it said, "there does not exist a justice system [in El Salvador] which combines the minimum requirements of objectivity and impartiality" to conduct trials. Instead, the commission called for a ten-year prohibition on holding public office for those named as committing serious human rights abuses, and their permanent exclusion from military posts. In any case, prosecution would have proved academic: Five days after the UN Truth Commission issued its report, the Salvadoran National Assembly adopted the last in a string of amnesty laws.

The work of the UN Truth Commission was complemented by the Ad Hoc Commission, a three-member body of Salvadorans appointed by the UN Secretary General. Its task was to review the Salvadoran officer corps and present recommendations for the removal or transfer of officers who did not meet three criteria: respect for human rights, professionalism, and a commitment to democracy. On

September 23, 1992, before the Truth Commission completed its work, the Ad Hoc group presented its confidential report to the UN Secretary General and to Salvadoran president Alfredo Cristiani.

The report stunned El Salvador's military leaders, who apparently had assumed little would come of the work of this commission made up of their countrymen. The commission called for the dismissal or transfer of 103 officers. Despite the confidential character of the report, it was widely known—and discussed in the press—that the list included General Ponce and General Zepeda, both subsequently named by the Truth Commission as being among those who plotted the murder of the Jesuits.

Under the peace accord, Cristiani was required to carry out the commission's recommendations by October 31, 1992. He ducked that date by arguing that the guerrillas had not complied with their agreement to demobilize all their troops. The UN worked out a new deadline for compliance: December 31, 1992. By this time, the FMLN had demobilized, and Cristiani reported to the UN that ninety-four officers had been transferred or dismissed. Of these, seven were appointed as military attachés abroad, a violation of the agreement involving the establishment of the Ad Hoc Commission. Even more flagrantly, Cristiani did not dismiss Ponce, Zepeda, and six other senior officers. On January 7, 1993, the UN Secretary General declared that the Salvadoran government had violated the peace agreement.

The UN declaration was one of the toughest stands it ever took on a human rights issue, creating a crisis for the Salvadoran government. After twelve years of war, the country desperately needed foreign assistance to rebuild. By this time, Bill Clinton had been elected president of the United States; shortly after taking office, he suspended $11 million in military aid for noncompliance with the Ad Hoc Commission. European assistance also depended on the willingness of the UN to certify compliance. Pressure mounted when the UN Truth Commission issued its report on March 15 naming Ponce and Zepeda as murderers of the Jesuits. Finally, the government cracked: On July 1, 1993, Ponce and Zepeda, along with Mauricio Vargas and Gilberto Rubios, two other generals named by the Truth Commission for covering up the Jesuit murders, were removed from their posts. (In late 1996, Vargas and an ex–guerrilla commander became co-hosts of a morning call-in radio program that quickly achieved wide popularity. The two men interviewed prominent individuals in El Salvador who had been on opposing sides in the war about many of the same issues that had been at stake in the conflict in which the hosts had fought each other.)⁹

Though no criminal penalties were imposed on the Salvadoran officers for their many crimes during twelve years of war in which more than 75,000 died, including 50,000 civilian victims of the armed forces, the UN did hold them accountable. It named names, told what crimes they had committed, and forced the dismissal of their top commanders. Because deniability had been such a crucial consideration in their crimes, official disclosure had a powerful impact. Except in countries where the armed forces were defeated militarily, or where a revolution had taken place, official disclosure had few precedents. Without the establishment of an international criminal tribunal, which was never even considered, it was the most that could be done.

In the end, the United Nations secured a measure of accountability in El Salvador because of a combination of a miscalculation by the military and the dedication to human rights of the UN negotiators. The miscalculation was the murder of the six Jesuit priests, their housekeeper, and her daughter on November 16, 1989, just a week after the fall of the Berlin Wall. Previously, the United States could be counted on to deny, explain away, or try to shift the blame for the crimes of the Salvadoran military. El Salvador was a pawn in the great struggle with the Soviet Union, and especially after the loss of Nicaragua to the Sandinistas a decade earlier, it was U.S. policy not to permit another leftist regime to take hold in Central America. But when the Jesuits were murdered, not only was America's enemy, world Communism, collapsing rapidly; at almost the same moment, the Sandinistas were under fire, about to be turned out at the ballot box, which meant Communism was about to lose its foothold in Central America. With the Cold War rationale for supporting the Salvadorans suddenly gone, the administration's defense of the Salvadoran military was halfhearted. Meantime, Congress was threatening to cut off aid to El Salvador unless the military was held accountable for human rights abuses.

The FMLN guerrillas had similar reasons at the same moment for seeking peace. Their aid from abroad also dried up with the end of the Cold War. The fall of the Sandinistas, in February 1990, meant they could expect no more help from Nicaragua. Their main regional backer, Cuba, was losing its support from the Soviet Union and was in no position to maintain aid to the FMLN.

Peace negotiations had begun in October 1989, and few placed much hope in a successful outcome. The murder of the Jesuits changed everything.

Despite shortcomings, what was achieved by the UN in El Salvador was dramatic. Peace was restored and a significant measure of respect for human rights was established in a country where the rule of law had never prevailed and where bloody abuses had made headlines for a decade. Except for isolated incidents of the sort that happen anywhere, violent, politically inspired abuses in that country have stopped. El Salvador has reverted to justifiable obscurity.

4

The Battle for Truth

Amnesty International, founded in Britain in 1961, helped to popularize human rights and, with 1.2 million members, remains the world's largest organization dedicated to the cause.

Amnesty first made its mark in its campaigns on behalf of "prisoners of conscience"—individuals who neither used nor advocated violence and who were imprisoned solely for their beliefs, expressions, or associations. The group's efforts have proved remarkably successful over the years, to the point where many countries that once locked up peaceful dissenters by the thousands no longer do so. But Amnesty's effectiveness, in one sense, fell victim to the law of unintended consequences, at least in one part of the world: Latin America.

Some recent history is instructive. Latin America, of course, is arguably where the United States has exercised its greatest influence—sometimes benign, from a human rights perspective, sometimes malign. A particularly noisome period began in the 1960s, when an America preoccupied with Fidel Castro and Cuban-inspired Communist insurgencies in the region promoted or cooperated with programs to counter them. But the military bosses of Latin American dictatorships had a decent sense of U.S. public opinion. They knew, for example, that such practices as large-scale political imprisonment of peaceful dissenters would cause waves north of the border—especially with groups like Amnesty stirring the waters—and probably would affect the congressional and White House financial support on which they counted to battle their real and imagined enemies.

The bully boys of Latin America needed a better mousetrap of repression, and soon enough they invented one. It was in Guatemala, in 1966, that the "disappearance"—the abduction of an individual or several individuals, usually followed by murder and denial of any knowledge of the missing people's whereabouts—was first noticed.[1] But during the seventies and eighties, the practice spread to other countries, including Chile, El Salvador, Honduras, Colombia, and Nicaragua. More than any other country, however, disappearances were associated with Argentina. Two related developments were responsible. First, it was in Argentina that a protest movement developed, effectively calling attention to the practice. Second, Argentina became the place where the most dramatic struggle was waged over accountability for such crimes.

The protest movement was the Mothers of the Plaza de Mayo, a group of women who assembled every Thursday afternoon in the square in front of the Casa Rosada (Pink House), the presidential palace in Buenos Aires. Occasionally joined by a few men, the middle-aged and elderly women walked around in a circle wearing kerchiefs embroidered with the names of their missing children or carrying their photographs in front of them. What they sought first, of course, was the return of their loved ones alive—and if not that, at least information about them.

But truth was anathema in what the Argentine military called "the dirty war." The phrase implied that opposing sides were struggling for control of the country and that dirty tactics were required by the very nature of the conflict. This was simply ludicrous. It imputed to the leftists a far greater threat than they actually posed and had nothing at all to do with the many innocent victims swept up and "disappeared" by the military or its agents.

In fact, the essence of the crime was deception. Typically, abductions were carried out by men in civilian clothes usually traveling in unmarked Ford Falcons, a car that unnerved many Argentines on sight because of its sinister reputation. The places to which the captives were taken were secret. Frequently, they were facilities of the armed forces ostensibly used for other purposes. In Buenos Aires, one site that became notorious for torture was the Naval Mechanical School. Disposing of the bodies secretly was also crucial. Sometimes fairly routine methods were used, such as burying them in unmarked graves in ordinary cemeteries. Others were drugged, put on planes, stripped of their clothes, flown out over the Atlantic Ocean, and tossed out—alive. Scheduled transports were flown weekly over a two-year period to eliminate traces of the disappeared.[2] The final stage of deception took place when courageous families sought information on their missing kin and were told by the military or another official agency that nothing was known or that their relatives had left the country or that they had gone into hiding with a terrorist group trying to overthrow the government. Learning what really happened acquired enormous importance to families. Many pursued every rumor and every possible lead in desperate and futile efforts to discover the truth.

But the ground already was beginning to shift, in Argentina and elsewhere. The United States began to pass laws in the mid-1970s banning military and economic assistance to human rights abusers and requiring the appointment of an assistant secretary of state for human rights. Suddenly, human rights was at the center of U.S. foreign policy. That seemed destined to change when the Reagan administration came to power in 1981, its leaders arguing that fighting terrorism was the larger issue in America's external relations. But one episode altered the balance. The confirmation of Reagan's first human rights assistant secretary had run into trouble, in part because disappearances in Argentina had become central to the Senate debate as a result of a new book by one of the rare survivors.[3] The victim, newspaper publisher Jacobo Timerman, turned up in the Senate chamber as nominee Ernest Lefever was being questioned. The standing ovation for the visitor made it clear that Lefever's nomination was doomed.

It also marked an about-face in the Reagan administration. Now the president's men and women were proclaiming their allegiance to human rights in foreign policy. But with a particular spin: None of the administration's favored lands—countries like El Salvador—were guilty of the abuses human rights groups were fighting. Conversely, those the administration opposed—like Nicaragua—were wholesale human rights abusers. Given this approach, Ronald Reagan effectively made truth the most important battleground in international human rights.

Nowhere was that battle fought more aggressively than in Argentina. If a date were to be chosen to mark the beginning of the modern global struggle for accountability for crimes committed by states, it would be December 10, 1983. On that day, Raúl Alfonsín was inaugurated the democratically elected president of Argentina, ending seven and a half years of exceptionally cruel military rule. Alfonsín immediately appointed a commission to investigate and disclose the truth about the disappearances. By then, the Reagan administration had been in office for nearly three years. During much of that period, the White House had tried to persuade Congress to assist the military regime in Buenos Aires. Leading the way was Jeane Kirkpatrick, the U.S. ambassador to the United Nations, whose doctoral dissertation had been on Argentina and who had established close ties to its generals.[4] The effort failed, but the debate it engendered helped to plant disappearances in the American consciousness—and conscience. Given Washington's long shadow in Latin America, that made the issue more critical in Argentina itself.

The commission established by Alfonsín and headed by novelist Ernesto Sábato did exemplary work. It obtained thousands of statements from witnesses, compiling more than 50,000 pages of documentation, and established the existence of 365 secret detention centers; 8,960 individual cases of disappearances were identified by the commission, which said, "We have reason to believe that the true figure is much higher." And the commission submitted to Argentine courts more than 1,800 cases for possible prosecution. Its findings were presented to Alfonsín on September 20, 1984, and its book *Nunca Mas* (Never Again), a classic of human rights reporting, was published that November.[5]

Alfonsín also ordered the prosecution of the nine members of the first three military juntas that had governed Argentina after the armed forces took power in March 1976, among them three generals—Jorge Rafael Videla, Roberto Eduardo Viola, and Leopoldo Galtieri—who had served as successive presidents. Their trial was long, and meticulous care was taken by the court to protect their rights. Much of the testimony from survivors was dramatic. It included accounts of "The Night of the Pencils," so named by the kidnappers because their victims on that occasion were high school students, and "The Night of the Neckties," a reference to a group of "disappeared" lawyers. Important testimony came from Clyde Snow, the forensic anthropologist who would exhume the mass grave at Vukovar nearly a decade later. Snow described to the Argentine tribunal his identification of a corpse buried by the military authorities as "unidentified." Liliana Peyrera, a twenty-one-year-old student, had been taken from her home by men dressed in civilian clothes. The scientific evidence presented to the court by Snow demonstrated conclusively that she had been killed by a single shot to the head fired at close range immediately after she gave birth.

During the trial, a new newspaper appeared in Argentina that published a daily transcript of the proceedings. As long as the trial lasted, it was the best-selling paper in the country.

Five of the nine defendants, including two of the former presidents, Videla and Viola, were convicted and sentenced to prison terms ranging from four and a half years for an air force general to life imprisonment for Videla. The remaining four defendants were acquitted.

Meanwhile, 2,000 private criminal cases were filed—a procedure impermissible in Anglo-American jurisprudence. Some of these cases were brought to trial. But when middle-level officers began facing prosecutions for their part in the "dirty war," they rebelled. Confronted with growing restiveness in the armed forces, Alfonsín pushed through Congress in December 1986 a Punto Final (Full Stop) law, setting a deadline of February 22, 1987, for new criminal complaints. That did not appease military men with prosecutions outstanding: In April, a group of younger officers seized a military compound and demanded an amnesty law. The rebellion was put down quickly, as hundreds of thousands of civilians poured into the streets of Buenos Aires to demonstrate support for democratic government, and fifty thousand surrounded the compound seized by the officers. Even so, Alfonsín took an extra step to mollify the rebels by sponsoring a Due Obedience Law, adopted in June 1987, that effectively exonerated officers below the rank of colonel for most crimes, including torture and murder, if they were following orders and acted in error about the legality of those orders.

That still left the highest-ranking officers who had already been convicted, as well as those against whom criminal complaints had been filed prior to the Punto Final law. They also got off, however, when Alfonsín was succeeded as president by Carlos Saúl Menem, who, in October 1989, pardoned those officers still facing trial. Fourteen months later, Menem pardoned the five junta members who had been convicted, including former presidents Videla and Viola, and two former police chiefs of Buenos Aires who had been serving prison sentences for mass murder. Finally, Menem pardoned the one Argentine officer who had fled the country when military rule came to an end, General Carlos Guillermo Suarez Mason, the self-styled "lord of life and death" in the detention centers over which he presided.

What, then, are we to make of Argentina and its pursuit of truth and justice? On the one hand, truth was served with the Sábato Commission report and the public trial of the nine junta members. On the other hand, the dispensation of justice was partial at best—partial because of the Punto Final, the Due Obedience Law, and most of all, the pardons ending prison sentences of convicted military leaders. Yet in the Latin American context, Argentina is considered to be a relatively successful instance of accountability for crimes against humanity. That judgment reflects the importance of truth in circumstances in which deception was of such enormous significance. Individual officers and their institutions were thoroughly disgraced, their claims to military virtues—honor, courage, sacrifice—demonstrably hollow when juxtaposed against the revealed details of the terrible crimes they committed and then tried to cover up.

No one could doubt the military's guilt, and on April 25, 1995, it was formally acknowledged, when General Martín Balza, chief of the Argentine Army, apologized to the nation for the crimes committed by the armed forces two decades earlier. Balza, who was out of the country during the years of the disappearances, had led forces loyal to the civilian government in putting down another military rebellion in 1990. His statement in 1995 was prompted by a controversy generated by a former naval officer who had revealed publicly his own role in the flights that dumped the disappeared into the sea. The army chief said that the military's seizure of power in 1976 had "unleashed a repression that makes us shudder today" and that he was in favor of "initiating a painful dialogue about the past that was never sustained and that acts like a ghost within the collective consciousness of the country, always returning from the shadows where it occasionally hides."[6] Balza's statement was unambiguous, reaffirming and even supplementing the truth process Argentina had undertaken in the 1980s.

•   •   •

The events in Argentina had a significant impact on Latin America. The military uprisings in the late 1980s helped to persuade political leaders in several countries that attempts to try those responsible for crimes against humanity might be imprudent at best and personally dangerous at worst. Attempts were made elsewhere to emulate Argentina's search for truth, with mixed results. In Chile, President Patricio Aylwin, inaugurated on March 11, 1990, after sixteen years of military dictatorship under General Augusto Pinochet, promptly established a National Commission on Truth and Reconciliation. Its report was meticulous, documenting 957 disappearances, as well as other clandestine abuses, and Aylwin took pains to make it meaningful to the families of victims by sending each a copy with a letter citing the page of their relative's case and apologizing on behalf of the state.

But the Chilean report suffered from sins of omission: Unlike the Sábato Commission in Argentina, its authors did not refer for prosecution those responsible for the crimes it detailed. Indeed, no attempt was made to attribute individual responsibility. Commission members said this was because naming names would violate the rights of the accused. In all likelihood, that explanation was simply protective cover for the real reasons. The military had already decreed an amnesty for its own and had refused to cooperate with investigators. Perhaps more important, Pinochet had seen to the continuing power of the armed forces by enshrining it in Chile's constitution and had threatened reprisals in the event of prosecutions.

Also, deception had not been so central to repression in Chile as it had been in Argentina. The transition to democracy played out over a longer period of time, and many of the crimes mentioned in the report were well known—the result of the Roman Catholic Church's staunch opposition to the military regime and its establishment of a Chilean human rights group that published information on abuses as they were committed. So it was hardly surprising that Pinochet did not even attempt to refute the findings of the commission when the report was published. Instead, he justified the abuses it recorded. "Its content reveals an unpardonable refusal to recognize the real causes that motivated the action to rescue the nation on September 11, 1973 [the date of the coup that brought him to power]," Pinochet told his military colleagues in an address on March 27, 1991. "The Chilean Army certainly sees no reason to ask pardon for having fulfilled its patriotic duty."

Four days later, a terrorist group assassinated a far-right senator, Jaime Guzmán, who was closely tied to Pinochet and the armed forces. The murder of Guzmán seemed to his supporters to punctuate Pinochet's point, and it abruptly curtailed public discussion of the Truth and Reconciliation Commission report. In sum, truth was not as well served in Chile as it was in El Salvador and Argentina, and justice was not achieved.[7]

AFRICA

South Africa differs from the rest of Africa in many ways, not least in its unusual sensitivity to public opinion in the West. This has been reinforced by massive press coverage, dwarfing that of any other sub-Saharan country. Indeed, except in times of great disasters, when countries such as Rwanda, Somalia, or Zaire (now, the Democratic Republic of Congo) have briefly captured world attention, it often seems that the column inches and TV time devoted to South Africa in the United States exceed the news reporting on the region's other forty-plus nations combined.

In effect, the South African government had two critical audiences during the years of apartheid—Western nations, among whom it sought acceptance, and its own white population, which ratified its legitimacy. Accordingly, though apartheid itself was completely open, many violent abuses against its enemies—murders by hit squads directed by the security services, for example—were conducted covertly. Commissions of inquiry were established from time to time, but their main purpose was to whitewash the government. Other covert actions attributed to South African security forces included deliberate efforts to foment "black-on-black" violence between supporters of Chief Mangosuthu Buthelezi's Inkatha Freedom Party and Nelson Mandela's African National Congress (ANC), which cost thousands of lives in the years before and after the fall of apartheid.

In 1990, under growing pressure from the West and in recognition that the end of the Cold War had reduced its capacity to resist that pressure, the South African government released Nelson Mandela, leader of the ANC, after twenty-eight years in prison. A year later, it established another of its commissions of inquiry to investigate violence in the black townships. This one would be different. Headed by Justice Richard Goldstone, who later would be appointed to lead the prosecution before the UN tribunals for ex-Yugoslavia and Rwanda, this commission dug much deeper than its predecessors, producing evidence that the military's intelligence agency had secretly funded private companies to provide weapons and training to Inkatha and to township gangs that engaged in violent attacks on other blacks. In April 1994, on the eve of South Africa's first nonracial elections, Judge Goldstone issued his most dramatic finding: A conspiracy to commit murder and to incite blacks to commit violent crimes against one another had reached the upper ranks of the South African police and was led by the second-ranking official of the national law enforcement agency.

Even before that startling revelation, however, President F. W. De Klerk had called for amnesty legislation, and a bill embodying his proposal was introduced in the South African Parliament on October 16, 1992. Encountering some unexpected opposition from Indian members of South Africa's racially organized tricameral Parliament, De Klerk still got his way: He circumvented Parliament by using the President's Council, a body established by the South African Constitution to deal with such eventualities, to enact the amnesty legislation. The amnesty not only exempted the security forces from prosecution for most abuses of human rights, it also allowed the government to bar disclosure of their crimes.

The ANC did somewhat better at disclosing its own abuses. Not long after his release, Mandela announced publicly that the ANC had detained and tortured some of its own members suspected of disloyalty. As De Klerk was pushing through his amnesty legislation, Mandela released a report by an independent lawyer commissioned by the ANC on brutality at camps the ANC maintained in Uganda, Tanzania, and Angola. Mandela condemned the abuses and said that the ANC leadership shared "collective responsibility" for them. A three-member commission established by the ANC to conduct a further inquiry issued a report in August 1993 providing gruesome details and named two high-ranking and several lower-ranking officials as particularly responsible. But the ANC declined to act against those it identified and allowed them to retain their posts. In addition, it gave its blessings to a Temporary Constitution, under which Mandela was inaugurated as president in May 1994, that superseded De Klerk's amnesty and granted amnesty to those on both sides of the struggle over apartheid who engaged in politically motivated crimes up to December 5, 1993.

On June 7, 1994, Mandela's minister of justice, Dullah Omar, announced the new government's policy on truth and justice. He reaffirmed the commitment to an amnesty but declined to extend it beyond the date provided in the Temporary Constitution. That meant the authors of such crimes as the assassination of Chris Hani, general secretary of the Communist Party, and a series of deadly bombings just before the April 1994 election could be prosecuted if they were caught. Omar also said that the government believed that there was a need to establish a Commission on Truth and Reconciliation "to enable South Africa to come to terms with its past. . . . If the wounds of the past are to be healed, if a multiplicity of legal actions are to be avoided, if future human rights violations are to be avoided—and indeed if we are to successfully initiate the building of a human rights culture—disclosure of the truth and its acknowledgment are necessary."

The stress placed on acknowledgment was significant. Those who sought amnesty were put on notice that the legislation the new government proposed to enact in compliance with the Temporary Constitution would not automatically abolish their crimes. It would be granted individually to those who came forward and acknowledged what they had done. If they failed to acknowledge their crimes, Omar suggested, they would not qualify for amnesty.

In January 1995, as the new law was submitted in Parliament, South Africa was racked by the disclosure that immediately prior to relinquishing power, De Klerk's government had secretly granted "administrative indemnity" to 3,500 law enforcement officials, including the minister of law and order, Adriaan Vlok; the former minister of defense, General Magnus Malan; and the commissioner of police, Johan van der Merwe. Mandela's cabinet ruled that the indemnities were not valid. For a period, the issue threatened to split the coalition government, with De Klerk saying he would have to "consider his position in the government of national unity if this decision [not to accept the validity of the secret indemnities] is firm." But Mandela didn't blink and De Klerk backed down and remained in the government.

Omar's legislation was enacted in July 1995. And later in the year, a Truth and Reconciliation Commission was formed, with Archbishop Desmond Tutu as its chairman, to conduct a wide-ranging inquiry and determine who should qualify for amnesty. The new law posed a quandary for many who committed crimes during the apartheid pe-

riod. Coming forward to acknowledge their crimes would be humiliating, and would make it impossible for many law enforcement officials to retain their jobs. Failure to come forward would expose
them to the risk of prosecution.

Even as the commission's labors were getting under way, another
test for the government of national unity was unfolding. Prosecutors
had brought criminal charges against twenty men, including Malan
and several other top officers of the Ministry of Defense, for organizing the hit squads during the era of apartheid. Under the law establishing the Truth and Reconciliation Commission, Malan and his
associates could escape punishment by confessing, disclosing the
crimes they committed, and seeking amnesty. They did not do so.
But after a lengthy trial in which the judge berated the chief prosecutor for his presentation of the case and the chief investigator who
assembled the evidence for the indictment criticized both the prosecutor and the judge, Malan and company were acquitted. Other cases
resulted in convictions. A leading assassin of antiapartheid activists,
former police colonel Eugene De Kock, was convicted in 1996 on
eighty-nine counts, including the murder of six people, and sentenced to life in prison. Following his conviction, De Kock revealed
many more crimes committed by the police and created a sensation
by alleging that a South African hit squad that operated internationally had murdered Swedish prime minister Olof Palme, an outspoken
critic of apartheid, in Stockholm.

While the Malan and De Kock trials were under way, De Klerk
appeared at a public hearing of the Truth and Reconciliation Commission, apologized for the crimes of the security forces, and acknowledged that officials in his National Party, which had ruled the
country for forty-two years, had approved "unconventional" actions
that "created the environment within which abuses and gross violations of human rights could take place." De Klerk claimed that these
actions "never included the authorization of assassination, murder,
torture, rape, assault, or the like" and that he had not "individually,
directly or indirectly, ever suggested, ordered, or authorized any such
action."[8] Who, then, was responsible for hit-squad killings and other
seemingly organized mayhem? Individual members of the security
forces acting on their own, the former president suggested.

The next day, Mandela's deputy president, Thabo Mbeki, also offered an apology—and, like De Klerk, also displayed moral obtuse-
ness. The crimes Mbeki acknowledged included the execution of

thirty-four men in ANC training camps. Yet he coupled his apology with the assertion that "it would be morally wrong and legally incorrect to equate apartheid with the resistance against it."[9] That missed the point. Apartheid and the resistance against it should not be equated. But Mbeki's attempt to justify ANC torture and murder of suspected traitors in its ranks by reference to the crimes of the other side was reprehensible in its own right.

Neither man had the last word. Top officials of the government who served with De Klerk, including Johan van der Merwe, his commissioner of police, applied for amnesty. In confessing that he directed the 1988 bombing of Khotso House, the headquarters of the South African Council of Churches, and the distribution three years earlier of booby-trapped grenades that killed eight student activists, van der Merwe said both acts had been approved by his superiors at the Ministry of Law and Order. His bosses, van der Merwe believed, had obtained approval from P. W. Botha, De Klerk's predecessor as state president. And that indirectly implicated De Klerk, since he was almost certainly a member of Botha's State Security Council, the secretive supreme body that guided government policy in the struggle to maintain apartheid. De Klerk refused to comment on van der Merwe's testimony. (An interim report by the Truth Commission in January 1997 accused De Klerk of lying to Parliament and covering up the involvement of high-ranking officers in murder and other crimes.)

As for Mbeki, the position he staked out on behalf of the ANC was denounced vehemently by Archbishop Tutu, the commission chairman. Tutu insisted that the arguments about the morality of ANC ends had no place in the consideration of ANC means used to pursue those ends. By placing his personal moral authority on the line on this issue, Tutu effectively cut the ground out from under the ANC stand.

As the Truth and Reconciliation Commission proceeded with its work, it became clear that the formula of granting amnesty individually for full disclosure and threatening prosecution of those who didn't step forward was even more powerful than its authors had imagined. Originally, December 14, 1996, had been set as the deadline for applications for amnesty. In the weeks leading up to that deadline, the commission was flooded with about a hundred new inquiries a day about amnesty. It was evident that much remained to be disclosed. For example, in the days immediately preceding the deadline, the commission started to hear from members of a military unit known as the 32 Battalion about the grotesque violence in the early 1990s that had caused hundreds of deaths on commuter trains bringing township residents to Johannesburg. Given the importance of obtaining testimony on such matters, the commission endorsed an extension of the deadline for amnesty applications to March 14, 1997. At the same time, it called for an extension of the period covered by the amnesty to May 10, 1994, the date that Mandela took office as president, to permit those who had organized the violence that took place just before the elections to come forward. Both recommendations were accepted by the Mandela government.

Truth got far less attention in the battleground to South Africa's west. In what would become known as Namibia, both South African security forces and the South-West Africa People's Organization (SWAPO) engaged in extensive abuses during a twenty-four-year struggle for independence. When independence finally arrived, in 1990, groups concerned about human rights pressed the new government of Sam Nujoma, the former SWAPO leader, for an accounting. None was provided. Instead, Nujoma, demonstrating a certain evenhandedness, appointed human rights abusers from both sides to top positions in the security services. On the one hand, for example, Colonel Gerritt Badenhorst, the South African officer in charge of interrogations and torture, got a key post—only to be suspended in March 1992 after demonstrators were beaten by police with *sjamboks* (whips made of hippopotamus hide). On the other, Solomon Hawala was appointed commander of the army. Hawala had been known as "the Butcher of Lubango" for his mistreatment of fellow SWAPO members detained on suspicion of treachery.

Among many other African countries where an accounting of the past would serve a significant role is Somalia, where crimes against humanity were committed by the government during the two decades of rule by Mohamed Siad Barre, as well as in the years of anarchy that followed his ouster in January 1991. Unfortunately, the United Nations created great confusion about accountability in the way its forces sought to capture or kill General Mohamed Farah Aidid, one of the warlords who devastated the country following the overthrow of Siad Barre. Aidid indiscriminately attacked the presumed civilian supporters of his rivals, killing thousands directly and creating conditions that led hundreds of thousands to starve. Rather than concern itself with the carnage, the UN in 1993 sought to punish Aidid for the deadly ambush of Pakistani soldiers deployed under UN auspices. Suddenly, the UN appeared to be taking sides between rival warlords and to be making the deaths of a relatively small number of UN troops seem far more important than the killing of many thousands of Somali civilians. The fact that Aidid was not killed or captured—he eventually died in 1996 of wounds suffered in factional fighting—and the fact that eighteen American soldiers were killed in the bungled attempt to apprehend him transmogrified a mass murderer into a folk hero. Moreover, the episode has had an unfortunate legacy. When the peace agreement for ex-Yugoslavia was negotiated at Dayton, the "Mogadishu factor" proved crucial. American military commanders of NATO troops in Bosnia seemed haunted by the memory of Somalia and determined to avoid "mission creep." The consequences were that their performance in Bosnia was extremely passive during the first year and a half of their deployment there and that they would insist they would arrest those sought by the tribunal only if they happened to encounter them. (Rumors have abounded that Bosnian Serb leader Radovan Karadzic and General Ratko Mladic, among others, were even permitted on various occasions to pass through NATO checkpoints unimpeded.)

Asia

In sharp contrast to Latin America, Asian nations that have committed barbarous crimes against their citizens rarely expose them to light. In twentieth-century China, for instance, the government has regularly visited horrors upon its people—chief among them the "antirightist" movement of 1957, in which hundreds of thousands of intellectuals were imprisoned or sent to the countryside, and the famine of 1959–62, caused by the Great Leap Forward, which resulted in 14 million to 30 million deaths. Deng Xiaoping was considered a reformer before the massacre in Tiananmen Square in 1989, and Deng himself suffered during the 1966–76 Cultural Revolution. Yet his government never disclosed the enormous crimes that killed millions during that period, and it greatly restricted efforts by individual victims to publish their own accounts. One of the outstanding memoirs of the Cultural Revolution is Nien Cheng's book *Life and Death in Shanghai,* which the author wrote in English and which was published first in the United States.[10] After a translation was published in China in 1987, I asked Nien whether she had noted any differences between the Chinese-language version and what she had written. Yes, she said, just one: Under the title of the book, the words "A Novel" had been added.

China is not a democracy, of course. But in Asia even democracies have trouble telling the truth to their people. Consider Japan. Japan's crimes against humanity during World War II—muted in the mind only when compared with the enormity of greater Nazi war crimes—included the enslavement, torture, rape, and murder of many millions of Koreans, Filipinos, Chinese, and other Asians, as well as the brutal mistreatment of prisoners of war from the United States, Britain, Australia, and other countries. All told, about 5,500 Japanese were tried for war crimes, though, unlike in Germany, none by the Japanese themselves; all those tried were judged by the victorious allies. Japanese judges never pronounced judgment on fellow Japanese for committing crimes against humanity.

The most notable defendants tried by the victors at the Tokyo tribunal were twenty-eight military and civilian leaders accused of principal responsibility for the "wholesale destruction of human lives, not alone on the field of battle . . . but in the homes, hospitals, and orphanages, in factories and fields." The tribunal handed down its judgment in November 1948, sentencing seven to death, sixteen to life imprisonment, and two to lesser terms. The remaining three were too ill to be sentenced. According to historian Arthur Tiedmann:

> Little moral opprobrium has attached [in Japan] to those convicted by the IMTFE [International Military Tribunal for the Far East]. A portion of the ashes of the seven executed leaders was surreptitiously obtained and placed in a shrine. . . . In 1959 a memorial stone reading "To seven patriots" was dedicated there by Yoshida Shigeru, the leading statesman of the occupation era. In 1978, Tojo and thirteen other war criminals were enshrined in a special corner of the Yasukuni Shrine [where those who died in the service of the emperor since the Meiji Restoration in 1868 are memorialized and where Shintoists worship their spirits; Japanese prime minister Ryutaro Hashimoto marked his fifty-ninth birthday in July 1996 by paying an official visit to the shrine, which also has a section commemorating the Kempeitai, Japan's counterpart to the Gestapo]. The case of Shigemitsu Mamoru, who received a seven-year sentence, indicates that conviction was not a political liability. In November 1950, he was released on parole; in the early spring of 1952, his rights were fully restored; in June 1952, he became president of the Pro-

gressive party, a major conservative group; and in December 1954, he became foreign minister.[11]

It was not until August 4, 1993, that Japan acknowledged publicly one of the ugliest practices during the war: the coercion of hundreds of thousands of women in occupied countries into brothels to service Japanese troops. The ostensible reason, postwar Japanese historian Yoshiaki Yoshimi learned from military documents he discovered, was to stop Japanese troops from committing rape in areas they controlled.

All across Asia, the issue of "comfort women," as Korean women were called by their captors, is still recalled with bitterness. Yet Japan's report and apology were grudging, with no accounts of individual suffering and no accompanying offer of compensation to surviving victims. A year later, in September 1994, in response to rising international criticism, the Japanese government announced establishment of a fund that could spend $1 billion over a ten-year period on a variety of projects that would include historical research on relations between Japan and its Asian neighbors. The purpose, according to the government's announcement, was to help Japan "look squarely at our history." But none of the money was earmarked to pay reparations to the Korean women or others who suffered at the hands of the Japanese. In June 1995, to mark the fiftieth anniversary of the end of World War II, Japan's legislature declined to go any further than a resolution of "remorse" for the suffering caused to other Asians during the war. In August 1996, a few women finally received compensation—about $19,000 each from the fund established two years earlier, contributed by "private donors" so the government could maintain its stance that any financial obligation had long since expired. Most of the eligible women, it should be noted, refused to accept what was offered them.

Another terrible chapter in Japan's World War II history was even less well known: the attempt to develop biological and chemical weapons by conducting painful and deadly medical experiments on Chinese prisoners in Manchuria. American occupation authorities had agreed not to prosecute Japanese leaders for the crimes committed by the experimenters, known as Unit 731, in exchange for information resulting from the experiments. In addition, Japanese authorities suppressed information about Unit 731. The story came to light in part because a Japanese Army surgeon who served with the unit, Ken Yuasa, in his late seventies at this writing, has been speaking out in Japan about his own experiences. According to Yuasa, "he drilled holes in the skulls of [live] prisoners to remove their brain tissue for study. He began bullet-removal demonstrations by shooting prisoners in the stomach."[12] It is estimated that at least twelve thousand prisoners were killed at Unit 731's main experimentation center, near Harbin, and that many more died at other locations where field tests were conducted.

Ian Buruma has cited what he says is "a typical textbook for high school students" that touches on the episode regarded by the rest of the world as the prime symbol of Japanese barbarism during World War II: the Rape of Nanking. In a matter of weeks, the Japanese murdered tens of thousands of Chinese civilians and raped, then mutilated or killed, an estimated twenty thousand Chinese women. Of this, the textbook says only: "In December [1937] Japanese troops occupied Nanking." A footnote adds: "At this time Japanese troops were reported to have killed many Chinese civilians, and Japan was the target of international criticism." No more.[13]

In part because of such selective history in textbooks, many Japanese feel little contrition for the acts of their leaders during World War II. Indeed, they see themselves more as victims than victimizers. Hiroshima, not Nanking, is the leading symbol of the war's cruelty in Asia, and the firebombing of Tokyo by American planes a mark of indiscriminate slaughter. John W. Dower, a historian at M.I.T., has described the indiscriminate character of American bombing of Japan during the final months of World War II:

> Precision bombing was abandoned dramatically on the night of March 9–10, 1945, when 334 aircraft attacked Tokyo at low altitude with incendiary bombs, destroying sixteen square miles of the capital city and making more than a million people homeless. Between eighty thousand and one hundred thousand died in the Tokyo raid—"scorched and boiled and baked to death" was how the mastermind of the new strategy, Major General Curtis LeMay, later phrased it. The heat from the conflagration was so intense that in some places canals boiled, metal melted, and buildings and human beings burst spontaneously into flames. It took twenty-five days to remove all the dead from the ruins. . . . [I]n the days and months that followed, incendiary attacks against urban areas became the primary U.S. aerial strategy against Japan. By May, incendiaries comprised 75 percent of the bomb loads, and in the final reckoning firebombs accounted for close to two thirds

of the total tonnage of explosives dropped on Japan. By the time Japan surrendered, 66 cities, including Hiroshima and Nagasaki, had been subjected to both precision raids and general urban-area attacks. The exact number of civilians killed by both incendiaries and the atomic bombs is uncertain, but probably was close to four hundred thousand.[14]

Buruma argues that the perception of Japan as more victim than perpetrator of crimes against humanity was one reason why the tribunal at Tokyo was less effective in creating public awareness than Nuremberg was in informing Germans. And the Japanese military, for all its brutality, never engaged in an enterprise remotely like the Nazi campaign to exterminate the Jews. Thus, while the majority of top Nazi defendants at Nuremberg were convicted of crimes against humanity, about half the top Japanese leaders tried at Tokyo were convicted only of the far more dubious crime of waging aggressive war. Furthermore, the rightful lead defendant, Emperor Hirohito, was never put in the dock, despite cries in America, Britain, China, and elsewhere that he be tried. It was General Douglas MacArthur's decision, because he considered Hirohito's authority critical to the successful occupation and reconstruction of Japan. But MacArthur's subsequent efforts to insulate the emperor from blame almost came unstuck during trial testimony. As Buruma reports it:

> During chief prosecutor Keenan's cross-examination of Tojo Hideki, the general agreed that the emperor had "consented, though reluctantly, to the war." He added that "none of us would dare act against the emperor's will." This was not at all in the scenario so carefully prepared by MacArthur. And Keenan was forced to prevail upon another defendant in the trial, Marquis Kido, keeper of the privy seal and the emperor's closest adviser during much of the war, to try to get Tojo to correct his statement. Tojo, ever a loyal subject, did so a week later. The emperor, he said, had been opposed to war. His "love and desire for peace remained the same right up to the very moment when hostilities commenced, and even during the war his feelings remained the same."[15]

By the time Hirohito died in 1989, his international image had been so completely sanitized that leaders everywhere paid tribute to him.

Europe

Who did what to whom, and when? During the five decades since the end of World War II, the issue of truth about systematic human rights violations has affected many nations across Europe. Debates have taken place in countries allied with Nazi Germany or ruled by its puppet regimes, in the countries of Central and Eastern Europe that were part of the Soviet empire, and to a lesser extent, in the countries of southern Europe that suffered under domestic Fascist rule for a time after the war.

Results are mixed. Most countries aligned with the Nazis have shied from telling the truth, some even falsifying history by portraying their own people as victims and not, as was the case with Fascist groups in several countries, as eager collaborators in criminality. Indeed, the absence of governmental efforts to disclose the culpability of their own citizens for the crimes of World War II has helped to produce a national amnesia in several countries. Hungarians know little about the extreme cruelty of the Arrow Cross. Romanians are largely unfamiliar with the viciousness of the Iron Guard, as are Lithuanians, Latvians, and Estonians about the part played by many of their people in the murders of Jews. Nor do Austrians know the extent to which their World War II antecedents were persecutors rather than victims.

Still, modest steps have been taken in some countries in Eastern Europe to acknowledge their part in Nazi crimes. On September 1, 1994, half a century after the event, the government of Estonia dedicated a memorial to two thousand Jews who were required by a force of Germans and Estonians to build their own funeral pyre before they were shot and set on fire. The prime minister of Estonia, Mart Laar, took part in the ceremony and expressed regret that Estonians engaged in "both red terrorism [that is, on the side of the Russians] and brown terrorism [as collaborators with the Nazis]." Later in the same month, Adolfas Slezevicius, prime minister of Lithuania, became his country's first high official to acknowledge collaboration with the Nazis. Discussing the murder of more than 200,000 Jews during World War II, Slezevicius said in a televised address to the nation: "Despite the fact that this Holocaust was the realization of Nazi policies in our country, we should recognize that hundreds of Lithuanians took direct part in this genocide. This obliges us to repent and ask the Jewish people for forgiveness." The reference to "hundreds"

understated Lithuanian culpability, making his statement an acknowledgment and a denial simultaneously; the same could be said
of the Estonian prime minister's use of the label "terrorism" in place
of "crimes against humanity" or "genocide."

In Western Europe, France has behaved almost schizophrenically
when it comes to acknowledging the sins of the past. Some French
artists, most prominently documentary filmmaker Marcel Ophuls
(*The Sorrow and the Pity* and *Hotel Terminus*), have unsparingly focused on French collaboration with the Nazis and the crimes committed directly by the Vichy government. Similarly, dedicated
researchers such as Serge and Beate Klarsfeld periodically unearthed
information that produced brief spasms of national discomfort. Yet
many French think of their country simply as one that suffered under
Nazi aggression and criminality and are only dimly aware of the extent to which France was an accomplice to those crimes. Even today,
many in France prefer to believe the myth of general resistance to the
Nazis. It is noteworthy that when Paul Touvier was tried and convicted in 1994 for executing seven Jews during World War II, thereby
becoming the first Frenchman ever convicted and sentenced for
crimes against humanity, the prosecution charged that he acted as an
agent of the Nazis. Actually, the evidence suggested that the Germans
were not directly involved. Touvier acted in his capacity as chief of
Milice intelligence for the Vichy regime in the Lyons region. He was
an agent of a French government.

In the Soviet empire, February 24–25, 1956, marks the first effort to
tell the truth about crimes against humanity—and may mark the beginning of the end of the empire as well. On those dates, Nikita
Khrushchev delivered his famous speech on the crimes of Stalin to
the Twentieth Party Congress in Moscow, attacking his predecessor's
"intolerance, his brutality, his abuse of power." Much of the speech
focused on the crimes committed during the years of the purge trials,
presented as excesses and as consequences of Stalin's megalomania
rather than as abuses that emerged from the nature of the Soviet system. Tens of millions had died as a result of forced collectivization or
the terrible conditions in the labor camps, and millions more were
killed during the deportations of whole peoples during World War II.
In essence, all this was attributed by Khrushchev to one evil man,
Stalin, and a few evil aides, such as secret police chief Lavrenti Beria.
"Stalin originated the concept 'enemy of the people,' " Khrushchev

told the delegates to the Congress. "This term automatically rendered it unnecessary that the ideological errors of a man or men engaged in a controversy be proved; this term made possible the usage of the most cruel repression, violating all norms of revolutionary legality, against anyone who in any way disagreed with Stalin. . . . The formula 'enemy of the people' was specifically introduced for the purpose of physically annihilating such individuals."

The content of the speech soon became known worldwide, but it was delivered only to the delegates to the Party Congress. The revelations about Stalin's crimes were made to them, not to the people of the Soviet Union, who learned about it from Western radio broadcasts. It was an acknowledgment, but only to an elite. Still, the repercussions were enormous. Thousands of prisoners from the labor camps were released and returned home. The speech helped to ignite rebellions that took place later in the year in what were known in those days as satellite countries—the uprising in Poznan, Poland, which produced unforgettable images of young men hurling stones at tanks, and even more dramatically, the Hungarian Revolution. The fallibility of those who based their claim to rule on the "scientific" character of socialism and on historical inevitability was revealed for the entire world to see. Then and there, the myth of Communism triumphant was permanently shattered.

Khrushchev's speech was not followed by further government revelations. Additional disclosures were the work of dissenters such as Alexander Solzhenitsyn, whose short novel, *One Day in the Life of Ivan Denisovich,* an autobiographical account of his own imprisonment in a labor camp, was published in 1962 in a Soviet magazine, *Novy Mir.* Solzhenitsyn's subsequent works could only be published abroad; his massive multivolume history, *The Gulag Archipelago,* began appearing in Paris in 1973 but could not be published in its author's homeland until Mikhail Gorbachev's final days as Soviet president.

In recent times, researchers have obtained access to the files of the Communist Party and the KGB, and as a consequence, additional information about the Soviet Union's repressive practices, not only during Stalin's time but also before and after, is now being revealed. But the Soviet Union under Gorbachev's glasnost never tried to produce an accounting of the crimes against humanity committed during more than seven decades of Communist rule. Neither has the Russian government under Boris Yeltsin. It would be a monumental and daunting task to compile such an accounting, and it could provide only a general outline; a comprehensive and detailed record of abuses, identifying the victims and their persecutors, seems too great a task. Nevertheless, the effort would be worthwhile. In a country that proclaimed its adherence to legality, albeit revolutionary legality, it would be important to put on the record what was done to people both in ways that conformed to the rules of the state and in ways that circumvented those rules. Only the crimes of the World War II aggressors, Germany and Japan, and those of Mao's China compare to those of the Soviet Union under Communism in the number of victims they claimed and the extent of their suffering. These warrant documentation, in Russia and the former Soviet republics and in the other East European Communist states as well.

The Communist systems of the region were built on deception. It was not the sort practiced in Latin America, where the aim was to deny that particular violent abuses were taking place or to deny that the government was culpable. Rather, the deception lay in the manner that words, such as *freedom* and *socialism,* were used; in the presentation of history and of local, national, and international events; and in the pretense of legality. All these were used to legitimize the imposition of suffering on tens of millions of people. The suffering itself requires acknowledgment, and the deceptions that were practiced in the effort to justify it require exposure. Though fixing individual responsibility may be the most difficult task of all in such situations, identifying those who were centrally involved in the administration of repression may be possible.

The United States

It should not go unremarked that America has its own history of crimes against humanity, of which the most significant, slavery and the massacres of Indians, ended in the nineteenth century.[16] In our own century, probably the darkest episode was the internment of Japanese Americans during World War II.

By now, the story is reasonably familiar to most Americans. The bombing of Pearl Harbor on December 7, 1941, produced a period of hysteria on the West Coast about the possibility of a Japanese invasion aided and abetted by Japanese Americans. Earl Warren, then attorney general of California, later to become an honored chief justice of the United States, testified at a congressional hearing that "every alien Japanese should be considered in the light of a potential fifth columnist." That no incident of sabotage could be attributed to Japanese Americans during the war's early days only proved, according to Warren, that they were biding their time.[17] Bowing to such pressure, Franklin D. Roosevelt signed an order on February 19, 1942, excluding Japanese Americans—native-born, naturalized citizens, and aliens alike—from the West Coast. About 120,000 were rounded up and taken to relocation centers. Their internment followed when the governors of states where the centers had been built refused to allow them to settle there. Accordingly, the federal government transformed the relocation centers into detention centers under the War Relocation Authority and ruled that the inmates of what Japanese Americans quickly labeled "concentration camps" could not leave without permission. Otherwise distinguished defenders of civil liberties on the Supreme Court—Harlan Fiske Stone, Hugo Black, and William O. Douglas—upheld this racially based assault on liberty.

As wartime passions faded over the years, a campaign by the victims of internment and their children and a growing sense of national embarrassment culminated in legislation, signed by President Reagan, that brought an official apology and appropriated funds to pay reparations. What happened to the Japanese Americans was a crime. Though disclosure was not critical, because there was nothing secretive about their treatment, acknowledgment of the wrongdoing mattered a great deal to the survivors, and though it took more than four decades, eventually it was forthcoming. The payment of reparations not only compensated Japanese Americans, at least partially, for financial losses, it also gave the acknowledgment of wrongdoing enhanced significance.

When the idea of a war crimes tribunal was first broached, some human rights advocates argued that accountability for the crimes in the wars in Croatia and Bosnia might be better served by a UN Truth Commission simliar to the one for El Salvador. But that seemed to miss the key point: A truth process for the Balkans would be irrelevant because there would be little to disclose. Indeed, there was no significant debate over truth. The crimes in Croatia and Bosnia were more widely and more promptly reported than ever before anywhere else, and in greater detail, by many international observers and the world's press corps. There was no precedent for highly detailed news reports almost daily over a period of years from a city under siege. Accounts of suffering from the bombardments and shortages in Sarajevo appeared in newspapers around the world, frequently on the front page, and for extended periods, powerful images were broadcast nightly on the evening news. At times, reporters managed to enter detention camps where civilians were held. They traveled with relief convoys that were turned back from towns lacking medical supplies and food. They filmed soldiers driving civilians out of their communities and burning their homes. And though they were kept out of places where torture, rape, and summary executions were then taking place, they reported extensively the testimony of survivors and, at times, the comparably horrifying accounts of those who took part in such atrocities. It was not disclosure that was lacking; what was missing was acknowledgment of their great crimes by the guilty and international insistence that they be punished. A truth report by the UN would have been disregarded.

Truth is a powerful weapon. Wherever it is lacking, it is essential that it should be provided. The identities of victims and perpetrators, the crimes committed, and the attempts made to explain them away or cover them up should all be revealed. Following a period of massive abuses, an essential part of the process of assessing responsibility and of demonstrating respect for those who suffered is the official disclosure of truth and acknowledgment of culpability. But a truth process derives much of its strength from the exposure of deception and the refutation of falsehood. When it does not serve these ends, more is required.

5

Purges and Criminal Regimes

ACCORDING TO THE *Oxford English Dictionary,* "lustration" is "the performance of an expiatory sacrifice or a purificatory rite." The ancient Romans lustrated their homes every five years by sprinkling water or rubbing objects in the house with various substances. The ancient Greeks practiced such rituals to purge entire communities of collective guilt for committing bad deeds. In our time, lustration has a particular meaning and resonance in Central and Eastern Europe, where it was the main tool used to hold accountable those responsible for human rights abuses in the former Soviet empire. Those allegedly associated with the repressive Communist regimes were purged from certain positions in government or the developing private sector.

The lustration process set off fierce debates in several countries where it was attempted, and some of its harshest critics were among the most outspoken dissenters during Communist rule. Adam Michnik, a Solidarity founder who became a legislator and newspaper editor in post-Communist Poland, was an eloquent opponent of Communist repression and spent several years in prison for his work organizing students and intellectuals. "My blackest dream," he told a conference in Salzburg, Austria, in March 1992, "is that we will take all our Communists and send them to Siberia. And then what will we have? Communism without Communists."

The lustration law of Czechoslovakia was adopted on October 4, 1991, two years after "the Velvet Revolution" that ended Communist rule peacefully and before the country split into the Czech Republic and Slovakia. It applied to agents of the state security police (known as the StB), informers and "conscious collaborators," officials of the Communist Party at the district level and up, members of the "People's Militias," and certain others with connections to agencies that implemented repression. The law defined a "conscious collaborator" as anyone listed in the files of the StB "as a confidant, a candidate of secret collaboration or as a secret collaborator of confidential contact and knowledge [who knew] he was in contact with a member of the StB and was giving him information through the form of clandestine contacts, or was implementing tasks set by him." It applied to those who held positions in the party between February 25, 1948, and November 17, 1989, the years of Communist rule, but it exempted those who held party posts between January 1, 1968, and May 1, 1969, a period that covered the "Prague Spring" of 1968, when Czechoslovakia went through rapid liberalization—crushed in August by Soviet tanks. Those covered by the law were banned from a wide variety of posts, including elective office, law enforcement, journalism, state enterprises, and senior positions in education and the military. The burden of proof was on the employee, and judicial relief was available only if a person suffered damages that caused specific harm.

In practice, lustration went further than the law provided, seemingly taking a page from the McCarthyite security purges in America in the late forties and early fifties. The minister of education, for instance, announced that he would require the lustration of all teachers and even school janitors and cafeteria employees—this despite the fact that only high-ranking academics were supposedly covered.

Opponents of the lustration law maintained that it presumed guilt by affiliation, ascribed collective guilt for Communist repression to hundreds of thousands, and lacked a fair-minded appeals process. Individual responsibility for human rights abuses should be the benchmark, the critics claimed, and the burden of proof should rest with the state. Some went even further: The very nature of the Communist system made repression so pervasive and implicated so large a segment of society that it was impossible to draw clear lines establishing individual guilt. Inevitably, grave new injustices would be done. In this view, it might be best to burn the files of the StB and start over—de facto amnesty.

Proponents of the law, on the other hand, insisted that the abuses of the past could not be wiped away. Many responsible for the suffering of others had benefited and continued to benefit in the post-Communist state. How could these advantages be justified? Moreover, it was not so much the individual acts they committed that harmed others but the entire system of Communist Party control. Accordingly, they should be penalized for holding certain positions in the party or other repressive institutions.

At the Salzburg conference where Adam Michnik spoke, I wanted to test this proposition. I asked Pavel Bratinka, a prominent member of the Czechoslovak Federal Assembly from Slovakia, whether Alexander Dubcek—the First Secretary of the Communist Party who presided over the liberal reforms of the Prague Spring and became a tragic hero in the West—would have been barred from executive office by the lustration law. Dubcek, after all, had been a party official for a decade or more before the Prague Spring. After the Soviet-led invasion, he was deposed and assigned to a lowly post as a forestry inspector in Bratislava. Two decades later, however, he returned to Prague triumphant and within a month was elected chairman of the post-Communist Federal Assembly, a position he held at the time of the Salzburg meeting. (In 1993, he died as a result of injuries sustained in an automobile accident.)

To my astonishment, Bratinka, a member of the Federal Assembly, responded that the lustration law should indeed apply to Dubcek: Party officials, to his mind, shared collective guilt for four decades of Communist repression regardless of what they had done individually.

The Federal Assembly, by this time, already had engineered a quiet purge of its own. Several months before the lustration law was enacted, in 1991, the assembly decided to vet its own members to see whether they were StB informers. Several resigned quietly when their names turned up in the files. But one refused to go without a fight, and his case came to epitomize the debate over lustration.

By the time he returned to Czechoslovakia in the midst of the Velvet Revolution, Jan Kavan had spent two decades abroad as an outspoken critic of Communist tyranny. Kavan had established the Palach Press Agency in London, which became a leading source of information on dissent in Czechoslovakia, and had promoted himself as someone who could deliver assistance to beleaguered dissenters inside the country and get information out. He also generated controversy among some human rights advocates who admired his zeal but found him truculent and competitive with others engaged in similar efforts. Even so, the human rights community esteemed Kavan as an essential source of information on one of the most tightly closed countries in the region. When he was accused of serving as an informer for the StB, most people who knew him were flabbergasted. Whatever reservations anyone had, this was inconceivable.

The Kavan case is complicated,[1] but it involves his student days in England shortly after the Prague Spring was crushed by Soviet tanks. As chairman of the association of Czech students attending British universities, Kavan had frequent contacts with the education attaché at the Czechoslovak embassy in London to discuss such matters as passport problems and scholarship issues. It turned out that the attaché was an StB agent, which Kavan says he did not know, and that the agent identified him in reports to Prague by what appeared to be a code name. Kavan's conversations with the attaché, as recorded in the files, also extended to such matters as public demonstrations by Czech students in Britain and the identities of British supporters of protests against the Soviets. Perhaps most damaging, the attaché recorded that he gave Kavan small sums of money.

Kavan, who was allowed to see only excerpts of the file containing this information, had explanations. He demanded a hearing, which was denied, then attacked the process in a flurry of articles, press statements, and lawsuits. Supporters of lustration countered by trying to discredit him. In defending the law, Petr Toman, chairman of a parliamentary investigative commission, dismissed the suggestion that anyone might have been registered as an StB collaborator unknowingly. "In the course of the *lustrace*," he told the Federal Assembly, "we asked a broad selection of StB employees whether they were familiar with the procedures. . . . All of them confirmed that a person registered as an agent knew he was in contact with an employee of the StB. . . . They excluded the possibility that a collaborator could be registered without his being aware that he was collaborating. They explained that the presence of the chief officer or his deputy was required during the binding action, and that meetings between StB officers and collaborators were supervised by superior organs."[2]

The file on Kavan dealt only with his student days and showed no further contacts with agents of the StB after 1970. His antagonists found more up-to-date ammunition, however. A videotape had been made of an encounter Kavan had with security agents when he landed at the airport in Prague in 1989 at the moment the Communists were being overthrown but before their principal instruments of repression had been dismantled. The tape showed him conversing pleasantly with the agents and, bizarrely, sharing a bottle of champagne with them. The episode might be explained away as Kavan attempting to outsmart the security police (an interpretation that also could apply to his conversations with the education attaché twenty years earlier) or the security police attempting to outsmart Kavan, or both. It was such murkiness that helped to inspire a comment by a Western writer who got to know Kavan well who told me, "I'm ninety percent sure that he is ninety percent innocent."

In November 1991, Adam Michnik went to Czechoslovakia to interview the country's president, Vaclav Havel, for his newspaper. Much of their conversation focused on the lustration process, and inevitably, they talked about Kavan. Michnik told Havel, "People gossip that last week you went with Kavan to a restaurant and you treated it as a demonstration, so that everyone could see it." Havel responded, "Indeed, I was at a restaurant with Kavan, but there was no question of any demonstration. I met with him because our mutual friend, Petr Uhl, asked me to talk to him and listen to his version of events. I did not see why I should not do it, particularly as I cooperated with Kavan during my dissident years. At that time he helped the Czechoslovakian opposition and he did a lot for us."

Havel said he had seen files on himself that listed the informers who reported on him, but he also said, "Not only did I lose this sheet of paper on the very same day, but I also forgot what names were on the list. This means that privately I opt for dropping this subject." Yet as president he could not drop it, "because people feel that the revolution has not been completed." He told Michnik:

> There are people whose lives have been destroyed by the regime, together with the lives of their families; people who spent their youth in concentration camps and who cannot easily come to terms with this.

Particularly in view of the fact that many of those who persecuted them are now better off than they are. This irritates people. Within our society there is the powerful need to face that past, to get rid of those who terrorized the nation and evidently violated human rights, to remove them from the posts they still hold. . . . I cannot deal with this problem with the same carelessness as I dealt with the fact that I had lost this list of "my own" informers.

Though Michnik expressed apprehension about the concept of an uncompleted revolution, he confessed to similar feelings of ambivalence, telling Havel:

I think that each of us must experience this unique dialectic. When I was still in prison, I made a vow concerning two things: First, that I would never join any combatant's organization that would give medals for the struggle against communism, and secondly, that I would never take revenge. But on the other hand, I kept repeating a fragment of Zbigniew Herbert's poem: "And do not forgive, as it is not within your power to forgive on behalf of those betrayed at dawn."

I believe that we are faced with this dialectic, that we can forgive only harm done to us, whereas it is not in our power to forgive harm to others. We can persuade people to do it, but if they want justice, they are entitled to get it.[3]

The distinction accepted by Michnik and Havel between their own willingness to forgive and their unwillingness to usurp the rights of others to forgive or to seek retribution is crucial. It is essential to the very idea of the rule of law. It is not up to the victims of criminality to seek vengeance; the state, acting on behalf of all, should demonstrate respect for sufferers from crime, and its seriousness about its own proscriptions against criminality, by punishing the transgressors. The victims count on the state not to overlook or forgive their victimization. They reserve this right to themselves. Yet what made the questions that the two former dissidents confronted so difficult in Eastern and Central Europe is that upon inquiry, other cases affected by lustration might turn out to resemble those of Alexander Dubcek or Jan Kavan. Neither the Communist Party posts of the former nor the purported identification of the latter as an StB informer demonstrated that they had carried out repression. While each may have been flawed, each contributed significantly to ending Communist tyranny. Eventually, on January 16, 1996, more than five years after Kavan was accused of collaboration with the StB, an appellate court cleared him of all charges.[4]

As Kavan's long ordeal and Dubcek's vilification in Czechoslovakia highlighted, presumptions of guilt based on police files and attributions of collective guilt based on party affiliations should be avoided by a state that is attempting to establish the rule of law and respect for human rights. The importance of probing the particular circumstances of each case before airing accusations in files based on informers seems especially great in states making a transition from Communist rule because an essential feature of that system was its collective judgment of those deemed to be class enemies. Even if the files based on reports provided by informers are used in good faith, there are dangers in relying on them. Much of what is contained in the files of police agencies worldwide, especially those concerned with political views and associations, is provided by people who lack accurate knowledge. Sometimes it is furnished to the police to serve the interests of the informer and is distorted for that purpose. Informers are frequently rewarded for providing data that cast a bad light on their targets. With this incentive, they may invent damaging information or present it in the way most calculated to arouse suspicions.

A further difficulty arises when informers are used by police agencies to infiltrate suspected conspiracies. Groups that are radically opposed to a regime or that conspire to subvert it tend to fear that their activities will be disclosed to the authorities. Accordingly, they limit the number of persons taken into their confidence. Knowing this, police agencies nevertheless attempt to penetrate to the core of any group of suspected subversives. Informers may be encouraged to demonstrate their trustworthiness, and therefore their entitlement to enter the innermost circles, by taking part in or even by instigating the most radical activities of the group. The route from informer to *agent provocateur* is fairly direct.

This aspect of informing has a rich history. Legend has it that two agents of Joseph Fouché, the durable police chief of the French Revolution and the Napoleonic era, unknowingly attended the same clandestine meeting and competed with each other in proposing schemes to overthrow the regime. By chance, they left at the same time, and as they reached the bottom of the stairs, they arrested each other. The informer as *provocateur* was treated satirically as early as 1908 in G. K. Chesterton's novel *The Man Who Was Thurs-*

day. Joseph Conrad's *The Secret Agent* and *Under Western Eyes* and Andre Biely's *St. Petersburg* are other novels from the early part of the century that deal with the same theme. The last of these was based on the career of a real-life informer known as Azev the Spy, who infiltrated a revolutionary group on behalf of the tsarist secret police and, in his revolutionary role, murdered leading figures of the tsar's court.

Even when informers report accurately and do not themselves instigate the offenses they disclose to police, there are inherent problems with the public disclosure of files based on their work. Inevitably, their reports are intrusions on the privacy not only of the subjects of those files but also of others identified in passing. If an informer reports that a suspected dissenter is having an extramarital affair—valuable information to the secret police for purposes of blackmail or simply to identify another possible dissenter—the disclosure will have an effect on others as well. Such personal information, accurate or not, is to be found in abundance in the files of secret-police agencies.

Much of the impetus for revealing secret-police files stems from the eagerness of the subjects of the files to know who informed on them, and from the eagerness of the general public to identify the informers. In a number of countries, political groups believe that disclosure will discredit their opponents as police informers. Others simply want to use disclosed information to condemn morally those who had betrayed them and their friends.

The question of moral condemnation has itself aroused debate among defenders of liberty who opposed the Communist system. Adam Michnik is not the only Communist-era dissenter who has argued that the entire period was one of moral ambiguity in which sharp distinctions between victims and victimizers are difficult. The Communist system, such former dissidents argue, coopted almost everyone; even many of those who are regarded as heroes for standing up against the system at certain times were collaborators out of necessity at other moments. Also, individuals adopted personal strategies to beat the system or at least to cope with it. Raw police files are too crude to allow readers to detect these subtleties so many years after the fact.

One human rights leader who has made this point is Arseny Roginsky, a Russian historian who spent the early 1980s in prison for his efforts to obtain access to archives of the state library in Leningrad (the once and future St. Petersburg) that would have shed light on Stalin-era repression. In 1989, he founded Memorial, an organization established to commemorate the victims of Stalin. Since then, Memorial also has become the leading citizens' group promoting human rights in the former Soviet Union.

At conferences on files that brought together researchers and human rights proponents from Eastern and Central Europe, Roginsky argued against indiscriminate disclosure and cited the case of the poet Anna Akhmatova, one of the giants of Russian literature. Akhmatova was fiercely anti-Stalin and at various times was denounced by the Communist Party's Central Committee and top Stalin aides. Yet her file, which Roginsky was able to see, was filled with reports by an informant—another writer, who was close to her—that maintained she was strongly patriotic, greatly admired Stalin, and had discussed with the man himself her plan to write an epic poem about him. In the period following World War II, when denunciations of Akhmatova by Communist Party officials reached a crescendo, according to Roginsky, the lies told by that informant saved Akhmatova's life.

When the Communist regime in East Germany collapsed, in 1990, its State Security Service, or Stasi, left behind political dossiers on 6 million people in a country of fewer than 17 million—files that would be 120 miles high if stacked on top of one another. When they were opened two years later, under a new law, the commission in charge, headed by Joachim Gauck, a Lutheran pastor, was stunned: The number of informers was huge. In East Berlin alone, for example, 80,000 householders submitted reports on fellow tenants and tenants' guests. It raised a definitional question: What, exactly, is an informer? In East Germany, many people had routinely collected information for various governmental agencies in a state where virtually all institutions were governmental, and the data eventually found their way into Stasi files. Some who had provided such information had surreptitiously gained the confidence of others and consciously betrayed them. Others had only elicited information that the subjects would have provided on their own, or had not known where information would wind up. Deciding how to categorize particular transactions is a complex matter; determinations often cannot be made merely by examining police files.

The larger debate in Germany, however, centered on another

question: Did the unified state have a right to sit in judgment on abuses committed in the fallen German Democratic Republic (GDR)? If so, should the institutions of the Federal Republic of Germany (FRG) be limited to condemning those acts that constituted abuses under the laws of the GDR? Or are there principles of natural law that may be invoked to judge the conduct of officials and their collaborators even when their actions did not violate the positive laws of the state in which they were committed?

Those who argued for holding informers and others responsible for abuses to account in the unified FRG defined the GDR as an *Unrechtstaat* (a state without law). Since a goal of unification was to create a *Rechtstaat* (a state under law), it was necessary to look beyond the laws of the GDR and judge the Stasi and its collaborators in accordance with universal principles of law. Klaus Kinkel, now Germany's foreign minister and previously the FRG's minister of justice, was a proponent of this point of view. Claims of being mere pawns in "systems, apparatuses, and organized collectivities" did not excuse criminal behavior, said Kinkel. Rather, each person should be held accountable for his own conduct because "even in a dictatorship, the individual's room for maneuver is just not as small as the perpetrators would like us to believe."[5]

Yet even Kinkel bent to other considerations. Prior to the fall of the Berlin Wall, relations between the FRG and the GDR had been good. Afterward, when the FRG's long-term goal of reunification was at hand, it was Bonn's policy to make the process as smooth as possible. In the end, the Unification Treaty of 1990—drafted in part by Kinkel—provided that the laws of the GDR should govern the adjudication of crimes committed in the territory of East Germany prior to the date it went into effect. This represented FRG acknowledgment of the legitimacy of the GDR and its laws, even though East German officials could have been morally condemned according to universal standards of justice.

The Unification Treaty, however, has not limited the use of non-criminal sanctions, such as disclosure of the Stasi files, to purge those identified as informers from various public posts. The files are being disclosed to schools, police departments, other government agencies, and various private bodies by Pastor Gauck's commission, which was provided with a staff of more than three thousand and an annual budget of 250 million DM (approximately $150 million) to undertake this assignment. Gauck has expressed no doubts about the probative value of the information in the Stasi files, calling them "a record of truth." There were no complexities in the GDR, as far as he is concerned.[6]

The opening of the Stasi files has had dramatic consequences. An important figure of contemporary world literature, Christa Wolf, disclosed that she had briefly served as an informer thirty years earlier. She had largely forgotten the episode but rediscovered it on seeing her Stasi file, and she published an article about it in the *Berliner Zeitung* in January 1993.[7] Gerhard Riege, a member of Parliament in unified Germany, committed suicide a few days after the files were opened, because he was identified as having been an informer in the 1950s. The chief minister of the state of Thuringia was forced to resign. Prominent athletes and coaches were stigmatized for informing on their colleagues. The number of people disgraced in this fashion has continued to grow.

In some cases, of course, they deserve to be exposed for spying on their friends and acquaintances. Others may have been tarnished unfairly. Might it have been possible to expose those who deserved exposure while protecting the innocent? One way would have been to establish a commission to examine the files confidentially. A commission could have identified informers who apparently did significant harm. The accused would then have been provided with *in camera* hearings at which they would have had a chance to defend themselves. Public disclosure would have taken place only in those cases where it was proved that such harmful informing took place and when the injured party agreed to disclosure.

This sort of case-by-case procedure would have been costly and time-consuming and, even if the German government were ready to bear the costs, might have been literally impossible given the vast number of investigations. But such considerations do not justify the disregard for due process and privacy that has occurred in the wholesale release of the Stasi files. Informing is a more morally complex matter than the summary executions and disappearances committed by some regimes. Even in cases of such violent crimes, the main arguments for identifying those responsible without hearings are that those named have threatened reprisals if efforts are made to try them and have forced the adoption of amnesty laws exempting them from criminal prosecution. In seeking to establish a *Rechtstaat,* the FRG failed to adhere scrupulously to principles of lawfulness.

•   •   •

The decommunization conducted in Germany since 1989 contrasts in nearly every respect with the denazification undertaken at the end of World War II. But understanding denazification is important because the method for carrying it out demonstrates how political considerations tend to dominate the implementation of purges.

What the Nazis did within Germany and in occupied Europe constituted crimes against humanity on a vast scale. In addition to 100,000 or so Germans who took a direct part in murder, many times that number participated in the roundups, transportation, and detention of Jews, Gypsies, and others to be slaughtered; the adoption and administration of laws and regulations stripping Jews of their jobs, their property, and their rights; and the construction of facilities where the killing took place. At the same time, literally hundreds of German industrial corporations, including many that enjoyed worldwide prestige at the time and that refurbished those reputations in the postwar years, requisitioned concentration camp inmates from 1942 until the end of the war. The corporate directors, managers, and other employees of these firms directly exploited their captive laborers, many of whom died as a consequence of the terrible working conditions. The sins of Communist East Germany, significant as they were, pale when compared with the collective crimes of the Nazis.

Even under Nazi rule, however, there were some complexities. Hannah Arendt pointed out that the denazification system, "devised to draw clear moral and political distinctions in the chaos of a completely disorganized people, actually tended to blur even the few genuine distinctions that had survived the Nazi regime. Active opponents of the regime naturally had to enter a Nazi organization in order to camouflage their illegal activities, and those members of any such resistance movement as had existed in Germany were caught in the same net as their enemies." Arendt conceded, however, that "the resistance movement . . . had so very little vitality in the first place."[8] Injustices were done in the denazification process to some anti-Nazis who felt obliged to join the party, but their numbers were small.

Under the circumstances, one would imagine that denazification would have involved far more sweeping purges than decommunization. It didn't turn out that way.

Denazification, in fact, was secondary to the main focus of the post–World War II effort—accountability in the form of thousands of criminal prosecutions before tribunals established by the Allies and, subsequently, before German courts. In contrast, the FRG prosecuted only a handful of East German officials, reflecting the fact that relatively few of their abuses of human rights in the last decades of Communist rule were defined as crimes under the domestic laws of the GDR, or under international law.

The allies agreed to denazification in August 1945 at Potsdam. A participant in the process, John H. Herz, recalled their thinking:

> [M]ost of those participating in the preparation as well as the subsequent implementation of occupation policies shared neither the so-called Henry Morgenthau ideology, according to which Germany, a nation of "aggressors through the ages," should be eliminated as an industrial entity and allowed to exist only as an agricultural country nor (as yet) the ideas of those who favored a policy of prosecuting and eliminating from office only the small number of Nazi "criminals and adventurers" who had intruded in the German elite so that a new-old Germany could be rebuilt as soon as possible. . . . The latter group foresaw the East-West split and wanted (hopefully) a united Germany as a strong Western bulwark. Those "in the middle" were anti-Morgenthau, knowing that the destruction of Germany as a modern state, even if it were desirable, would require, if not splitting the country into small and weak units, indefinite occupation by troops ready to squash the expected revanchism. But they also knew that eliminating the few Gauleiters and similar top Nazi elite would not be enough to build a democratic Germany. Too many other Germans had participated in the Nazi venture and reconfirming them in their positions would prevent the establishment of democracy on a firm basis.[9]

All three sides in this debate, according to Herz, regarded denazification as a way to shape the future Germany. Their primary concern was not accountability for past wrongdoing. Rather their intent was to use the process to create the kind of state that they hoped to see emerge from defeat. Those who prevailed, the group in the middle, sought "democratization through denazification."

Democratizing a totalitarian state responsible for a war of aggression that engulfed much of the world and committed crimes against humanity on an unprecedented scale is a worthy purpose. Yet is it compatible with an effort to establish accountability? It seems grossly unfair to subordinate the interests of those directly affected by the crimes of the Nazis to a geopolitical calculation of the future. Punishment commensurate with the crime, or with the abuse of human rights committed, concerns the past.

The forward-looking purpose of denazification was stated in the first paragraph of the preamble to the Law for Liberation from National Socialism and Militarism promulgated in the American-controlled sector of Germany on March 5, 1946: "The liberation from National Socialism and Militarism is an indispensable prerequisite to political, economic and cultural reconstruction." Article 1 developed the theme:

> To liberate our people from National Socialism and Militarism and to se-cure a lasting base for German democratic national life in peace with the world, all those who have actively supported the National Socialist tyranny, or are guilty of having violated the principles of justice and hu-manity, or of having selfishly exploited the conditions thus created, shall be excluded from influence in public, economic or cultural life and shall be bound to make reparations.

The sanctions provided under the law included fines to be used to pay reparations to victims of the Nazis, prohibitions from certain categories of employment, and in the case of "major offenders," as-signment to a labor camp for between two and ten years, permanent ineligibility to hold public office, and other restrictions. Classification of those subjected to denazification under the law was to be deter-mined by tribunals that would hear evidence presented by a prose-cutor, and the person could be represented by defense counsel. Unlike the present-day decommunization process, rules required fair proceedings, and an appellate process was provided.

Because many millions of Germans had been members of the Nazi Party or such groups as the Hitler Youth, the task was enormous. To cope with the numbers, Germans were required to fill out a ques-tionnaire (*Fragebogen*) with 131 questions. Some questions were di-rect in seeking evidence of involvement in Nazi repression. For example, question 123 asked: "Have you ever acted as an adminis-trator or trustee of Jewish property in furtherance of Aryanization decrees or of ordinances?" Others sought general biographical infor-mation such as annual income and whether the person spoke any foreign languages.

The questionnaires were used by the prosecutors to determine which cases to pursue. Most who acknowledged participation in Nazi repression characterized themselves as followers (*Mitlaeufer*—liter-ally, someone who runs along). Those found to be in this category were required to pay small fines—in worthless currency—and were denazified. Denazification was the equivalent of rehabilitation. *Mitlaeufer* could be employed in any position. According to John Herz, those found to be more deeply involved in Nazi abuses

> subsequently tried to prove that they should have been placed in the *Mitlaeufer* category or at worst judged "lesser offenders." In those cases (or also in the ones in which designated *Mitlaeufer* appealed to be exonerated), the local or appeal boards were presented with a rich array of whitewashing documents (popularly known as *Persilscheine,* after a well known brand of German soap) obtained not only from friends but also from clergymen testifying to their loyal church attendance, from fomer employees testifying to their generous attitudes as employers, and so on. On the other hand, there occurred what amounted to a "witness strike" observed by persons who might have incriminated the defendants. None of the defendants was ready to take the stand for his Nazi convictions anymore; they all claimed to have joined the party or its organizations for opportunistic reasons, to keep their jobs, and so on. While this was done in many cases involving small fry, one usually failed to differentiate between them and the big shots; all who could prove the barest of extenuating circumstances were classified followers, and the whole procedure soon became known as *Mitlaeuferfabrik* (followers factory).[10]

Herz attributed the failure of denazification to the fact that the boards were swamped and the occupation authorities became more concerned with other matters—notably, the developing Cold War. But there were other reasons, too. Victims of Nazi repression almost surely would have come forward to testify against their persecutors if they could have. They did not for obvious reasons: The Jews, Gypsies, homosexuals, mentally retarded, and others of Germany itself were dead or, in the case of most surviving Jews, had fled the country. Some returned to testify at war crimes trials, but it was not worth the burden and expense of travel to appear before denazification tribunals. Similarly, the Poles, Russians, Dutch, Belgians, and others who had suffered in Nazi-occupied Europe did not go to Germany to appear in such proceedings. At the conclusion of the war, Germany was almost entirely populated by those the Nazis considered Germans. In the event, the "witness strike" was no cause for surprise.

Perhaps even more important was the focus on creating a new Germany. The defeat of Nazi Germany and the exposure of its grotesque crimes had discredited National Socialism as an ideology, resulting, as Herz pointed out, in the absolute unwillingness of anyone to come before the tribunals and defend Nazi beliefs. Accordingly, it was easy for the occupation authorities and the Germans who administered denazification to conclude that they were succeeding in their purpose—to eliminate Nazism and to build democracy. Moreover, the Cold War and the Iron Curtain made the United States and its allies eager to portray the sectors of Germany that they occupied as part of the free world. Germans, at least West Germans, needed to feel aligned with the West in the new global struggle that loomed ahead. Purging Nazis simply was less important than proclaiming denazification a success.

The program was effectively ended by March 1948, two years after it began and three years after the end of the war. In contrast, decommunization continues nearly a decade after the fall of the Berlin Wall.

Denazification was even less serious in the French- and British-occupied zones of Germany. A more comprehensive effort to remove Nazis from significant offices was undertaken in the Soviet occupied zone, the future GDR. There too, however, it played according to the postwar script: The main purpose was to shape the future—in this case, to put Communists into the key positions of government.

It is worth noting one consequence of the failure to remove Nazis from key positions—the impact on the postwar judiciary in Germany. Among the institutions that had a particularly shameful record during the years of Nazi rule were the courts. Ingo Müller, a German law professor who was an official of the Justice Department of Bremen, has written a scathing book on the manner in which judges and lawyers served the Nazi regime,[11] pointing out that

> no matter how hard one searches for stout-hearted men among the judges of the Third Reich, for judges who refused to serve the regime from the bench, there remains a grand total of one: Dr. Lothar Kressig, judge of the Court of Guardianship in Brandenburg. . . . The degree to which the judiciary became a smoothly functioning part of the National Socialists' system of intimidation—today they prefer to say they became "enmeshed" or "entangled"—becomes clearer when one looks at the number of death sentences passed. There are no exact statistics, but Martin Hirsch, a retired judge of the federal Constitutional Court, has es-

timated that the courts handed down "at least 40,000 to 50,000 death
sentences," not counting the verdicts in the summary proceedings of the
military and the police, and that approximately 80 percent of these were
carried out.[12]

In all, Müller estimates, approximately eighty thousand judicial
death sentences were carried out during the Nazi era.

One of the trials convened by the Allies at Nuremberg focused on
Nazi jurists. Sixteen defendants were tried; four were acquitted, ten
received prison sentences of five or six years, and two were sentenced to life. There was no follow-up. "Before the mass of prosecutions of Nazi criminals came to an abrupt halt in the 1950s," according
to Müller, "German postwar judges had managed to sentence 5,288
people. Members of their own profession were not among them."[13]
Denazification had little effect on the judiciary. Müller has assembled
a mass of information demonstrating that judges who presided in
Nazi race-law trials and handed down death sentences for trivial offenses against the state were again appointed to judgeships following the war. Even the judges who were convicted at Nuremberg not
only got their pensions, but the payments they received covered the
time they spent in prison.

The contrast between what took place after World War II and
what happened after the fall of the Berlin Wall has led to some curi-
ous comparative analysis. For example, Rudolf Wasserman, a former
Higher Regional Court president, has argued that the more rigorous
approach to decommunization, compared with denazification, was
entirely appropriate, because Communism was worse. "The one
group disregarded human rights from the standpoint of race while
the other did it from the class standpoint," he has written. "The oppression in [East Germany] was even more tangible than under national socialism, because communist rule had no legitimacy at all and
people had to be forced to go along, while almost to its end, the national socialist system was based upon the broad consent of much of
its population."[14] That is, popular support for Hitler gave the Nazi
regime a measure of legitimacy. This reasoning reflects the unrecon-
structed character of a significant part of the German judiciary.

In recent years, the German judicial system has reappeared on
the radar screen of conscience. To their credit, tens of thousands of
Germans have taken part in street demonstrations to denounce the
racist assaults against foreigners committed by neo-Nazi "skinheads."

But until their performance became so notorious that it created an international scandal, German judges showed extraordinary lenience toward the thugs arrested for these crimes. Sentences of probation were handed down for those found guilty of setting fire to a hostel housing Vietnamese workers. The premeditated murder of an Angolan or a Mozambican resulted in no more than a two-year prison sentence.

Purges elsewhere after World War II were mixed. In Japan, it was an echo of Germany, with MacArthur and his associates choosing what they perceived as the more important objective—preserving Japanese institutions as a bulwark against Communism. More sweeping purges took place in countries of Nazi-occupied Europe such as France, Holland, Belgium, Denmark, and Norway, but most of these had little to do with crimes against humanity. Rather, they were assaults on people considered traitors—Nazi collaborators. And there was no shortage of witnesses: Many French and Dutch stepped forward to testify against their fellow nationals who administered the country on behalf of the Nazi conquerors. Feelings of vengeance ran so high that thousands of Frenchmen and French women were killed by other French settling scores in the year after liberation.

In our time, purges and debates over purges have not figured so significantly in other parts of the world. One reason is the differences between repression in the right-wing military dictatorships of Latin America and East Asia and the party dictatorships of Communist countries. In the former, specific crimes were committed by a limited number of military men and a few civilian allies; in the latter, great numbers took part in a pervasive system of repression. Tina Rosenberg, who has written perceptively about Latin America and, subsequently, about Central and Eastern Europe,[15] has called the military dictatorships that held power in countries such as Argentina and Chile "regimes of criminals" and the Communist dictatorships in Eastern Europe "criminal regimes" (a term that echoes Karl Jaspers's characterization of Nazi Germany as a *Verbrecherstaat*—a criminal state). Purges have become significant in dealing with regimes of criminals mainly where that remedy is a substitute for prosecutions, as in El Salvador. In contrast, the criminal regimes of the Communist system operated in a way that has made it difficult to attribute particular crimes to particular officials who might be prosecuted.

• • •

It is too early to tell whether purges will play a major part in accountability for great crimes in the former Yugoslavia. A small beginning was made at Dayton with the agreement to bar those indicted by the tribunal from holding office, thus excluding Radovan Karadzic and General Ratko Mladic from government posts. But many less notorious individuals among those indicted have continued in their public posts. Except as a way to appease the tribunal in an attempt to forestall arrests and additional indictments, the parties to the conflict are unlikely to purge their own ranks of these mass murderers, torturers, and rapists. It will be necessary to await the emergence of new political leadership in the countries of ex-Yugoslavia before a more general effort is made to bar those responsible for war crimes from government positions.

6

Doing Justice Abroad and at Home

IN THE YEARS after Nuremberg, the governments of the world signed and ratified several treaties that oblige each of them as a member of the international community to prosecute and punish those who commit great abuses of human rights. The obligation is not limited to the wartime situations covered by the 1949 Geneva Conventions and the 1977 Protocols. The 1948 Genocide Convention, for example, requires that "persons charged with genocide . . . shall be tried by a competent tribunal of the State in the territory in which the act was committed, or by such international penal tribunals as may have jurisdiction." The International Covenant on Civil and Political Rights, adopted by the United Nations in 1966, requires states to provide "an effective remedy" to "any person whose rights or freedoms . . . are violated." And the Convention Against Torture and Other Cruel, Inhuman or Degrading Treatment or Punishment, adopted by the United Nations in 1984, requires states to seek out torturers, take them into custody, and bring them to trial.

Nations have honored these obligations largely in the breach. And in some countries, what pretends to be justice is anything but.

The violent revolutions that overthrew dictators in Cuba in 1959 and in Nicaragua twenty years later swept up the innocent as well as the guilty in the trials that followed the fighting. Justice requires due process as well as accountability; in both cases, special courts failed the test, dispensing revolutionary justice, not justice. Torturers and murderers went to prison or, in Cuba, were executed, but others wrongly convicted suffered similar fates.

In the half century between the tribunals of the forties and the tribunals of the nineties, perhaps the best example of justice being done in dealing with state-sponsored crimes is Greece. The collapse of the colonels and their military dictatorship in July 1974, after seven years in power, resembled what would happen in Argentina nearly a decade later. Both regimes had practiced cruelties. Neither had been able to articulate a persuasive ideological rationale for its rule beyond a crude anti-Communism; neither had been able to manage the economy competently. And in both countries, a military adventure abroad—pursued in accordance with Henry IV's advice to his son, the future Henry V, to "busy giddy minds with foreign quarrels"— failed, and sparked the downfall.

Under Demetrios Ioannides, who succeeded George Papadopoulos as prime minister in 1973, Greece had attempted to seize control of Cyprus, where elements of the Greek majority had long agitated for union with Greece (*enosis*). Turkey invaded the island in response, raising the prospect of a war in which Greece would have fared badly. Greek and Turkish Cypriots, who had lived together peacefully in much the same way Serbs, Croats, and Muslims had in Bosnia, were forced to flee to separate parts of the island—the Greeks to the South, the Turks to the North. Many lost their land, homes, and possessions. This disaster-in-the-making, coming just as Turkish tanks were landing, provoked sharp dissension within the Greek armed forces. A group of officers forced Ioannides out, and an agreement to turn the government back to democratic control was reached quickly, with civilian leaders freed from prison. A new government was formed under Constantine Karamanlis, a former prime minister who returned from exile in Paris.

Karamanlis moved rapidly to dismantle the repressive apparatus of the dictatorship and to restore democratic institutions. Although the military dictatorship was ended by military men, Karamanlis initiated a process of "dejuntafication" that included the forced retirement of officers involved in abuses of human rights. His government also prosecuted more than a hundred public figures, military and police officers, and others for crimes such as the torture of political prisoners. Among those prosecuted were Papadopoulos and Ioannides themselves, along with thirty other officials who had ruthlessly put down student protests at Athens Polytechnic University in November 1973, killing scores of students and wounding hundreds.

Amnesty International sent observers to the leading torture trials. Their report points out that many defendants claimed, as German officers had at Nuremberg and in subsequent prosecutions, that they were only following orders.[1] These included the soldiers who actually administered torture. Other defendants were superior officers who claimed that they did not know of the tortures that were being carried out. Had both groups of defendants succeeded, no one would have been held to blame.

They did not succeed. According to Amnesty:

> If the officers' strategy was to win their subordinates' silence in court they were not highly successful. The soldier Alexander Lavranos said, "We served under them, and now they haven't the courage to take responsibility for what they ordered." "Now I'm in the dock," said soldier Dimitrios Stambolidis bitterly, "and that's because none of those in the front row [i.e., the officer defendants] will take responsibility and say, 'Yes, Sirs, they were carrying out our instructions.' . . . Our reward was to be ruined and get a bad name which will stick throughout our lives; to help them carry out their crazy ideas. They ought to have killed themselves. Instead they try to throw the blame on us."
>
> It was of course in the soldiers' interest to accuse their superiors and to shield themselves behind the position of having to obey orders. By placing officers and soldiers together in the dock at the same trial—a procedure to which some officers took exception—the prosecution prevented each group from shifting blame to the other and then trying to escape their own individual culpability.

The question of whether a soldier had to obey orders was explored at the trial. Some officers refused orders to engage in abuses and suffered harsh reprisals. One officer was severely beaten, and a guard who assisted a prisoner was "disappeared." Ordinary soldiers had more leeway, according to Major Ilias Menenakos, who refused to carry out an order to attack the students taking part in demonstrations at Athens Polytechnic. Menenakos was arrested and deported to Yaros, the site of one of the island detention centers operated by the colonels' regime. He was cross-examined by an attorney for some of the soldier defendants:

COUNSEL: Could a soldier not execute orders?

MENENAKOS: I think he could.

COUNSEL: And wouldn't he suffer for it?

MENENAKOS: I think not. But he would be transferred.

COUNSEL: But surely a soldier must execute orders.

MENENAKOS: Certainly—as far as they are legal.

COUNSEL: Has a soldier the discrimination to judge whether an order is legal or not?

MENENAKOS: Yes.

PROSECUTOR: Do not all soldiers know that it is illegal to beat someone?

MENENAKOS: Of course.

Amnesty had a few criticisms of the trial. The organization thought the attorneys did not pursue cross-examinations in sufficient depth. And it criticized the prosecution's decision not to try certain defendants in exchange for their testimony against former colleagues. (Giving witnesses immunity in exchange for testimony, a routine practice in the United States that most law enforcement officials consider essential to the criminal justice system, is rare in European trials.) On the whole, however, Amnesty evaluated the trial favorably:

[T]he overall impression is that the prosecution was fair. The defendants had the offer of representation and the opportunity to cross-examine and state their case. Moreover, if during a prosecution witness's oral evidence his testimony differed from his deposition before the examining magistrates, the prosecutor declined to question him further and placed no reliance on his previous evidence. . . . [The trial] generally met high standards of jurisprudence while apportioning blame for individual acts of physical injury and abuse of authority. Primarily, the trial has established a truth and proved a point: torture was practiced by the junta's military police on a systematic scale as a means to enforce authority, and torture can be punished by the ordinary criminal process.

Many officers were sentenced to prison terms as long as twenty-three years for torture and for operating a notorious detention center. The most severe punishments—death sentences for Papadopoulos and two other officers who led the coup that brought the colonels to power—were imposed for mutiny and high treason. Papadopoulos received a further twenty-five-year sentence for the attack at Athens Polytechnic University, and his successor, Brigadier Ioannides, was sentenced to life in prison for that massacre.

Argentina also maintained high standards in trials held before the justice phase of accountability was interrupted by Raúl Alfonsín's Punto Final and Due Obedience laws and terminated by Carlos Menem's pardons. Defendants included the highest officials in the country, men who previously had put themselves above the law. The truth process exposed them as torturers and murderers, and the justice process stripped them of their ability to avoid facing their accusers or to escape having to defend themselves. Doing justice not only signaled that the generals had lost their cloak of impunity, it also disclosed truth in a particularly powerful way. "The public presentation of truth is much more dramatic when done through a trial with the accused contributing to the development of the story," insisted the late Carlos Niño, a legal philosopher and adviser to Alfonsín. "Furthermore, the quality of narration in an adversarial trial can not be fully replicated by other means. Even when an amnesty or pardons are issued at the end of a trial, they do not counteract the initial effect of such emphatic public disclosure."[2]

But Argentina's bow to a still-restive military and its failure, in the end, to complete the justice process had an impact—and not for the good. One of its neighbors, tiny Uruguay, had been ruled by the military since 1973, with torture and political imprisonment—six thousand jailed in a country of only 3 million—all too common.

Torture, in most countries where it is practiced, occurs almost exclusively during the first two or three weeks of detention, as the police or military try to extract confessions and get detainees to identify others, or as they dispense summary punishment. In Uruguay, torture often lasted much longer, because the country's rulers wanted to break suspected Tupamaros, members of a left-wing guerrilla movement. The deliberate infliction of extreme pain did not end when detainees were remanded to regular prisons. Torture in prisons is rare, in part because inmates and their warders share the same space for extended periods, in part because guards fear reprisals and, in any event, lack the political incentives of the police and military. Again, Uruguay was different. Uruguayan correctional authorities had adopted some theories about behavior modification popularized in the 1950s and 1960s, and they employed doctors and psychologists to apply particularly nasty variations of "aversion therapy" in an attempt to remold inmates. (In the United States, where behavior modification also had its vogue, a series of lawsuits in the 1970s ended practices such as electroshock treatment and the injection of drugs that cause a sensation of suffocation as a way of modifying prisoner conduct.)

In September 1986, eighteen months after the restoration of civilian rule, President Julio Sanguinetti proposed a law to bar prosecutions of military officials for human rights abuses. At the time, private complainants already had pressed a number of criminal cases, and the Uruguayan courts were nearing a decision on how to handle them. The law submitted by Sanguinetti was quickly adopted by the Uruguayan Congress, and the possiblity of prosecutions was terminated. The Sanguinetti government's refusal to allow justice to be done fulfilled an earlier secret agreement—known as the Naval Club Pact, because of the negotiating site—between the civilians about to take power and the armed forces about to give it up. After the amnesty law was adopted, opponents attempted to overturn it through a nationwide referendum. Eventually, a vote was held on April 16, 1989. Though the amnesty law was unpopular, 53 percent of the electorate voted to uphold it. A critical factor, by all accounts, was neighboring Argentina, where military revolts against prosecutions had occurred. Many Uruguayans apparently were reluctant to risk comparable turmoil in their country; the prudent course for them was to forgo justice.[3]

Chilean lawyer José Zalaquett is one of the world's best-known and most-admired human rights activists. A large, outgoing, and generous-spirited man, with a broad knowledge and love of the arts, especially painting, Zalaquett first became prominent as a human rights defender in the mid-1970s, when he was in his thirties. He was appointed legal director of the Vicaria de la Solidaridad (Vicariate of Solidarity), an office established in the Santiago Archdiocese by Cardinal Raúl Silva Henríquez to defend victims of the Pinochet regime. In April 1976, Zalaquett, known universally as "Pepe," was arrested for the second time in a year and expelled from the country. In exile in the United States and Britain, he kept up his work for human rights and held various positions with Amnesty International. Eventually, he returned to Chile while Pinochet was still in power, because U.S. ambassador Harry Barnes interceded personally with the military government.

In November 1988, Zalaquett took part in a small meeting sponsored by the Aspen Institute on efforts to promote accountability for state crimes. A paper he presented became an influential document and served as something of a blueprint for the Truth and Reconciliation Commission in Chile established eighteen months later by President Patricio Aylwin. Zalaquett served as a member of the commission and was a principal author of its report.

In his Aspen paper, Pepe Zalaquett argued that "a policy to deal with past human rights abuses should have two overall objectives: to prevent the recurrence of such abuses and to repair the damage they caused, to the extent that is possible. Other objectives, such as retribution or revenge, cannot be considered legitimate in light of contemporary international values." To promote the legitimate objectives of accountability, he asserted, "the truth must be officially proclaimed and publicly exposed. . . . The policy must represent the will of the people," and "the policy must not violate international law related to human rights." He also called for "reparative measures" and "preventive measures" and discussed the questions of punishment and clemency.

Zalaquett never explicitly opposed punishment, but it was clear to those who read his paper and listened to him talk that the lessons he derived from Argentina had persuaded him that punishment should not be attempted in Chile. He said that he considered the capitulation of the Argentine government under military pressure a great setback not only for human rights but for the future of democratic government. It would have been better, Zalaquett argued, if the Alfonsín government had moved from the start down a different path, placing even more reliance on the truth process. "For those who would have remained unconvicted," he said, "exposure of their involvement in the crimes committed would have meant a measure (however tenuous) of punishment."

I had taken a different tack, arguing in *The New York Review of Books* that it would have been better if Argentina had limited prosecutions to the top commanders. "Punishment of officers at the higher level who were responsible for crimes would likely have been accepted by most of the Argentine population, and many in the military," I wrote. "If subordinates are prosecuted, commanders who ordered, approved or tolerated their abuses have little choice except to rally to their side. On the other hand, a commander's subordinates have no such obligation. Their loyalty is to the nation, and to the institution of the armed forces. They may defend their commanders, but as was shown in Argentina [where no signs of unrest by the military were evident so long as prosecutions focused on the commanders], this is far from certain if the state lays the groundwork for prosecuting the people ultimately in charge."[4]

Juan E. Méndez, a prominent human rights lawyer of Argentine origin, took exception to my argument in *The New York Review of Books* and to Zalaquett's report. He argued that the Alfonsín and Menem governments themselves damaged democratic authority by their timorous response to the military rebellions. Had they held firm, they would have prevailed, the judicial process would have gone forward, and democratic government would have been strengthened. In his view, "Support for trials and effective punishment grew with every step taken in the direction of accountability and with every rumbling of objection by the military." Méndez contended that exempting middle-rank officers from prosecution undermined civilian rule and that "there was no legal or moral basis to restrict prosecutions to the top officers without violating the principle that obedience to these orders is not a defense in these crimes. The ability or inability to resist a manifestly illegitimate order is a matter of proof that should have been left to courts to decide on a case-by-case basis."[5]

Zalaquett espoused a more cautious approach than either of us. A new democracy, born or reborn after an extended period of dictatorship, establishes the rule of law slowly and incrementally, he said. Such an approach was required in a country such as Chile, because "the forces that were part of or supported the government have neither lost control of armed power nor do they suffer from a lack of cohesiveness or low morale in their ranks. They are thus a formidable factor to reckon with. Experience shows that the outgoing ruling forces have stated or assumed that they will not respond for the human rights violations committed (which they either deny or attempt to justify as acts of war)." Another reason for not prosecuting in Chile, Zalaquett asserted, was that the worst forms of human rights violations ceased or subsided during the slow-motion transition from dictatorship to democracy. "The course of events facilitates a degree of popular forgiveness."[6]

But the two objectives articulated by Zalaquett—preventing recurrence and repairing damage—are potentially at odds with each other. One way to repair damage is to acknowledge the seriousness of the harm that has been done and insist that the state will act commensurately against the perpetrators. In other words: Prosecute human rights abusers and punish them if they are found guilty. How does that square with a judgment that the best prospect of preventing a recurrence lies in forgiveness?

I also dissented from Zalaquett's contention that "retribution or revenge cannot be considered legitimate in light of contemporary international values." It is true that retribution as the basis for punishment had an extended period of disrepute that reaches back to the publication of the *Essay on Crimes and Punishments* in 1764 by the Italian enlightenment philosopher Cesare Beccaria. According to Beccaria, "the object of punishment is to prevent the criminal from injuring anew his fellow citizens and to deter others from committing similar injuries." In contemporary criminology, this is "incapacitation" of the criminal—keeping him in prison for an extended period so that he cannot commit additional crimes. In *Genealogy of Morals,* Nietzsche identified eleven distinct purposes served by punishment, described his list as incomplete, and argued that utilitarian thinking could not be disentangled from the various approaches that were pursued. Continuing disdain for retributionist punishment two centuries after Beccaria is reflected in the views of a leading contemporary legal philosopher, H.L.A. Hart, who wrote that the argument for it is "a mysterious piece of moral alchemy, in which the two evils of moral wickedness [that is, criminality] and suffering [that is, punishment for purposes of retribution] are transmuted into good."[7]

In the past two decades, however, the pendulum has moved in the other direction. If punishment is based on what the criminal did, rather than on the impact on others, a determination of actual guilt becomes crucial. A retributive theory of justice turns on the arguments that society punishes to restore the equilibrium of benefits and burdens in a society unfairly disrupted by crime and that it needs to demonstrate the seriousness with which it regards its laws against criminality, its condemnation of transgressions, and its respect for victims. It follows, then, that the punishment should be proportionate to the crime. Such an approach, grounded on the thinking of Beccaria's contemporary Immanuel Kant, is fairer to criminal and victim alike, since it isn't based on speculations about the impact on others or, in the context of the debate on whether to punish the authors of state crimes, on predictions of future political developments.

Proportionality does not mean *lex talionis*—an eye for an eye, a tooth for a tooth. It does mean that the most severe punishments should be imposed on those with the highest level of responsibility for the most egregious crimes. Apprehending, prosecuting, and punishing such people should be the main goal of a policy of accountability. Those who "only followed orders" should be held responsible for their own actions and punished as well. Otherwise, a single-minded focus on the commanders moves into dangerous territory: Hitler, in this formulation, becomes single-handedly responsible for the Holocaust. Proportionality based on a theory of retribution merely holds that foot soldiers, and those who committed less serious crimes, deserve to be punished more leniently.

In Chile, doing justice was less important to many advocates of human rights than consolidating democracy, which would restore the rule of law and ensure the protection of all. The problem with this as a general proposition is that it fails to recognize in other circumstances that the victims of great crimes may be members of a despised minority, such as the Jews in Nazi Germany, the Gypsies in Romania, the Tibetans in China, or the Chechens in Russia. Should the question of punishing the perpetrators be determined by Germans, Romanians, Chinese, or Russians generally? If the will of the people governed accountability in Rwanda, where 85 percent of the population was Hutu before the genocide and a much higher percentage after it, nothing might have been done.

Questions about whether doing justice should be settled democratically have a rich history, argued most famously in the United States as the central issue in the Lincoln-Douglas debates. Stephen Douglas contended that the question of slavery was too important to resolve in any manner except through "popular sovereignty"— that is, the settlers in each of the Western territories should decide democratically whether slaveholding was to be permitted. Abraham Lincoln had said in his speech accepting the Republican nomination to run for the Senate against Douglas that "this government cannot endure permanently half slave and half free." Slavery was morally wrong, he insisted in debate against Douglas, and should be abolished nationally, not left to the will of the people in each state or territory. As president, he dealt with the issue not by referendum or even by the vote of Congress, but by means of the Emancipation

Proclamation. (Subsequently, of course, slavery was outlawed by the Fourteenth Amendment.)

For the most part, civilian governments in the other Latin American countries that underwent transitions from military rule in the 1980s also failed to do justice. Guatemala, for one, still hasn't come to grips with its past, although a modest attempt is now being made with the formation of a Clarification Commission, which is not allowed to name those who committed abuses. But its neighbor to the south is an exception. In Honduras, which has democratized in stages, some civilian officials now seem ready to deal with the crimes of the past and to end military impunity.

Honduras's human rights history isn't as notorious as Guatemala's or El Salvador's, but it isn't pretty. After the Nicaraguan revolution in 1979, the CIA had recruited Argentine military officers to help organize the opposition force that came to be known as the contras, which operated from camps across the border in Honduras. The Argentines also educated Honduran military thugs in the ways of "disappearances" and helped them establish a unit known as Battalion 3–16 to execute what they had learned against opponents of the contras. At the same time, Honduras was a place of refuge for supporters of a left-wing insurgency in another neighboring state, El Salvador. Suspected partisans of the Salvadoran guerrillas became targets of Battalion 3–16, too.

In 1988, the Inter-American Court of Human Rights ordered Honduras to pay damages to relatives of men murdered by Battalion 3–16, and after a long delay, the compensation was ultimately paid. Though this embarrassed the Honduran government, it had enacted an amnesty law and took no action against the military men involved—another case, it seemed, of justice insulted. But in 1994, a lawyer long active in the human rights cause, Carlos Roberto Reina, became president. The following year, Honduran prosecutors brought criminal charges against officers of Battalion 3–16 for kidnapping and torturing six leftist college students thirteen years earlier. What about the amnesty? Prosecutors pointed out that international law prohibits the application of amnesties to such crimes. Though the outcome of the prosecution is not known at this writing, the fact that it was brought so long after the crimes that the officers are accused of committing is a portent for the future. It suggests to military men throughout the region—in Guatemala, El

Salvador, and elsewhere—that their amnesties may not confer impunity indefinitely.

South Korea, half a world away, is another country where the armed forces acted as though they were above the law, especially in a tragic and bloody 1980 incident in the southern city of Kwangju. Students protesting the coup that had brought General Chun Doo Hwan to power were confronted by South Korean troops. In the aftermath of what came to be known as the Kwangju massacre, hundreds of students lay dead. Chun's government claimed that fewer than two hundred died in the military's violent suppression of the demonstrations. The families of some of those killed, and other critics of Chun's dictatorship, said the number was closer to two thousand.

Chun still ruled with an iron hand, but Kwangju had achieved a significance as symbolic and enduring as the Tiananmen massacre in China did nearly a decade later. The beginning of the end of military rule came in 1987. In Seoul, South Korean students began to demonstrate for democratic reforms; over several weeks, the crowds grew steadily larger. South Koreans are obsessed with college education, and student demonstrations matter more there than they do in most other countries. What made them especially important in 1987 was that Chun was unable to use lethal force to suppress them. The Seoul Olympics were scheduled for the summer of 1988, and Koreans from all walks of life saw them as an unparalleled opportunity to display their country's accomplishments to the world. A bloodbath in the streets of Seoul, a vivid reminder of Kwangju beamed everywhere by CNN, was unthinkable.

The students knew they had chosen a moment of unique security and pressed their advantage. Chun could respond only with phalanxes of police carrying full-length plastic shields to defend themselves against objects thrown by the students, and with tear gas and water cannon. Even that provided striking visual images flashed worldwide, threatening the Olympics. Unable to maintain control without ruining an event on which the entire country was fixated, Chun resigned, opening the way for a transition to democratic government.

General Roh Tae Woo won a three-way race for the presidency later in the year. But even though he was a former colleague of Chun's, Roh could not blunt mounting demands for a reckoning. Chun's critics charged him with human rights abuses and widespread corruption. He and members of his family, it was said, had amassed great wealth during his years in power.

The former military dictator's attempt to mollify public opinion was distinctively Korean: On November 23, 1988, Chun went on national television to apologize for corruption and his abuses of human rights, said that he would return certain funds to the nation, and announced his retirement to a Buddhist monastery. His apology and the money he returned fell short of expectations, but his self-abasement temporarily quelled demands for his prosecution. Subsequently, from time to time, press accounts appeared on his life in the monastery, where, it seems, he led a Spartan existence for a substantial period.

In December 1992, Kim Young Sam became the first civilian elected president of South Korea in decades. Suddenly, the possibility of prosecuting Chun was on the table again. In October 1994, however, the Seoul Prosecutor's Office announced that Chun, Roh, and other military officers who collaborated with them in seizing power in 1979 would not be prosecuted for treason, in the interests of allowing old wounds to heal. The decision seemed to foreclose a prosecution for the Kwangju massacre. But the case was reopened in 1995, when it was discovered that Roh, Chun's close associate and successor, had amassed a $650 million slush fund while he was president. After Roh was indicted for corruption, Chun finally was indicted for the Kwangju massacre. Both men were indicted for the military coup that had brought Chun to power in 1979. Chun was sentenced to death, and Roh got a prison term of twenty-two and a half years. An appeals court commuted Chun's sentence to life imprisonment and reduced Roh's sentence to seventeen years.

Then, in December 1997, Kim Dae Jung, a longtime opponent of Chun and Roh, was elected president of South Korea. During Chun's presidency, Kim had been sentenced to death, imprisoned, and eventually sent into exile allegedly for fomenting the demonstrations at Kwangju. In a gesture aimed at promoting national unity during South Korea's financial crisis, Kim announced just two days after his election that he would pardon Chun and Roh, freeing them from prison.

Among former Communist countries, Romania probably ranks second only to East Germany in the number of officials of the former regime prosecuted, but it ranks near the bottom in accountability. If anything, the trials that have taken place covered up the abuses of the Ceauşescu era.

A five-day revolution in December 1989 had toppled Ceauşescu after twenty-four years in power. I traveled to Bucharest a month later to look into the way that the new government would deal with the repression of the past, particularly how it would handle the impending trial of four top associates of the ousted dictator.

Ceauşescu and his wife had fled Bucharest after a rally in the city's main square, intended to demonstrate support for the regime, turned into a violent protest against the killings in Timisoara, the Transylvanian city where the revolution started, and against Ceauşescu rule generally. A couple of days later, the Ceauşescus were captured by Romanian troops who had joined the uprising. They were summarily executed by firing squad on Christmas Day 1989. Five weeks later, on January 27, 1990, the trial began of Tudor Postelnicu, the former interior minister; Emil Bobu, a member of Romania's Politburo; Ion Dinca, former deputy prime minister; and Manea Manescu, former vice president. The charge? Complicity in genocide, a crime defined by Romanian law as any case of mass killing. International law, in contrast, defines genocide more narrowly, restricting the crime to killing with the intent to exterminate members of a particular racial, religious, or ethnic group.

Genocide was the most serious charge that could be leveled, which helped to satisfy public expectations of tough justice. But in one critical sense, the trial was a sham. Given the positions of the defendants and the repressions of the Ceauşescu regime, diligent prosecutors could have made a strong case based on crimes committed over many years. Instead, the charge referred solely to conduct during the five-day revolution. The defendants were accused of responsibility for 689 deaths and the wounding of more than 1,200—the casualties, according to the new government, suffered during the struggle to overthrow Ceauşescu. No testimony was permitted about events prior to December 17, 1989. Most of the evidence focused on two meetings of the party executive committee in which the defendants had discussed how to crush the uprising.

The four readily acknowledged their guilt, ridiculed their former leader, and apologized for their crimes. One defendant told the court that the Romanian revolution had been fully justified. After two hours of deliberation, all four were found guilty and were given the maximum penalty: life imprisonment. Other trials followed. In the next, twenty-one officers of the Securitate, Ceauşescu's secret police, were tried in Timisoara for the violent suppression of the protests in that city. Again, no other crimes were charged, and the outcome was similar to what happened in Bucharest.

In launching quick trials and in imprisoning top officials of the previous regime, the successor government of President Ion Iliescu, which was voted out of office in 1996, did more than appease public opinion: It also did effective damage control. Iliescu and other members of his Front for National Salvation who had previously held office under Ceauşescu might have been implicated if broader charges had been brought and defendants had begun to name names. Iliescu had a long history of participation in repression, going back to his student days. "The most feared, the most extreme, of the triumvirate of YCL [Young Communist League] leaders heading the purge [of those from "bourgeois" or "anti-Communist" families] was Ion Iliescu, a young student who gave unmistakable signs of relishing his powers and his tasks as inquisitor. . . . [H]e was singled out for lightning promotion within the RCP [Romanian Communist Party]," according to a biographer of the Ceauşescus, "becoming one of the hand-picked young men owing their careers to Nicolae Ceauşescu."[8] Indeed, it was almost impossible in the Ceauşescu era for anyone in Romania to occupy a prominent position without being implicated in corruption or repression.

Prosecutions for past abuses have taken place in several other countries of Eastern and Central Europe, but without much consequence. The most significant efforts were made in Bulgaria, Albania, and East Germany, where those charged with crimes included some of the not-so-grand old men of state repression. Todor Zhivkov's rule in Bulgaria, for example, spanned the same period as General Alfredo Stroessner's in Paraguay. Both held power from 1954 to 1989, and when they fell, only Kim Il Sung of North Korea ranked ahead of them on the longevity list of the world's dictators; his forty-six-year rule, until his death in 1994, was even longer than that of Enver Hoxha in Albania, whose forty-one years in power made him the previous record holder in a Communist regime. Erich Honecker's tenure in East Germany was brief by these standards: He fell in 1989, after twenty-two years in power.

On September 4, 1992, Todor Zhivkov was convicted for misappropriating $24 million for his own use and sentenced to seven years in prison. Because of ill health, he was not jailed and was permitted to serve his sentence under house arrest until 1996, when the Bulgarian Supreme Court reversed his sentence. Zhivkov still faces charges for two episodes in which gross abuses of human rights were committed. One was the campaign that his government initiated in the mid-1980s to Bulgarianize forcibly the country's principal ethnic and religious minorities: Turks, Pomaks (ethnic Bulgarians who embrace Islam), and Gypsies. Hundreds who resisted Zhivkov's bizarre demands—Slavicizing all names, for instance—were killed in government-inspired pogroms. Some 300,000 ethnic Turks fled the country. (Most eventually returned, and since the fall of the Communist regime, relations between the Bulgarian majority and the Turkish minority have been largely amicable. Gypsies—or Roma, as many prefer to be known—continue to suffer many abuses.) The other charge against Zhivkov involves the establishment in the late 1950s of two labor camps in which many detainees died from their mistreatment. Given the passage of time and Zhivkov's age and health, the chances that these accusations will ever come to trial are remote.

Even though the Unification Treaty severely limited the scope of prosecutions, reunited Germany did manage to prosecute some officials in the East. Erich Honecker, of course, was at the top of the list. After the collapse of East Germany, Honecker fled to Moscow, in April 1990. But after the attempted coup in the Soviet capital sixteen months later, the Russians turned against him. On December 11, 1991, Honecker took refuge in the Chilean embassy in Moscow, where the ambassador was Clodomiro Almeyda, a prominent leftist who had served as foreign minister in the government of President Salvador Allende. Following the overthrow of Allende by a military coup in September 1973, Almeyda went into exile and spent several years in East Germany. In effect, Honecker sought repayment for his hospitality. Honecker also had a daughter in Chile and no doubt was aware of the Latin American tradition of allowing deposed heads of state to obtain asylum in embassies. It was a kind of professional courtesy among dictators: Given the frequent coups in the region, leaders offering asylum might need it themselves sometime later.

But Chile now had a democratic government and did not relish sheltering another dictator. Eventually, Honecker was required to leave and return to Germany, where he stood trial on forty-nine counts of manslaughter and twenty-five counts of attempted manslaughter for the shoot-to-kill policy he had ordered against any-one attempting to leave the East without permission. The trial was never completed: Honecker had cancer and in January 1993, six months after his return, he was allowed to leave Germany to join his daughter in Chile. He died there sixteen months later, on May 29, 1994.

The departure of Honecker left Germany in the embarrassing po-sition of having tried and convicted two border guards who shot and killed a young man fleeing over the Berlin Wall while having released the chief of state who established and oversaw the policy they car-ried out. In the border guards' case, decided in January 1992, the judge rejected the defense that they were following orders but handed down relatively light sentences because the defendants were "at the end of a long chain of responsibility."

Over time, many more low-level officials were prosecuted for shooting deaths at the Wall. Most of the more than fifty who were convicted got short prison terms or suspended sentences. Eventually, however, a top official paid a more serious price. Egon Krenz had been the East German Politburo member in charge of security policy before he succeeded Honecker as GDR leader. Krenz was convicted on August 25, 1997, and sentenced to six years in prison—one of the few cases of a top Communist official held criminally liable for severe human rights abuses.

What explains the scarcity of prosecutions for repressive prac-tices in the countries that were part of the Soviet empire? The list of reasons is long—the sense that many crimes are ancient history; the gradual transitions to democracy in some countries, such as Poland and Hungary; the huge number of people who shared responsibility; the flawed prosecutorial systems. Adam Michnik and other former dissenters opposed reprisals against past human rights abusers be-cause they feared a blood lust that might have led, as one of them put it, to "Robespierre justice." In Latin America, there were risks in pursuing justice: principally, the overthrow of a freshly minted civil-ian government. The countries of the former Soviet bloc, had they in-stituted trials for state crimes against their citizens during the Communist era, faced no such threats.

When it comes to initiating prosecutions long after state crimes were committed, Ethiopia joins South Africa as an exception in Africa in much the same way Honduras and South Korea are exceptions in

Latin America and Asia. The Dergue, or Provisional Military Adminis-
trative Committee (*dergue* is Amharic for "committee"), had ruled
Ethiopia between 1974, when it overthrew Emperor Haile Selassie,
until 1991, when its dictatorship was defeated by insurgent forces.
For most of that time, the Dergue was headed by Lieutenant Colonel
Mengistu Haile Mariam. Mengistu and his associates in the Dergue
professed to be Marxists, and from the time of the Ogaden War with
Somalia in 1977–78, they obtained extensive support from the Soviet
Union. In seventeen years of Dergue rule, more than 100,000 people
were killed in summary executions and disappearances. Far larger
numbers died during indiscriminate bombing of predominantly civilian communities in the wars with the insurgent groups that eventually defeated Mengistu's regime. The greatest number of civilian
deaths took place during forcible relocations of peasant populations,
and as a result of famines deliberately created by Mengistu for ideological and counterinsurgent purposes.

Mengistu himself fled to Zimbabwe when his regime fell in May
1991, and continues to live there, reportedly in comfortable circumstances, protected against extradition by the one-party government of
President Robert Mugabe. Hundreds of other Dergue officials weren't
so lucky and were arrested by the successor government of President
Meles Zenawi and held for trial. In August 1992, a Special Prosecutor's Office (SPO) was established, and more than two years later, in
December 1994, proceedings began against seventy-three top officials. By then, seven had died and twenty, including Mengistu, were
out of the country and were to be tried in absentia. Forty-six were actually present in court to hear the charges against them. To give them
time to prepare their defense, the Ethiopian court adjourned the trial,
which resumed in 1995 but has not concluded at this writing.

More than 2,000 people were detained following Mengistu's
ouster, 1,300 of them held in prison until October 1994 before being
charged. Another 3,000 or so were charged in absentia. Three additional trials began in March 1997 but ran into delays similar to the ones
that marked the first Dergue trial. Until the trials were recessed, the
defendants lacked adequate representation. Despite these shortcomings, however, the Ethiopian government, at least for a time, has made
a good-faith effort to conduct proper trials. A substantial attempt was
mounted to launch soundly based prosecutions with the creation of
the SPO; more than $1 million in international contributions helped
the SPO to recruit forty-five Ethiopian prosecutors, eight foreign ad-

visers, and a total staff, including investigators, of more than four hundred. The availability of large quantities of documents, meanwhile, made it possible to provide the court with detailed evidence.[9] Prosecutors presented to the court testimony about government radio broadcasts of long lists of those executed as "antirevolutionaries," "reactionaries," and "feudalists" and of such gratuitously cruel practices as prohibitions against mourning for executed loved ones and requirements that their families pay for the bullets used to kill them before they could recover the bodies for burial. The Ethiopian trials set a precedent of great importance for other African countries—among them Rwanda—that have suffered from crimes against humanity.

During the war in Vietnam, Americans came face-to-face with a difficult truth: Their countrymen were capable of war crimes too. Journalists were reporting stories of rape, the deliberate killing of civilians, and indiscriminate air attacks by U.S. forces. The most decorated American soldier of the Korean War, Anthony Herbert, a lieutenant colonel in Vietnam, publicly accused fellow officers of complicity in war crimes—an accusation that caused Herbert to receive a punitive reassignment. But the only Vietnam war crimes trial was the prosecution of Lieutenant William Calley and Captain Ernest Medina for the massacre at My Lai on March 16, 1988. Telford Taylor summarized what happened:

> It appears certain that the troops had been told to destroy all the structures and render the place uninhabitable; what they had been told to do with the residents is not so clear. However that may be, the accounts indicate that C Company killed virtually every inhabitant on whom they could lay hands, regardless of age or sex, and despite the fact that no opposition or hostile behavior was encountered. There were few survivors, and based on the prior population of the area, the deaths attributable to C Company in Xom Lang and Binh Dong, together with other killings said to have been perpetrated a few hours later by a platoon of B Company a few miles to the east in the subhamlet of My Hoi, amounted to about 500.
>
> There was certainly nothing clandestine about the killings. About 80 officers and men went into the Xom Lang area on the ground. Above them, at various altitudes, were gunships, observation and command helicopters. There was constant radio communication between the various units and their superiors, and these were monitored at brigade headquarters. A reporter and a photographer from an Army Public In-

formation Detachment went in with the troops and witnessed and recorded the course of events virtually from start to finish. The pilot of an observation helicopter, shocked by what he saw, reported the killings to brigade headquarters and repeatedly put his helicopter down to rescue wounded women and children. Command helicopters from the divisional, brigade and task force commanders were assigned air space over the field of action and were there at least part of the time.[10]

The military had no intention of bringing charges against those responsible for the massacre, despite widespread knowledge of the incident in the Pentagon and the Vietnam high command. But a former soldier in Vietnam heard about the incident more than a year later and finally got the attention of Representative Morris Udall (D-Ariz.), who prodded the army to investigate. Initially, the investigation proceeded in secret. It went public only when journalist Seymour Hersh found out, conducted his own investigation, and made My Lai a front-page story in papers all across America.

Three years after the massacre, Calley's court-martial began at Fort Benning, Georgia. One of the charges against him specified that he caused the deaths of "an unknown number, but no less than thirty oriental human beings, males and females of various ages" and another dealt with the deaths of "not less than seventy oriental human beings." It was alleged that Calley told his troops to "waste them." He kept urging on hesitant soldiers. In one episode, according to the indictment, "he [Calley] attempted to do bodily harm to one oriental human being, approximately two years of age, whose name and sex is unknown; that he did so by shooting at this described person."

Captain Medina, Calley's immediate superior, was charged before a court-martial at Fort McPherson, Georgia, six months later for dispatching the troops to My Lai, maintaining radio contact throughout the operation, seeing and hearing the killing, having a continuing duty to control his troops, and declining "to exercise his command responsibility by not taking necessary and reasonable steps to cause his troops to cease the killing of noncombatants." There was contradictory evidence on the question of whether the orders issued by Medina authorized the killing of noncombatants, perhaps reflecting ambiguities in those instructions.

Had Medina been convicted, it would have been logical to inquire whether his superiors also should have been prosecuted on the basis of what they knew and failed to stop. It did not come to that. Only Calley was convicted. The military court's sentence was life imprisonment, but President Richard Nixon intervened. Calley's sentence was reduced to three years, of which only about three days was spent in prison; he spent most of the rest of his sentence under house arrest at Fort Benning. His girlfriend had unrestricted visiting rights.

Calley got off much easier than one Captain Howard Levy. An army doctor, Levy was court-martialed for refusing to train Green Berets on the ground that they would use the medical skills he taught them in the commission of war crimes. He was convicted and served most of his three-year sentence under harsh circumstances in the military prison at Fort Leavenworth. In other words, refusal by Levy to obey a lawful order on the ground that this would allegedly make him complicit in war crimes was punished much more severely than the actual commission of such crimes.

7

The Trouble
with Amnesty

Aᴄᴄᴏʀᴅɪɴɢ ᴛᴏ *Black's Law Dictionary,* an amnesty is the "abolition
and forgetfulness of the offense; pardon is forgiveness. The first is
usually addressed to crimes against the sovereignty of the nation, to
political offenses; the second condones infractions of the peace of
the nation." An amnesty that meets this definition was proclaimed by
President Andrew Johnson in 1865, exempting from criminal punishment former Confederates who took an oath of unqualified allegiance to the United States. They had rebelled against the United
States, and it was the prerogative of the United States to abolish their
crimes in the interest of national reconciliation.

In our time, amnesties have been granted in a manner that
stands this definition on its head. Instead of abolishing or forgetting
crimes against their sovereignty—by those who attempt to secede
from or overthrow them, for example—states have purported to
abolish and forget the crimes of their own officials against their
people. Those decreeing amnesties, as we have seen, often manage
to be the main beneficiaries. This became popular sport in Latin
America, a tragic twist on Follow the Leader. General Augusto

Pinochet's military regime led the way in Chile by issuing an amnesty in 1978 for crimes committed by the armed forces during the previous five years. Brazil's military followed suit the next year. Then came General Efraín Ríos Montt in Guatemala (1982), the generals in Argentina (1983), Uruguay (1986), the government of President José Napoleón Duarte (1987), the Sandinistas in Nicaragua (1990), the Fujimori government in Peru (1995), and Guatemala yet again (1996).

Defending the right of a state to declare an amnesty for its own officials as well as for their opponents, President Julio Sanguinetti of Uruguay argued that

> [t]he State's obligation to administer justice cannot be performed without taking into account other State functions, of which the most important are to ensure that its citizens live together in peace. . . . The severity of the law in prescribing a penalty must be attenuated when its application would result in a greater social ill than that of allowing a crime to go unpunished. . . . In a word, the renunciation of the power of punishment is merely another way of administering justice, since the political basis of the amnesty is the same as that on which the exercise of punitive power is based: the intention underlying both of these elements, amnesty and punitive authority, is ultimately to bring peace and tranquillity to all members of the community.[1]

It's certainly true that prosecutors must be free to choose which cases to bring. The reasons for this are manifold. Criminal laws cannot be drawn to anticipate every eventuality, resources must be allocated to the prosecution of cases that seem particularly important at a given moment, and the evidence in some cases is not strong or may be difficult to develop. The judicial process also needs to demonstrate evenhandedness in law enforcement and promote to the extent it can the goals cited by Sanguinetti—peace and tranquillity. In short, there are no formulas.

But Sanguinetti makes it seem that an amnesty law or decree benefiting government officials is an exercise in prosecutorial discretion. It isn't. To the contrary, what is everywhere condemned are determinations not to prosecute because of political connections between the prosecutor and the potential defendants, because certain defendants are considered beyond the reach of the law, or because some defendants have intimidated the prosecutor with threats to retaliate by violent or other means. The peace and tranquillity that Sanguinetti expected as a consequence of the failure to prosecute the Uruguayan armed forces for their crimes was that the military would not take reprisals against its civilian institutions and would permit the maintenance of civilian rule. He could not be blamed for wanting to avoid another military coup. Acknowledging this rationale for supporting an amnesty is quite a different matter, however, than arguing that an amnesty in such circumstances is another way to administer justice.

Characteristically, amnesty laws such as Uruguay's apply to opponents of the government as well as to the military and the police. This is intended to create an illusion of symmetry and, in fact, is an affront to common sense, since—in most cases—a great many more crimes will have been committed by government forces than by the opposition. Most important, such amnesties imply moral equivalence—that the crimes of the enemies of the state should be equated with those of the state itself. This, of course, is nonsense: It is the state that is supposed to be the embodiment of the rule of law.

There seems little question that successor governments enjoy the legal authority to repudiate amnesties. Even without explicit nullification, amnesties are invalid when they conflict with international treaties that obligate states to prosecute and punish. The Geneva Conventions require states to seek out those who have committed grave breaches, the Genocide Convention demands that genocide be punished, and the Convention Against Torture mandates that cases of torture be prosecuted.[2] The usual criteria for the exercise of prosecutorial discretion may be validly invoked to determine whether particular cases are pursued, but these requirements of international law cannot be reconciled with the abolition of crimes to which they apply.

Yet another treaty binds nations in the region where amnesties have become notorious. In Latin America, most governments are parties to the American Convention on Human Rights, a treaty adopted by the Organization of American States in 1969 that entered into force in 1978, when the requisite number of states had ratified it. The OAS has established two bodies to enforce the treaty: the Inter-American Commission on Human Rights and the Inter-American Court of Human Rights. The court's decisions are binding on governments that have accepted its jurisdiction.

The court decided its most important case, *Velasquez-Rodriguez,* in 1988.[3] It involved the disappearances conducted by Battalion 3–16 of the Honduran armed forces earlier in the decade. Families of some of the victims sued, and eventually the court found the government responsible for the abduction and murder of two of the men and ordered a number of remedies, including payment of damages to the families. In addition, the court established that the Honduran government had engaged in a practice of disappearances.

The court also heard arguments over whether Honduras had a duty to punish those responsible. There is such a duty, the Inter-American body decided. The convention that the court enforces provides that the parties shall take "such legislative or other measures as may be required to give effect to those rights or freedoms" it sets forth. Though this provision of international law is not as explicit as the Geneva Conventions or the Genocide Convention in asserting an obligation to punish, the court considered that it is sufficient to require action. "Subjecting a person to official, repressive bodies that practice torture and assassination with impunity is itself a breach of duty," the court said. "If the State apparatus acts in such a way that the violation goes unpunished and the victim's full enjoyment of such rights is not restored as soon as possible, the State has failed to comply." The court also held that the provision of the convention requiring the parties "to ensure to all persons . . . the free and full exercise of those rights and freedoms" requires them to "prevent, investigate and punish any violation of the rights recognized by the Convention." It was not until seven years later, in 1995, that Honduran civilian authorities demonstrated the courage and will to prosecute military officers connected to Battalion 3–16. The Inter-American Court's decision was undoubtedly a factor.

Amnesties for state officials who committed crimes against humanity may also be invalid under national constitutions and in states with unwritten constitutions that have a common-law tradition. Francis Bacon discussed the issue nearly four centuries ago: "The King [and, therefore, anybody exercising the power that once belonged to the king] can by no previous License, Pardon or Dispensation, make an Offense dispunishable which is *Malum in se* [inherently or essentially evil]; as being against the Law of Nature, or so far against the Public Good as to be indictable at Common Law, and that a Grant of this kind tending to encourage the doing of Evil, which is the chief End of Government to prevent, is plainly against Reason and the

Common Good, and therefore Void."[4] Genocide, crimes against humanity, and war crimes meet the test of *Malum in se* and are, therefore, not "dispunishable."

Conflicts with international law or higher domestic law are not the only grounds for a successor government to invalidate exemption from punishment crimes committed under state authority. In most cases, such amnesties have been decreed by self-benefiting military regimes that usurped power. Once legitimate government is established through a democratic process, its obligation to respect the laws decreed by its dictatorial predecessor is negligible under any circumstances, least of all when that regime promulgated laws for the personal advantage of its officials. Many successor regimes do not hesitate to invalidate laws providing outsize pensions or vast properties to their military predecessors. Exemption from prosecution and punishment for great crimes is even more dubious in its legality as a corrupt act of self-interest. Democratically chosen governments intent on adhering to the rule of law have every right to refuse to go along.

Two Republican administrations in the 1980s embraced the many transitions from military dictatorship to democracy in Latin America as a great achievement of American foreign policy. Though the United States looms large in the affairs of Latin America, the self-congratulation is open to some dispute. Still, the global campaign to promote democracy launched by President Reagan in mid-1982, a year and a half after he took office, and sustained by President Bush after he succeeded Reagan in 1989, clearly played a part. Unfortunately, the concept of democracy promoted by Reagan and Bush was narrow, focusing mainly on free and fair elections. Throughout, U.S. policy did not include significant attention to the rule of law.

One of the failures of the Reagan and Bush policies in Latin America was that their administrations almost never spoke out against amnesties. Though many European governments denounced the self-amnesty proclaimed by the Argentine military in October 1983, the United States was silent. The only exception was when the Reagan administration criticized the application of El Salvador's 1987 amnesty law to the killers of Americans—the military men who murdered four U.S. churchwomen and the left-wing guerrillas who attacked an outdoor café popular with U.S. embassy staff, killing four U.S. marines in the process. The main reason successor governments in Latin America respected amnesties promulgated by dictatorial regimes was fear of a military coup if they did not. The United States might have made a big difference. If American policy in the region carried sufficient weight to foster transitions from military dictatorship to elected civilian government, it could also have bolstered civilian efforts to insist that the rule of law did not exempt military mass murderers from prosecution and punishment. Yet these concerns were ignored.

The Clinton administration did not diverge from the practices of its predecessors. Its biggest test case in the region was Haiti. In September 1991, the first freely elected president in the country's bloody history, Jean-Bertrand Aristide, was ousted by a military coup after just a few months in office. Aristide is something of a demagogue, but his brief tenure as president was marked by a dramatic reduction in human rights abuses. During the coup, however, and over the three years before he was reinstated, abuses proliferated. Reliable statistics are difficult to obtain, but it is widely estimated that the number killed in violent rights abuses during that period was between 3,000 and 4,000, making Haiti one of the most dangerous places in the hemisphere to express dissent.

The Bush administration sought Aristide's reinstatement as president, a cause taken up with vigor by the Clinton administration when it took office in January 1993. The priority Clinton gave the matter reflected his embarrassment over the flow of Haitian boat people to the United States. As a candidate for president in 1992, Clinton had criticized Bush for interdicting boats on the high seas and turning them back to Haiti. When Clinton won, there were predictions that a flotilla carrying many thousands of Haitians would be ready to set out for the United States on the day of the new president's inauguration. The prospect brought back memories of the Mariel boatlift of 1980, when more than 100,000 Cubans—many of them former inmates of prisons and mental hospitals—sailed to the United States, sparked widespread public resentment, and did considerable political damage to President Carter. Clinton reversed himself. He directed that the interdictions should continue but pledged that democratic government would be restored so that Haitians would not have to flee political persecution. Under international law, refugees fleeing because of a well-founded fear of persecution are entitled to asylum in other countries; those migrating for economic reasons have no such rights. Accordingly, the restoration of

Aristide would validate exclusion of Haitian migrants from the United States.

Negotiations with Haiti's military bosses proved difficult. They feared Aristide's oratorical powers and knew he enjoyed enormous support among Haiti's impoverished millions. If Aristide were to call for a popular uprising, it was possible that the relatively small, poorly equipped armed forces would be overrun. As long as Aristide was barred from the country, nothing of the sort was imaginable. One of the demands of the Haitian armed forces as part of the price for Aristide's return was an amnesty. Aristide himself was reluctant to agree. But the Clinton administration, like the Bush administration before it, insisted. Eventually, Aristide gave way and, along with other measures designed to reassure the military that they would be safe, a deal was concluded for the ousted president's return in October 1993, a little more than two years after he had been thrown out.

That deal was abrogated by the Haitian military, eventually leading the United States in July 1994 to seek United Nations authority for an invasion. Though the Clinton administration had lost patience with the Haitian military, the United States never abandoned its insistence on an amnesty as part of any arrangement to restore Aristide.

On September 15, 1994, President Clinton delivered a televised address to the American people to explain why the United States would invade Haiti. Human rights abuses by the military rulers of the country, headed by General Raoul Cedras, were high on the list. "Cedras and his armed thugs have conducted a reign of terror," Clinton said, "executing children, raping women, killing priests. As the dictators have grown more desperate, the atrocities have grown ever more brutal. . . . International observers uncovered a terrifying pattern of soldiers and policemen raping the wives and daughters of suspected political dissidents—young girls, thirteen, sixteen years old. People slain and mutilated, with body parts left as warnings to terrify others. Children forced to watch as their mothers' faces are slashed with machetes."

The speech implied an invasion was imminent, but Clinton made a last attempt to avoid force. A delegation headed by former president Carter that included General Colin Powell and Senator Sam Nunn of Georgia was dispatched to Haiti to negotiate with Cedras and his associates. When it was reported that U.S. troops were on their way to begin the invasion, a deal was struck by Carter and Cedras that included an amnesty—though its terms were left unclear. Despite the litany of horrors he had recited publicly, Clinton accepted the deal, and the invasion was transformed into a largely bloodless occupation. The Haitian Parliament dutifully enacted an amnesty law, but avoided specifying its elements, leaving the details to Aristide, who returned to Haiti in October 1994 to take up his duties.

Though he did not say so explicitly, it appeared that Aristide was inclined not to pursue prosecutions. He had previously resisted the efforts of the Bush and Clinton administrations to get him to agree to an amnesty. But by the time he returned to Haiti, inspired by the example of Nelson Mandela, who had taken office as president of South Africa a few months earlier, reconciliation had become the main theme of his public statements. (Mandela subsequently made plain that his concept of reconciliation did not preclude prosecutions.) One factor in Aristide's decision probably was his awareness that the Haitian judiciary lacked the capacity to conduct fair trials or even the lawyers needed to bring credible prosecutions. Critics would doubtless complain about denial of due process, and that might cost Haiti the international assistance the Clinton administration was promising (though ultimately failed to deliver) as part of the deal for Aristide's return.

At this writing, no prosecutions have been brought against Haitian military leaders or the organized thugs who were allied with them. Moreover, in mid-1996, the Clinton administration blocked a move to deport Emmanuel Constant. The founder and leader of the Front for the Advancement and Progress of Haiti (FRAPH), a paramilitary group blamed for a reign of terror during the three years of military rule, Constant had entered the United States illegally when Aristide was reinstated and, after his whereabouts were discovered, was confined in a Maryland jail for a year pending deportation. Apparently, the Clinton administration freed him as further recompense for his services to the CIA, which had paid him all the time he led FRAPH.

The case of Haiti typifies the considerations involving amnesties. There are almost always prudent reasons for going along with them, yet the effect has been to create a culture of impunity. In country after country, especially in Latin America, the armed forces have believed that they will not be held judicially accountable for torture, murder, and disappearances. The more countries that adopt amnesties and allow them to stand unchallenged, the more difficult it is to end the practice. Haitian military officers were well aware that their Latin American counterparts were amnestied just before civilian governments took over. Under the circumstances, the difficulty of denying them exemption from prosecution and punishment for thousands of killings became all the greater. Bush, Clinton, and Carter all pressed for an amnesty because it had become de rigueur in such circumstances.

In South Africa, in contrast, some proponents of human rights were themselves outspoken advocates for an amnesty. "If there is a general amnesty and it brings democracy and peace to our country, I would be thrilled," Albie Sachs said prior to the transition to majority rule. "Even if the amnesty extends to the people who tried to kill me."[5]

Albie Sachs is a white lawyer who was prominent in the African National Congress. In 1988, he had been severely injured in Mozambique, where he was then living in exile, when a bomb planted in his car tore off most of his right arm, blinded him in one eye, and caused multiple additional injuries. Following the transition to democratic government, Sachs was appointed to serve as a member of South Africa's Constitutional Court by President Mandela. Despite his personal history, he supported an amnesty and in 1996, as a judge on the Constitutional Court, joined with his colleagues to uphold its validity.

Sachs wasn't alone. Many other longtime campaigners for human rights and true democratic rule in South Africa echoed his position, arguing that an amnesty was a price the black majority needed to pay for a more or less peaceful transition. The alternative, they feared, was a sharp increase in bloodshed. Military men and police who faced prosecution and punishment for assassinations and the torture of detainees were expected to fight to the death against a transition. An amnesty was required to persuade them to allow the transition to majority rule without still more bloodshed, and so a provision for it was duly incorporated in the Transitional Constitution under which Mandela was elected.

South Africa made the best of the situation. Amnesty was granted only individually—both for officials of the apartheid regime and for activists in the movements that sought its overthrow. Each person seeking amnesty had to apply by completing a prescribed form that required detailed information on the crimes for which amnesty was sought (the commission's Amnesty Committee diverged from this requirement by granting amnesty to ANC officials who had not individually acknowledged their crimes, but the full commission took the matter to court and invalidated those grants of amnesty). Crimes had to be fully disclosed. Following submission of the form, the applicant appeared at a public hearing of the Amnesty Committee of South Africa's Truth and Reconciliation Commission to answer questions on such matters as the comprehensiveness of the disclosure, the objective of the abuse, and whether it was committed with the knowledge and approval of the agency or organization with which the applicant was associated. Amnesty was denied when the commission determined that the crime was committed for reasons of personal malice or for personal gain.

These proceedings complemented the other work of the Truth and Reconciliation Commission in disclosing and compiling a record of severe abuses of human rights during the long period covered by its mandate, from March 1960, when the Sharpeville Massacre of fifty-nine blacks took place, until May 1994, when Mandela was inaugurated as president. The required individual disclosures meant that those who planned, directed, and carried out abuses all had to acknowledge them directly to benefit from amnesty.

The South African Constitutional Court, with Sachs as one of its members, upheld the amnesty against legal challenge. As Justice John Didcott asserted, "The amnesties made available to individuals are indispensable if an essential object of the legislation is to be achieved, the object of eliciting the truth at last about atrocities committed in the past and the responsibility borne for them. The primary sources of information concerning those infamies, the perpetrators themselves, would hardly be willing to divulge it voluntarily, honestly, and candidly without the protection of exemptions from liability."[6] Elsewhere, amnesties granted to all without the requirement of individual disclosure impeded the discovery of truth; in South Africa, the process encouraged truth.

It also served to shame the perpetrators. For example, South Africans heard the confessions of the police officers who killed Steve Biko in 1977. They learned that the masked men who wreaked havoc on the commuter trains to Johannesburg in the early 1990s were not black revolutionaries, as had been believed at the time, but military agents intent on discrediting the antiapartheid struggle. And they discovered the many crimes committed under the direction of Winnie Mandela, formerly an icon of the revolutionary struggle.

•   •   •

From the moment the proposal for a war crimes tribunal for ex-Yugoslavia began to gather momentum, many proponents of prosecution and punishment feared that the process would be aborted by an amnesty. Their concern was that the parties—especially the Serbs—would decline to sign a peace agreement unless they were assured they would not face prosecution.

After indictments were issued, however, it became more difficult to make amnesty an element of a peace agreement. Early on, it might have been done with little notice; later, it would have created an uproar. It would have meant that named individuals were freed from accountability for particular crimes with which they had already been charged. When Radovan Karadzic and Ratko Mladic were reindicted for Srebrenica while the Dayton peace talks were under way, it ended any possibility of an amnesty. The public credit the United States obtained for brokering the agreement at Dayton would have been nullified if part of the deal was that the Bosnian Serb leaders escaped any penalty for a crime of that enormity.

After Dayton, Mladic continued to seek an amnesty, at least for himself. When NATO bombed Bosnian Serb positions a few months prior to Dayton, two French pilots were shot down and captured. Mladic informed the French that he would release them only if the charges against him were dismissed. Andrei Kozyrev, the Russian foreign minister who supported the proposed deal, even sought cooperation from the prosecution in The Hague. It was a nonstarter. When the pilots were released anyway, rumors abounded that the French had made a secret deal with Mladic not to arrest him. Paris vigorously denied any such thing, but suspicions have persisted to this day.

Where no indictments have been issued, general amnesties are seductive. The alternative is the potential for more conflict. To reject an amnesty may seem to manifest lack of concern for those who would suffer the consequences of a new military takeover or a prolonged war. Yet the grounds for resisting an exemption for great crimes are compelling.

That justice should be done and the appearance of justice maintained are the most important reasons to reject amnesties. But there are others—most prominently, that civilian successor governments and the international community should not yield to the equivalent of terrorist demands by ousted generals or rogue warriors. In a given situation, such as an airplane hijacking, submitting to terrorist demands may save many lives. But a consensus has developed worldwide that giving in to the demands of terrorists only inspires more terrorism. The way to stop terrorists is to ensure that they derive no profit from their acts.

Standing up to terrorism is painful. It is the same with standing up to demands for an amnesty, only more so.

PART TWO

Bosnia, Rwanda, and the Search for Justice

8

Calling for
a Tribunal:
The Right Deed
for the Wrong Reason?

O~N~ FEBRUARY 22, 1993, the Security Council of the United Nations, by unanimous vote, decided that "an international tribunal shall be established for the prosecution of persons responsible for serious violations of international humanitarian law committed in the territory of the former Yugoslavia since 1991." Resolution 808 directed the secretary general of the United Nations to submit to the Security Council a specific proposal to constitute such a tribunal. A few weeks later, on May 3, the secretary general delivered a 48-page proposal, and on May 25, again by unanimous vote, the Security Council approved it, launching an effort to appoint judges and a prosecutor. The designation of a prosecutor took a long time, for reasons that will become clear, but the judges were appointed in reasonably prompt fashion and the tribunal held its first session at The Hague, on November 17, 1993.

It would be comforting to believe that the international community, having countenanced atrocities all over the world in the decades since Nuremberg and Tokyo, had finally reversed course and said, *Enough! From now on, those who commit great crimes will pay*. The facts are more complex. Good and bad reasons led to the decision by the Security Council to deal with ex-Yugoslavia in the manner it did. The bad evoke T. S. Eliot's dictum "The last temptation is the greatest treason: To do the right deed for the wrong reason."[1]

The wrong reason for the United Nations Security Council's decision to establish a tribunal was that it was a substitute for effective action to halt Serb depredations in Bosnia-Herzegovina. Time and again, it appeared that international outrage had boiled over and might push the Security Council to employ substantial military force against the Serbs to make them stop bombarding civilian communities, wantonly destroying ancient cultural monuments, and forcibly deporting and interning noncombatants in detention camps, and to put an end to torture, rape, summary executions, and the massacres euphemized as "ethnic cleansing." But each time, until August 1995, the major powers that run the Security Council backed away from significant armed intervention. Facing domestic criticism for allowing the slaughter to continue unchecked, some governments seemed to feel obliged to show that they were doing *something*. It was in this vacuum that the proposal for a tribunal advanced until its establishment was formally approved.

The war in Bosnia began on April 6, 1992. As in Croatia ten months earlier, the outbreak of war coincided with Bosnia's declaration of independence and its recognition internationally. The critical elements in launching the war were similar as well. As in Croatia, the Serbian population in Bosnia suddenly went from being part of a dominant plurality in Yugoslavia to being a minority in a new state. At the same time, Bosnian Serb leaders such as Radovan Karadzic exploited nationalist aspirations that had been raised to fever pitch by Slobodan Milosevic, the leader of the Serbs in Serbia, during the previous five years. Still, there was an important difference between the Serbs in Croatia and the Serbs in Bosnia. In Croatia, the Serbs were a relatively small minority and the Croatians were an overwhelming majority. In Bosnia, however, the Serbs were a significant minority, nearly a third of a total population of 4.3 million prior to the war. The breakdown was 43.7 percent Slavic Muslims, 31.3 percent Serbs, and 17.3 percent Croats. Of the remainder, the largest number were Yugoslavs (mixed heritage), and the rest included the usual assortment of ethnic groups in the Balkans.

Like their counterparts in Croatia, the Serbs in Bosnia had a history of persecution that exacerbated—and exaggerated—their concerns. In some measure, that historical memory focused, as in Croatia, on World War II. In addition, a more remote history, and more distorted in popular memory, permitted leaders like Milosevic and Karadzic to fan resentment against a state dominated by Muslims. Both history and perceptions of history played a large part in the events of the 1990s.

During World War II, Bosnia was ruled by the Ustasha Croats, and many Ustasha crimes took place there. Some Muslims were Ustasha, though the great majority of Bosnian Muslims were not identified with their crimes either as perpetrators or as supporters. The leader of the Muslims in Sarajevo, a businessman named Uzeir-aga Hadzihasanovic, drafted a petition signed by a hundred prominent Sarajevan Muslims denouncing Ustasha violence against Serbs and Jews. Elsewhere in Bosnia, some Muslims allied themselves with Serb Chetniks, others with Tito's Partisans, but especially in parts of southeastern Bosnia, some Muslims did take part in Ustasha crimes. These led to massive reprisals when Chetniks overran the area, and thousands of Muslims were massacred in the region in the latter part of 1942 and early 1943. This, in turn, aroused Muslim antagonism to the Chetniks. "A terrible system of mutually fueled enmities was now at work" in the region, according to British historian Noel Malcolm. "The more Muslims there were joining the Partisans, the more the Chetniks regarded Muslims as such as their foes; and the worse the killings of Muslims by the Chetniks became, the more likely local Muslims were to cooperate with Partisan, German, Italian or NDH [Ustasha] forces against the Chetniks."[2]

The victims of the Ustasha in Bosnia and Croatia were Jews and Gypsies, as they were in most of Nazi-occupied Europe. But Serbs in Bosnia died in far greater numbers, with Ustasha criminality horrifying even their Fascist allies. Italian troops stationed in coastal areas frequently intervened to save intended victims of the Ustasha, which meant they sometimes found themselves on the same side as Serb guerrillas, their ostensible enemies in the war. That some Jews survived the Ustasha is attributable primarily to the Italian troops, who sheltered them and prevented them from being butchered.

German forces on the scene were content to see the Jews slaughtered, but they were appalled by the massacres of the Serbs and by the cruelty with which they were carried out. A 1941 SS report stated:

"The Ustasha units have carried out the atrocities not only against male Orthodox of military age, but in particular against unarmed men, women and children." Edmund Glaise von Horstenau, the German plenipotentiary general on the scene, put it more directly in another report: "According to reliable reports from countless German military and civilian observers during the last few weeks, in country and town, the Ustasha have gone raging mad."[3]

Jasenovac, the Ustasha death camp in Croatia that warrants designation as the Yugoslav Auschwitz, began operation in 1941. Poison gas was used at Jasenovac, as it was at Auschwitz, although the great majority of the tens of thousands killed there were hanged, clubbed, stabbed, burned, or buried alive. The killers included several Franciscan priests, who apparently considered that they were engaged in a holy war for the triumph of Catholicism over Eastern Orthodoxy. They seemed to respond to the crude mathematics of a leading NDH official, Mile Budak, a writer of popular nationalist novels before the war. Budak argued that a third of the nearly 2 million Serbs in Croatia and Bosnia should be converted to Catholicism, a third should be expelled, and a third should die. Budak's call was published in the newspaper *Hrvatski List* on June 26, 1941. The same day, the conference of Catholic bishops met in Zagreb under the leadership of Archbishop Alojzije Stepinac and resolved to meet with the leader of the Ustasha state, Ante Pavelic, to express their support. Stepinac told Pavelic, "We, the legitimate representatives of the Church of God in the NDH, give you, its Head of Government, our heartfelt greetings, with the promise of our loyal and true cooperation."[4]

There were atrocities, of course, on all sides. One of the bloodiest incidents, for example, took place at Foca, a mountain town in southeastern Bosnia. In 1941, in reprisal for Muslim participation in Ustasha atrocities, Serb Chetniks who overran Foca reportedly rounded up more than three thousand local Muslims, tied them, and threw them off a bridge to drown in the river below.[5] (Foca was also the site, a half century later, of some of the most severe abuses by Serb forces during the "ethnic cleansing" of the region in 1992.)

For all the great crimes committed, there were few trials in postwar Yugoslavia. The principal Ustasha leaders—among them Pavelic, Budak, the commander of the Jasenovac death camp, and the archbishop of Sarajevo, who led the forces in the Catholic Church urging on the slaughter of Orthodox Serbs—all fled the country. Political factors came into play as well, with Marshal Tito's newly established Communist regime concerned that trials would stoke hostility between Croats and Serbs.

The most important trial that did take place was the prosecution of Archbishop Alojzije Stepinac. It was controversial from the beginning. Others had participated directly in the killings of Serbs and were not tried because they fled, were summarily executed, or were simply neglected. Stepinac's prosecution also did not begin until a year after the end of the war. Against that backdrop, Stepinac's sympathizers concluded with much justification that the real motive was to silence an opponent of a Communist state rather than to punish him for complicity in war crimes.

To Catholics in many countries, Stepinac was a hero and a martyr. By 1943, his support for the Ustasha regime had waned and he was speaking out forcefully against racism—statements cited by his partisans as evidence he had been wrongly judged. (One of his most outspoken champions was New York's Francis Cardinal Spellman, who had a Westchester County Catholic school named for Stepinac.)

At the least, however, Stepinac deserved to be condemned for serving so long as the most prominent apologist for one of the cruelest regimes of a cruel era, and despite his public positions from 1943 on, he never explicitly denounced Ustasha criminality. Yet the manner of his prosecution allowed the Catholic Church to avoid acknowledgment that much of its hierarchy in wartime Croatia—the bishop of Mostar was an honorable exception—collaborated with the Ustasha. On October 11, 1946, Stepinac was convicted of welcoming the establishment of the Ustasha regime while Yugoslavia was at war and of persecuting Serbs in the interest of the Vatican. He was sentenced to sixteen years in prison at hard labor.

Stepinac himself was elevated to cardinal by Pope Pius XII after his conviction. Within Yugoslavia, he retained a strong following among Croats and, to appease them, was released from jail after serving only five years. He died in 1960, still under house arrest, and his funeral service was held at Zagreb Cathedral. Following his death, a movement to canonize him attracted a substantial following, especially among Croats in the United States, Canada, and Australia. When Pope John Paul II visited Zagreb in September 1994, he lauded Stepinac as "a true pastor of his flock" at the airport welcoming ceremonies, spoke of him again at evening vespers at Zagreb Cathedral, and knelt at his grave. The pope's tributes drew applause from the assembled priests and lay worshipers in Zagreb Cathedral, but they undoubtedly inflamed anti-Catholic and anti-Croat sentiment among Orthodox Serbs, who recalled his service to the Ustasha state.[6]

In 1986, six years after the death of Tito, an Ustasha leader, NDH minister of the interior Andrija Artukovic, was deported to Yugoslavia by the United States to face trial. Though Catholic groups in many countries, including the Knights of Columbus in America, took up his case, Artukovic was sentenced to death. He died in prison in 1988 before he could be executed. Artukovic was the only top Ustasha official ever brought to trial. (In 1998, Dinko Sakic, commandant of Jasenovac, was discovered in Argentina. Argentine president Menem said the seventy-six-year-old Sakic would be extradited to a country that wished to try him, but at this writing, no government has sought to put him on trial.)

The most prominent defendant in a postwar trial in Yugoslavia other than Archbishop Stepinac was the Serbian Chetnik leader Draza Mihailovic. During the war, Mihailovic acquired celebrity in the West as a formidable opponent of the Nazis. Though sometimes likened to Charles de Gaulle as a Resistance leader, he was tried on charges of collaborating with the Germans. Indeed, in the shifting alliances in Yugoslavia, there were times when Mihailovic's forces made common cause with those he fought against throughout most of the war in an effort to defeat Tito's Partisans. Mihailovic was convicted and executed by firing squad. The execution was widely condemned in the West and was seen as further proof that opposing a Communist state, rather than responsibility for crimes against humanity, motivated the prosecution. In combination, the Stepinac and Mihailovic cases vitiated any sense in Yugoslavia that legal process could be relied upon to do justice in the wake of great crimes.

During World War II, the Muslims in Bosnia-Herzegovina were not yet considered a distinct ethnic group. "Muslim" was still a religious designation. Indeed, until the second half of the nineteenth century, when Darwinian thinking fostered heightened consciousness of race and ethnicity in many countries, their fellow Bosnians were not generally known as Serbs and Croats; rather, they were considered by themselves and others to be Bosnian Orthodox and Bosnian Catholics. According to Robert J. Donia and John V. A. Fine, Jr., "Encouraged by similar developments in neighboring lands, Bosnia's Catholics gradually came to think of themselves as Croats and Orthodox Bosnians came to regard themselves as Serbs. This process accelerated in the late decades of Ottoman rule and was well advanced—particularly in urban areas—by the time Austrian rule began in 1878."[7] Identification of Muslims as a distinct ethnic group did not begin until the 1960s. The main impetus came from Tito's Communist regime, which opposed identifying any segment of the Yugoslav population by religion and promoted the idea that the label "Muslim" had a secular connotation. In the late 1960s, censuses in Yugoslavia began to use "Muslim" as an ethnic designation. Tito also adopted a policy of distributing various public posts proportionately among members of different ethnic groups. Designating Bosnian Muslims as an ethnic group was meant to ensure that they were allocated their fair share of official patronage. Though identifying them ethnically was intended to be benign, the ultimate consequences were disastrous. If the Bosnian Muslims had been mindful of the history of the Jews, the only other people in Europe, and one of only a handful worldwide, whose religious and ethnic identity are the same, they might have resisted Tito's benevolence in attributing an ethnic component to their religious designation.

The Serbs of Bosnia in the 1990s may not have had much cause to harbor grievances against their Muslim neighbors for the crimes of their fathers during World War II, but they thought they had older scores to settle. The defining moment in Serbian history was the battle of Kosovo, on June 28, 1389, when Serbian knights under the leadership of King Lazar were defeated by a Turkish army on the "field of blackbirds," inaugurating nearly five centuries of subjugation to the Ottoman Empire. The emergence of contemporary Serb nationalism was punctuated by a series of rallies in Kosovo, regarded by Serbs as the southern part of Serbia, at which Slobodan Milosevic linked Muslim Albanians and Muslim Bosnians to the Muslim Turks. One rally on June 28, 1989, marking the 600th anniversary of the battle of Kosovo, was attended by a million Serbs, most of whom traveled long distances to hear Milosevic revile the enemies of Serbs.

The actual history is murky and open to dispute. Some ancestors of Bosnia's Muslims were Bogomils, members of a heretical Christian sect persecuted by both Catholics and Orthodox. Turkish administrators offered Bogomils the opportunity to convert to Islam and, as rewards, appointed them to civil service positions to help administer their colonies in what would become Yugoslavia. In short, the Bogomils managed to transform themselves from victims to victimizers—or at least collaborators with those regarded by the Serbs as their oppressors.

Ottoman rule in what became Yugoslavia was not generally characterized by forcible conversions to Islam, but it was marked by
many episodes that gave rise to lasting grievances. In the historical
imagination of the Serbs, Muslims bear the blame. Their Muslimness
embodies a central feature of purported ancestral Serb suffering—
that is, a Christian people was subjected to Islamic rule. But as
historians of Bosnia have pointed out, "Orthodoxy was the Christian
group favored by the Ottomans," with the result that it gained many
converts from Catholicism. As Donia and Fine write, "One can easily
see why the Ottomans preferred the Orthodox to the Catholics. The
Orthodox head, the patriarch of Constantinople, lived in the Ottoman
capital, where he was easily controlled. His whole hierarchy lived
within the empire. The Pope lived in Rome, outside the empire, and
was the main sponsor of crusades against the Ottomans."[8]

Whatever the actual history, the most intense nationalist feelings
in Serbia derive from the sense of being wounded as a people, and
these feelings express themselves in the attribution of collective guilt
to those, such as the Muslims—often called "Turks" by Serb militants
in Bosnia—considered historically culpable. Contemporary Serb nationalism also took a particular anti-Muslim cast, because the sacred
soil of "Old Serbia" in Kosovo, where the most important Serb historical and religious monuments are located, is now populated
mainly by the despised Albanian Muslims.

Class hatreds have played a big role in Bosnia as well. Most Serbs and
many Muslims in Bosnia-Herzegovina are village dwellers or rural
people, and there is no significant class distinction between the two
groups. But a segment of the Muslim population in Bosnia became
more affluent, better educated, and more cosmopolitan than any
comparable portion of the Bosnian Serb population. Some of these
worldly Muslims are descendants of those who held civil service positions under the Ottomans. They were concentrated in cosmopolitan
cities such as Mostar and the capital, Sarajevo.

What happened in both places underscored the Serbs' sense of
injustice. The siege of Sarajevo, which commenced at the beginning
of the war in Bosnia, in April 1992, astonished world opinion by its
unrelenting viciousness. Residents, largely deprived of electricity,
water, and fuel, had to depend on the United Nations to supply
food—the quantities, under the circumstances, often insufficient to
feed them adequately. The city's cultural treasures in particular

seemed targeted for destruction. Those sniping at the city's residents and shelling them from the nearby surrounding hills aimed to cause as much grief as possible by bombarding Kosevo Hospital and by lobbing mortar shells into bread and water lines, markets, and groups of children playing ball or riding bicycles.

It is almost impossible to comprehend a sustained attack of this nature on a near defenseless civilian population unless it is fueled by intense class hatred. Milosevic, Karadzic, and their henchmen were the principal avengers, in their own eyes, of supposed historical injustices during the centuries of Ottoman Muslim rule over the Christian Serbs, symbolized in the 1990s by the cosmopolitan residents of Sarajevo.

Mostar got hit even harder, its Muslim section on the east bank of the Neretva River suffering enormous destruction. The villains of the piece were the Bosnian Croats, many of them mountain people from Herzegovina noted for their class resentments, who destroyed or severely damaged the majority of Mostar's structures. Once a great tourist attraction, the city lost a graceful sixteenth-century bridge of Turkish design across the jade-green Neretva River—its destruction making headlines around the world.

Class resentments influenced the way "ethnic cleansing" was carried out in the countryside, too. In interviewing Bosnian Muslims who had fled from provincial towns and villages, or who survived confinement in detention camps, I asked them to tell me what had happened in their communities. In virtually every case, they said that those designated for particularly cruel treatment—including, but not limited to, murder—were the educated Muslim elite: the mayors, the doctors, the teachers, the clerics, the engineers. (The tribunal's indictments against Karadzic and Mladic cite their targeting of intellectuals and professionals.) The accounts were reminiscent of those by survivors of the killings a decade and a half earlier by the Khmer Rouge in Cambodia. There, eyeglasses marked a member of the intelligentsia, and wearing them could be a death warrant. In Bosnia, class distinctions could be made almost as easily, since the killers often included acquaintances of their victims. In Phnom Penh, Cambodia's capital, residents were required to abandon the city en masse on a moment's notice, the forced departure a certain death for many of them. In Sarajevo, Bosnia's capital, residents were exterminated slowly within the city. One difference is that the Khmer Rouge did not destroy the cultural monuments and architectural heritage of Phnom Penh: ancient temples did not symbolize the class under attack. Pol Pot's forces were like a neutron bomb, killing the people but leaving the buildings intact. In Bosnia, the destruction of such renowned structures as the historic mosques of Banja Luka, the national library in Sarajevo, and the old bridge at Mostar seemed as important to the ethnic cleansers as driving away or killing their ethnic and class enemies.

If the wrong reasons were an important factor in the United Nations Security Council decision to create a tribunal for ex-Yugoslavia, the proposal to establish it did not originate in cynical considerations. Rather, the provenance was the international human rights movement that had struggled, particularly during the previous decade, to hold government officials accountable for their crimes.

In the forefront was Human Rights Watch, of which I was a founder and then director. The organization had been deeply involved in efforts to ensure that democratically elected governments in Latin America disclose and acknowledge the crimes committed against civilians by the displaced military dictatorships, and that they punish those principally responsible. Attempts to secure accountability had been at the top of our agenda since the transition from military rule to democratic government in Argentina in 1983. We had also been engaged in struggles over military accountability in Chile, Brazil, Uruguay, Colombia, Peru, Haiti, Nicaragua, Honduras, El Salvador, Paraguay, and Guatemala, in several East Asian and African countries, and in Eastern and Central Europe. No organization anywhere had campaigned more, had published more, or was more committed to holding accountable officials responsible for great abuses of human rights.

Yet neither Human Rights Watch nor any other prominent human rights group had ever before campaigned to establish an international war crimes tribunal. Why ex-Yugoslavia? One reason was that as a matter of international law, the provisions of the Third and Fourth Geneva Conventions of 1949 and of the First Additional Protocol of 1977 setting forth "grave breaches," or war crimes, were applicable; Bosnia-Herzegovina and Croatia had been internationally recognized, and the armed forces of another internationally recognized state, the Federal Republic of Yugoslavia (Serbia and Montenegro), were directly involved.[9] That made the wars in Bosnia and Croatia international armed conflicts, as the Security Council recognized when it established the tribunal. In contrast, the other circumstances in which we had sought accountability either did not involve armed conflict at all (Chile, for example) or involved internal armed conflict (Guatemala). A different legal regime could be invoked in the case of ex-Yugoslavia.

The other consideration that drove me, as director of Human Rights Watch, to push for a war crimes tribunal was that the war in Bosnia was avowedly fought in furtherance of an abhorrent principle: that persons of different ethnic groups may not live together. There had been many other ethnic conflicts. Yet the unabashed assertion that driving people away or killing them is justified on these grounds was different and inevitably evoked comparisons to Nazi doctrines. We began—tentatively, at first—to use the term *genocide* to describe the slaughter in Bosnia. The word didn't come easily, given our fears of exaggeration and the word's almost sacrosanct historical association. But we thought it fitting to call for a tribunal like the one that tried the Nazis to hold accountable those engaged in Nazi-like crimes.

The word *genocide* was coined not long before the Nuremberg trials by Raphael Lemkin, a Polish-Jewish scholar working for the United States War Department. In a 1944 book, he argued that a new term was needed to describe what the Nazis were doing to Jews, Gypsies, and Slavic peoples in territory that they conquered. Lemkin defined the crime as

> a coordinated plan of different actions aiming at the destruction of essential foundations of life of different groups. . . . The objectives of such a plan would be the disintegration of the political and social institutions of culture, languages, national feelings, religion, and the economical existence of national groups, and the destruction of personal security, liberty, health, dignity, and even lives of the individuals belonging to such groups.[10]

The crucial factor in establishing that genocide was committed, as Lemkin described the crime, was not the complete extermination of the target group. At the time he wrote, he did not know the full extent of the slaughter of the Jews of Europe, and many more Jews were killed in the months between publication of his book and the end of the war. His estimate in the book was that 1.7 million Jews had been killed by the Nazis. The gravamen of the crime of genocide was killing with the *intent* to destroy a national group. Such destruction involved not only mass murder but also a variety of acts that in combination were carried out for the purpose of ending, or ending in significant part, a distinct group's continued existence.

Lemkin discussed precedents, citing the extermination of the Carthaginians by the Roman legions in 146 B.C. as the first historical example of genocide. The siege of Carthage was intended to end once and for all the power of Rome's most formidable rival for Mediterranean hegemony. Roman fears about Carthage's power were exemplified by Cato the Elder, who concluded every speech he made after he visited the city with the warning *Delenda est Carthago* (Carthage must be destroyed). It is estimated that 150,000 of Carthage's 200,000 residents died during the siege and the capture of the city. The survivors were enslaved, and Carthage and the Carthaginians were wiped out. The Romans even rubbed salt into the ground where Carthage stood so that it would remain infertile and no attempt could be made to occupy it again.

Lemkin might have gone back even further to the slaughter of the residents of New Carthage (Cartagena, Spain) several decades earlier by the forces of Scipio Africanus, or even to the extermination of the Melians by the Athenians in 416 B.C., an episode known to history because of "The Melian Dialogue" that concludes Book V of Thucydides' *The Peloponnesian War.* The Melians were the residents of the island of Melos, a Spartan colony, who resisted demands that they join the Athenian empire in its war against Sparta. Athens sent representatives to Melos to negotiate, and Thucydides reported their diaglogue. The Melians ask, "So you would not agree to our being neutral, friends instead of enemies, but allies of neither side?" To this, the Athenians responded, "No, because it is not so much your hostility that injures us; it is rather the case that, if we were on friendly terms with you, our subjects would regard that as a sign of weakness in us, whereas your hatred is evidence of our power." To demonstrate Athenian power, according to Thucydides, "siege operations were now carried out vigorously and, as there was also some treachery from inside, the Melians surrendered unconditionally to the Athenians, who put to death all the men of military age whom they took, and sold the women and children as slaves." The Melians' survival as a distinct group was extinguished.

Historical examples of large-scale slaughter include the conquests by Genghis Khan in the thirteenth century, by Tamerlane in the fourteenth, and the persecution of heretical religious sects in Europe in the same era. In more recent times, the ages of discovery and colonial settlement were marked by the intentional destruction of many of the Indian nations of the Americas, the Hottentots of southern Africa, and other distinctive groups, such as the Tasmanians, an aboriginal people who were wiped out in the nineteenth century.

It was in the post-Darwinian era that racial thinking assumed its current importance. Genocide, defined as the intentional attempt to exterminate a racial, religious, or ethnic group, acquired its contemporary character in 1915, with the Turkish massacres of the Armenians, became indelibly associated with the Nazi Holocaust that inspired the word, and touched a gut-wrenching nadir with Rwanda in 1994.

At Nuremberg, it was proved that the Nazis had murdered Jews with the intent to exterminate them as a people. Accordingly, Nuremberg made it possible for Lemkin, who waged a one-man crusade, to persuade the United Nations to adopt the Genocide Convention on December 9, 1948, and to submit it to member states for ratification. Three years later, it had been ratified by a sufficient number of states to become binding international law. (The United States, where suspicion of international law has remained a potent political force, did not ratify the Genocide Convention until 1988. I vividly recall going, as a student at Stuyvesant High School in New York City in the early 1950s, to the United Nations building to meet Lemkin to arrange for him to speak at a History Club forum at school on the need for U.S. ratification, then a forlorn cause.)

Though the crimes at Vukovar and elsewhere during the Croatian War clearly met the definition of grave breaches under the Geneva Conventions, and the scale of killing warranted labeling them crimes against humanity, neither Human Rights Watch nor any other significant group responded then by calling for the establishment of an international tribunal. The crimes did not meet the definition of genocide, since they were not characterized by an intent to destroy the Croats as a national group; rather, the goal of the Serb authors of those crimes was to control territory. Furthermore, no international criminal tribunal had been convened since Nuremberg and Tokyo; accordingly, the prospects for persuading the Security Council to establish one seemed remote.

The war in Bosnia-Herzegovina that began in April 1992 quickly superseded the conflict in Croatia in the scale, ethnic character, and horror of the carnage. Even to the most hardened observer of atrocities in ethnically driven conflicts, not only in ex-Yugoslavia but worldwide, the reports on Bosnia were shocking. It seemed appropriate not only to refer to what was happening as crimes against humanity but even to use the name for the ultimate crime: genocide.

Alerted to what might develop by our experience monitoring the war in Croatia, Human Rights Watch's investigators were on the scene in Bosnia at the beginning of the war. We expected a conflict, but even the crimes committed in Croatia did not prepare us for what we would see. Three months later, in July 1992, we published a book-length report. To signal that something extraordinary was going on, we cited the provisions of the Geneva Conventions dealing with international armed conflict that designate certain abuses as grave breaches. I decided to entitle our report *War Crimes in Bosnia-Hercegovina*. Although Human Rights Watch and its regional divisions had published hundreds of reports, many focusing on abuses in armed conflicts, it was the first time we referred to war crimes in a title. Seeking a commensurate response to the crimes we documented, we called on the United Nations Security Council to establish a tribunal to bring to justice those responsible, and we named ten Serbian and Bosnian Serb political, military, and militia leaders against whom we had collected sufficient evidence to warrant their investigation for committing war crimes.

Our call to establish an international criminal tribunal was immediately picked up by many others in the human rights movement, the U.S. Congress, and the press. It also was electric within ex-Yugoslavia, where it was broadcast by the international radio services that were the main sources of news in cities cut off from most media by the war. Commissions to document war crimes were established in such Bosnian cities as Zenica and Sarajevo. The call for a tribunal also attracted the interest of the U.S. State Department, where Lawrence Eagleburger, deputy secretary of state under James Baker, had become acting secretary when his boss moved to the White House to direct George Bush's ailing campaign for reelection.

Eagleburger had once served as U.S. ambassador to Yugoslavia and knew the country well—so well that he had acquired the sobriquet "Lawrence of Yugoslavia." Out of government during a part of the Reagan presidency, he became a principal in Henry Kissinger's consultancy, Kissinger Associates, and his unequaled contacts and status in Yugoslavia brought substantial business to the firm. One of his business ventures was an effort to promote the "Yugo" automobile as a low-priced import.

His excellent ties to Yugoslavia made Eagleburger the target of considerable criticism over the disastrous armed conflicts engulfing the states emerging from the country where he was formerly posted. He was accused of being too understanding of Serbian strongman Slobodan Milosevic, the former Communist turned nationalist and the principal architect of the wars in Croatia and Bosnia. It had been the policy of the United States to prevent the dissolution of Yugoslavia. The nationalist passions aroused by Milosevic had doomed that policy, and the consequences were these horrifying wars. Eagleburger needed to demonstrate that he was not as accommodating of Milosevic as his detractors inside and outside the State Department were claiming. He seized upon the idea of a United Nations effort to deal with war crimes.

A crucial factor was the publication, at that moment, of the first press accounts of the horrifying conditions in Serb detention camps in Bosnia. Though Eagleburger did not immediately advocate establishment of a tribunal, reflecting traditional State Department hostility to an international criminal court, he called on the United Nations to establish a commission to investigate war crimes in ex-Yugoslavia. A commission could be terminated if a settlement was reached; a tribunal could take on a life of its own, and prosecutions, once initiated, could be difficult to stop. In September 1992, the United States introduced a resolution in the Security Council to form a Commission of Experts to collect information on war crimes in ex-Yugoslavia, and on October 6, the Security Council adopted Resolution 780, calling on the secretary general to establish such a commission. Three weeks later, on October 26, 1992, a five-member Commission of Experts was established by the secretary general. Just three months from the moment Human Rights Watch had initiated the call for an international war crimes tribunal, a United Nations body was formed to collect evidence that could be used in prosecutions. For the UN, it was something of a record.

Eagleburger's endorsement of a war crimes investigation was crucial in the rapid pace of developments, but his next move on the issue was a misstep, at least in timing. On December 16, the eve of elections in Serbia pitting Milan Panic, an idiosyncratic American businessman of Serb origin, against Milosevic, Eagleburger endorsed establishment of a tribunal and named Milosevic as one of those who warranted prosecution. Just as Human Rights Watch had named ten potential defendants in war crimes prosecutions several months earlier, Eagleburger now named his own list of ten, including several of the same people—Milosevic, for example. He made his accusation while he was attending a peace meeting on Bosnia in Geneva also attended by Radovan Karadzic, who was on his list. Eagleburger subsequently insisted his statement was triggered by a conversation with Holocaust survivor and Nobel laureate Elie Wiesel, who had persuaded him that it was important to name those responsible for war crimes, but the timing made it seem that he was trying to help Panic defeat Milosevic. That had the unfortunate effect of seeming to transform a moral condemnation by the senior foreign-policy spokesman of the United States government into a political gesture. It is difficult to sort out what impact Eagleburger's statement had on the elections in Serbia, but if it had any effect, it wasn't good: Milosevic was reelected by a wide margin and emerged stronger than ever.

Though Eagleburger's timing suggested an attempt to influence the Serbian elections, other factors were also at work. Along with leaders such as Milosevic, Karadzic, and General Ratko Mladic, the secretary of state named a twenty-one-year-old Bosnian Serb soldier, Borislav Herak, as a war criminal.

Herak was special to Eagleburger, someone to be bracketed with the others, because a month earlier, he had taken a wrong turn while driving in the vicinity of Sarajevo. As a result, he had been captured by the city's defenders. They allowed John Burns, a reporter for *The New York Times,* to interview Herak in detention. The *Times* put Burns's story on page one under a three-column headline and continued it for a full page inside.[11] If there is one newspaper story from 1992 that will be remembered for years to come, it is John F. Burns's account of his interview with Borislav Herak. The story helped Burns win a Pulitzer Prize for his reporting on Bosnia, which he shared with Roy Gutman of *Newsday,* who also was rewarded for his coverage of atrocities by Serb forces.

Burns told the story of a young man who had committed twenty-nine individual murders over five months, including ten members of a single Bosnian Muslim family—from a ten-year-old girl to her elderly grandmother. Eight others were Muslim women held prisoner at an abandoned motel, where Herak raped them before he murdered them. Herak told Burns that he and other Serbian troops were encouraged by their commander to commit such rape-murders. He also described the way young fighters were trained to wrestle pigs to the ground and cut their throats and said that he used this skill to kill three Muslims captured by Serb forces.[12]

The international tribunals at Nuremberg and Tokyo focused on the top German and Japanese war criminals. Young defendants like Herak were tried in less publicized proceedings before military judges and, in the case of Germany, before domestic courts after international trials ended. In fact, the Bosnians made plain that they intended to try Herak themselves; they did the following March before television cameras—the trial was broadcast in the United States on Court TV—and sentenced him to death. Eagleburger was undoubtedly aware that bringing foot soldiers to account was not the real purpose of convening the first international criminal tribunal in nearly a half century, even when they have committed crimes as ghastly as those to which the young Bosnian Serb confessed. Yet he apparently was driven to name Herak by the storm created by the *New York Times* coverage.

One other factor almost certainly played a part in the secretary's December 16 statement: George Bush had lost the presidential election in November, and his presidency would end in little more than a month. Following his defeat, Bush made the dramatic decision to send American troops to Somalia. This was a bold act for a lame-duck president, but as Eagleburger knew as well as anyone, it ensured that there would not be a comparable initiative in Bosnia. In his final days in office, the president could not commit American troops in two different parts of the world. Though Bush would get the credit (and later the blame) for intervening in Somalia, Eagleburger's past association with Yugoslavia made it likely that the secretary of state—he was promoted after the election, and was no longer "acting" secretary—would be vilified for allowing that conflict to become so catastrophic without any significant American effort to stop the bloodshed. He had little time left to clear his own record for the history books, and not many options. Calling for a war crimes tribunal and naming those who should be brought before it was one of the few things the secretary of state could do without enlisting the support of anyone else—not the Congress, or the armed forces, or America's European allies. "It was my best opportunity to do it," Eagleburger told *The Wall Street Journal*. "I did it on my own."[13]

At that point, the State Department had invested few resources in collecting evidence of war crimes—itself an indication of how impulsive Eagleburger's move was. Several young foreign service officers within the department had been pressing for a systematic effort but had been rebuffed by their superiors. Over time, some of them resigned publicly to protest this and other elements of American inaction. Indeed, the number of such public resignations was unprecedented in State Department history and embarrassed the secretary. A desire to appease the dissidents at State and head off further resignations may have played a role in Eagleburger's decision, but he made clear that his main concern was his own image. Doing the right thing for the wrong reasons, the United States became a proponent of an international criminal tribunal for ex-Yugoslavia.

Eagleburger's boss, of course, had just lost his job. George Bush's opponent during the presidential campaign had castigated the administration for failing to take meaningful action against "ethnic cleansing." Now, the question of what should be done in Bosnia was one of the first major foreign policy issues Bill Clinton faced. The U.S. military, according to a story making the rounds in Washington, was sending a signal to the White House: "We do deserts, we don't do mountains." The words may have been apocryphal, but they conveyed the Pentagon's view under Colin Powell, chairman of the Joint Chiefs of Staff. Of the choices available to him, Clinton settled on a carefully circumscribed program for intervention called "lift and strike."

"Lift" referred to lifting the arms embargo on the government of Bosnia-Herzegovina, which, like the other parties to the conflict, was prohibited from arms sales by the UN Security Council. The embargo, however, lopsidedly favored Serbian forces, which could draw on the large reserves of weapons and ammunition of the Yugoslav armed forces and on ex-Yugoslavia's domestic arms-production industry, which was located mainly in Serb-controlled territory. In contrast, the ragtag army of the Bosnian government had little weaponry, making it unable to counter the steady bombardment of Sarajevo and other Bosnian towns by mortars, howitzers, and tanks. The equal application of the embargo did not have equal consequences. It crippled Bosnia's capacity to defend itself without seriously interfering with the ability of the Serbian forces to attack.

The other half of the president's plan meant air strikes aimed at Serb artillery. Clinton had taken flack during the campaign for his avoidance of the draft during Vietnam and had begun his presidency in a battle with the Pentagon over gays and lesbians in the armed forces. "Strike" would forestall another outright confrontation with the military and Colin Powell, its enormously popular leader, who opposed deployment of American ground troops in ex-Yugoslavia. The Clinton people even worried that Powell might resign in protest if his views were disregarded.

To win backing for lift and strike, Secretary of State Warren Christopher was dispatched in March 1993 on a tour of European capitals. The effort was halfhearted, apparently reflecting Christopher's and his president's lack of enthusiasm. Christopher probably knew the plan would not go over well, and it didn't. America's allies were not persuaded that lifting the arms embargo was a good idea, and they found even more appalling the prospect of air strikes on Serbian artillery positions without deployment of American ground troops. Britain, France, and other European countries had supplied troops to the United Nations for a number of services in Bosnia, including protection of the delivery of humanitarian assistance to besieged communities. The Serbs threatened that if they were attacked from the air, they would retaliate against these lightly armed ground troops. The American attacks would take place from an altitude above the range of anti-aircraft fire, the Europeans said, while their own troops would run all the risks on the ground. If the United States proposed to strike from the air, they demanded, it should also deploy ground troops.

Caught between American military resistance to using ground troops and European insistence on them, the Clinton administration backed away from its plan to intervene. Then, in October 1993, the Somalia factor reappeared when eighteen Americans were killed in a battle with the loyalists of a Somali warlord, General Mohamed Farah Aidid; horrifying TV footage showed an American pilot's body being dragged through the streets of Mogadishu by a Somali mob. Amid cries that America could not be policeman to the world, the episode gave Washington an additional reason not to deploy Americans in Bosnia. (Somalia was invoked repeatedly two years later by those who feared that sending American troops to Bosnia following the Dayton peace agreement would result in "mission creep.") In the circumstances, however, retreat from the plan to intervene with force in Bosnia left the new president looking weak and inept. Accordingly, supporting the idea of a war crimes tribunal became as opportune to the Clinton administration as it had been to Lawrence Eagleburger. It was a way to do *something* about Bosnia that would have no political cost domestically.

Similar considerations were at work in Europe. Though France and Britain opposed military intervention, and would support such action only if the United States provided strong leadership, as it had in Kuwait, popular opinion in Europe sympathized strongly with the Bosnian victims of Serbian atrocities. As in the United States, press coverage was extensive and aroused outrage: European governments felt strong public pressure to act, or to appear to act. A surge of racist violence in Germany during the same period was seen as the same scourge as "ethnic cleansing" in ex-Yugoslavia, and both had to be resisted.

Other governments also had reasons of their own to support, or not to oppose, a tribunal. Many Islamic governments were among those with strong cause to resist a permanent international criminal tribunal, or an ad hoc tribunal that could lead to a permanent court, for fear it might someday turn its attention to them. Yet they were angry over the failure of the international community to respond to aggression by a Christian nation against a Muslim country. Intent on demonstrating strong international condemnation of the Serbs, and denied the opportunity to support military intervention, they too were ready to go along with a tribunal. During the period when proposals for a tribunal came before the Security Council, Pakistan was a member, and though its government might not have been enthusiastic about an international criminal court in other circumstances, it wanted those responsible for slaughtering Muslims in Bosnia put on trial.

Another strong advocate of a tribunal on the Security Council was Venezuela, reflecting the personal commitment to human rights by its ambassador to the United Nations, Diego Arria. While he served as president of the council, Arria had been a leading advocate of UN intervention in Somalia to alleviate famine. He also was a passionate advocate of forceful efforts to halt "ethnic cleansing" in Bosnia—and to dramatize the need for a stronger stand by the United Nations, he personally led a group of Security Council members on a visit to Sarajevo and other besieged communities.

To block the tribunal, either Russia or China would have had to exercise its veto. Strong U.S. support for the measure would be crucial in preventing these permanent members of the Security Council from standing in the way. In addition, a new factor had come into play: President Clinton had appointed Madeleine Albright as ambassador to the United Nations. A native of Czechoslovakia with a particular interest in Central and Eastern Europe, a commitment to human rights, and strong personal feelings about developments in ex-Yugoslavia (whose language she speaks), Albright was the administration's foremost advocate of intervention. Bitterly disappointed by her government's retreat, Albright acted as forcefully as she could on any matters involving Bosnia where she could get Washington's backing. The tribunal was such a matter. When creation of the tribunal came before the Security Council in 1993, China was awaiting a decision from President Clinton on whether its Most Favored Nation trading status would be renewed or, as the president had suggested the previous year during his electoral campaign, whether it would be withheld on human rights grounds. Ambassador Albright signaled to the Chinese that it would not help their human rights image if they blocked establishment of a tribunal to judge war crimes in ex-Yugoslavia.

Potentially, Russia was an even greater obstacle. When the decision to establish a tribunal came up on February 22, 1993, Boris Yeltsin was facing a referendum that could end his presidency. Within Russia, nationalist sentiment favored the Serbs, with whom Russians had historic ties and shared an alphabet. The Serbs also were fellow Orthodox Christians. The Clinton administration had delayed announcement of its "lift and strike" plan for intervention in Bosnia—subsequently abandoned—to assist Yeltsin. In comparison to that, the question of a tribunal was a small matter, and Russia did not block it. By the May 1993 vote adopting a specific plan, the referendum in Russia was history. Yeltsin had prevailed, and his own domestic political considerations did not require obstruction of the tribunal. A year and a half later, in December 1994, Russia launched its military campaign in Chechnya and committed gross human rights abuses, including the indiscriminate bombardment of civilians. By the time the Chechen war began, Russia also had voted in the Security Council to establish the Rwanda tribunal, thereby endorsing the internationalization of jurisdiction to try those responsible for war crimes in internal armed conflicts. If he had anticipated the war in Chechnya, and the legal significance of the statutes establishing the two tribunals, Yeltsin might have declined to go along with their establishment.

Four of the five permanent members of the Security Council had been unenthusiastic and perhaps unclear about the ramifications of their action; the fifth permanent member had initially endorsed a tribunal because of opportunistic personal considerations by a brief occupant of the post of secretary of state. Still, the votes in the Security Council on February 22, 1993, to establish the tribunal for ex-Yugoslavia and on May 25, 1993, to approve a specific plan for its operation, were both unanimous.

It would take another fourteen months before the UN managed to approve a choice for the tribunal's chief prosecutor—a period of embarrassing stalemate and obstruction that threatened to undermine the enterprise's seriousness of purpose. Pakistan had objected to the selection of a former attorney general of India because of the long enmity between the two countries. Britain balked at the appointment of the chairman of the UN War Crimes Commission because it feared he would challenge any attempt to drop prosecutions in exchange for a peace settlement. And Russia said it might veto any nominee from a NATO country.

The selection, in the end, of South African judge Richard Goldstone on July 8, 1994, put to rest many of the concerns. Goldstone had won renown, inside and outside his own country, for his work heading a commission investigating South African violence and had just been appointed by President Mandela to serve on South Africa's new Constitutional Court. Those who saw the tribunal as a pawn to be traded away for a peace agreement soon realized that the new prosecutor had other ideas. Goldstone was a credible and authoritative advocate for the proposition that any peace would be diminished if it did not include justice—a reckoning in an international court of law for those accused of committing war crimes in the former Yugoslavia.

Still, the idea of a trade—peace for a de facto amnesty—would not disappear. Two factors blew the idea away, guaranteeing the tribunal's continued work and even strengthening its hand. The first came barely a year after Goldstone's appointment, when Bosnian Serb forces overran the UN "safe haven" at Srebrenica and massacred as many as eight thousand Muslim men and boys over a twelve-day period in mid-July 1995. On July 25, Bosnian Serb leader Radovan Karadzic and his top general, Ratko Mladic, were indicted by the tribunal. In early August, when details of Srebrenica began to emerge, several survivors reported that Mladic had personally supervised the executions—but not before he had assured his captives they wouldn't be harmed.

Karadzic and Mladic could not attend the Dayton peace talks in the fall of 1995 because their indictments left them susceptible to arrest, so they obviously were in no position to make a case for dropped prosecutions in exchange for a settlement. The slaughter of Srebrenica, meanwhile, concentrated minds like nothing that had preceded it. "Srebrenica was the low point in the history of the United Nations since 1945 and the Western alliance in the post–Cold War era," former assistant secretary of state Richard Holbrooke told *The Washington Post*. "It was the point at which we either had to give up or turn it around. It was the shock to the system that forced the United States to get heavily involved." The tribunal's work, under tragic circumstances, was assured.

9

The Return of
the Concentration
Camp

On August 2, 1992, *New York Newsday* reported that Bosnian Muslims held at the Omarska detention camp near Prijedor were being slaughtered by their Serb guards. The following day, the U.S. State Department press spokesman, Richard Boucher, responded to questions about the article at his noon press briefing by suggesting the United States knew about Omarska and effectively confirming *Newsday*'s report. In the next few days, Roy Gutman, the *Newsday* reporter who broke the story, filed other vivid accounts detailing further horrors.[1] Gutman's reporting caused a sensation. Journalists from many countries flocked to Bosnia, and within a week, newspapers around the world carried accounts of "concentration camps" and television screens everywhere showed pictures of emaciated inmates behind chain-link fences, staring in silence at the cameras.

Gutman's articles on Omarska and other detention camps appeared just at the moment that Human Rights Watch was issuing its call to establish a war crimes tribunal, and they created a climate of public opinion that made it possible for the call to be taken seriously. The news stories also brought intense pressure on the Serbs to open the camps to inspection to try to refute Gutman's reports. As Ed Vulliamy of the British newspaper *The Guardian* recalled: "Radovan Karadzic was in London for the latest peace conference when the allegations surfaced, and went on ITN to denounce them as fabrications. Pinned by cameras on a live broadcast, he said that if those making the allegations insisted, they could come and *see for themselves*. We insisted."[2] Vulliamy was held up in Belgrade for three days by Serb authorities before being allowed to proceed to Omarska. In the meantime, hasty attempts were made to disguise conditions at the camps. Facilities were painted and cleaned, inmates were warned not to disclose to journalists what they had seen and what had happened to them, and those journalists who were admitted were allowed only into designated areas. Language impeded communication, but some foreign journalists were accompanied by local translators. (One of Human Rights Watch's investigators, Vlatka Mihelic, got into the camps by translating for *Washington Post* reporter Peter Maass).[3] And some prisoners spoke English or German and found opportunities for hurried communications with the journalists. Among the first journalists to get in along with Vulliamy was Penny Marshall, with a camera crew from ITN. Because of the August heat, some prisoners stripped off their shirts, enabling Marshall and her crew to obtain memorable footage of their emaciated chests. ITN's pictures were everywhere that summer. The association was unmistakable: Shown repeatedly on TV all over the world, the images of men with protruding rib cages couldn't help but remind viewers of the inmates of Nazi concentration camps freed at the end of World War II.

It was a coincidence that the stories about the camps, and the photographs and television scenes, appeared at the very moment we were petitioning for a war crimes tribunal. The timing proved crucial. Though Human Rights Watch had backed its call with a litany of horrors, its accounts were not as evocative as the newspaper articles and TV pictures. Camps and starved prisoners meant the Nazis and the Holocaust, reinforcing powerfully the analogy to Nazi practices made by reports of ethnic cleansing. In popular opinion, Nuremberg was a response to the camps, the foremost symbol of Nazi cruelty. (In fact, the Allies' initial decision to convene a war crimes tribunal at the conclusion of World War II was made before the death camps became infamous and with little thought to dealing with what had happened in them.) Editorial writers, columnists, political leaders, and diplomats searched for ways to express their outrage about the camps, and some eagerly seized on the proposal for a tribunal. Overnight, the call for a war crimes tribunal acquired momentum and legitimacy as a fitting response to revelations that had struck a nerve.

As Roy Gutman described Omarska, it was a mining complex where large numbers of men and some women were held in pits, warehouses, and metal cages in an ore loader. The prisoners, who had been held since the early weeks of the conflict, were severely malnourished, and in disregard of the Geneva Conventions and Protocols, the International Committee of the Red Cross was not permitted to see them. At night, guards entered the darkened halls of a warehouse where hundreds of men were packed in so tight that they could not lie down to sleep and pulled out a few at random and executed them. The next day, other prisoners were selected to bury the corpses of the victims, who had been shot in the mouth or had their throats slit. Many more prisoners, such as those forced into the mine's open pits, died of starvation, exposure, or diseases contracted because of the absence of toilets, clean drinking water, and medical attention. Gutman reported that "more than a thousand civilians have been executed or starved and thousands more are being held until they die" at Omarska and another camp at Trnopolje.

The United Nations felt compelled to act. Just two days after Gutman's articles began to appear, and the day after the U.S. State Department spokesman had given credence to Gutman's story, the Security Council adopted a resolution demanding the camps be opened for inspection. That resolution, of August 4, 1992, was followed by another the following week,[4] in which the Security Council made its most comprehensive statement up to that point on human rights abuses in the Bosnian conflict. The new resolution expressed the Security Council's grave alarm over the reports of mass forcible expulsions and deportations of civilians; deliberate attacks on civilians and on medical facilities; interference with the delivery of food, medical supplies, and other forms of relief; the wanton destruction of property; and of course, the imprisonment and abuse of civilians in the camps. The resolution laid the groundwork for subsequent efforts to establish accountability by calling on member states of the UN and other organizations to collect substantiated information on violations of international humanitarian law and grave breaches of the Geneva Conventions. Though not spelled out at the time, the Security Council's reference to grave breaches constituted recognition that war crimes were being committed and implied there would be a day of reckoning.

The August resolutions were inspired largely by press accounts—just as nineteenth-century conventions to codify the laws of war were inspired by the pioneering work of the war correspondents of the era—and by the reports of human rights groups. They set the world body on the path that subsequently led it to adopt its resolution of October 6, 1992, establishing the War Crimes Commission, and its resolutions the following February and May establishing the tribunal and specifying its mandate. *Newsday* was not one of the world's major press institutions, but a determined reporter and the willingness of his editors to back his investigations and display them prominently played a critical role in what would become an effort without precedent since the end of World War II to bring to book the authors of crimes against humanity.

There was some irony in the part played by Roy Gutman's accounts of conditions in Serb detention camps as a precipitating factor in the establishment of the tribunal. The foremost justification by Serbs for their conduct in Croatia and Bosnia was their determination not to permit a repetition of the persecution they claimed they had endured over the six centuries since their defeat at Kosovo by the Ottoman Turks in 1389. The most grievous suffering inflicted upon them in that entire period was in a concentration camp at Jasenovac in Croatia.

A phenomenon of the twentieth century, concentration camps were invented at its outset by Lord Kitchener to confine noncombatants during the Boer War in South Africa. Many of those confined by Kitchener were the wives and children of suspected Boer guerrillas. About 20,000 inmates of the camps died in them, mainly from hygiene-related diseases. Especially since the end of World War II, when it became widely known that the Nazis had established some of their camps as genocidal killing centers, such places have evoked images of horror. Jasenovac, forty-five miles southeast of the Croatian capital of Zagreb, was one of the worst. As Michael Ignatieff wrote, "If the new Croatian state, proclaimed in 1990, made one central mistake on the road to war, it was its failure publicly to disavow the Ustasha state and what it did at Jasenovac. The President of free Croatia, Franjo Tudjman, fought the Ustasha as a young partisan, but in the euphoria of independence, he tried to unite all of Croatia's tortured past into what was called a national synthesis. So he never came to Jasenovac. He never got down on his knees, as Willy Brandt did at Auschwitz. If he had done so, Serbs and Croats might have begun the process of ending the past, instead of living it over and over."[5] Now, as a consequence of Omarska and other camps like it, the world knows Serbs not as they see themselves—as the victims of Jasenovac—but rather as the masters of death camps.

By allowing television cameras into Omarska and some other camps in a vain effort to demonstrate that conditions were not as horrendous as portrayed by Roy Gutman, the Serbs sought to exculpate themselves. Yet in the process they furnished evidence that subsequently proved valuable to the prosecutors designated to try them for war crimes. "Unlawful confinement of a protected person" is a grave breach under Article 147 of the Fourth Geneva Convention. The convention defines a protected person as a noncombatant who has fallen into the hands of a party to the conflict or an occupying power and who has not been detained as a spy or saboteur or on suspicion of engaging in activities hostile to the occupying power. Even those detained legitimately must be treated in a humane manner, but detention of civilians who have taken no part in hostilities, even if they are treated decently, is a war crime. The television footage broadcast around the world when the camps were exposed, even though most of it only shows men standing around behind the camp fences, is valuable evidence. The prosecutors have located some of those detainees and, by showing that they were noncombatants, can demonstrate that their detention was a crime. The TV pictures also corroborate their testimony about what happened in the camps by proving that they were there.

Prijedor is a municipality in northwestern Bosnia near the predominantly Serb city of Banja Luka, where Omarska and several other notorious detention camps were located. Before the war, it had a population of 112,470—44 percent Muslim, 42.5 percent Serb, 5.6 percent Croat, 5.7 percent "Yugoslav," and 2.2 percent "other" (including Ukrainians, Russians, and Italians). "Ethnic cleansing" took place with great speed in Prijedor because the local Muslim population was easily overwhelmed by the numerically superior Serbs who lived nearby and who were reinforced and well supplied with weapons by JNA (Yugoslav Army) troops from their regional headquarters in Banja Luka. By June 1993, according to figures published in the Serb-controlled media in the region and subsequently cited in a UN War Crimes Commission report, the number of Muslims in Prijedor had declined from the 49,454 counted in a 1991 census to 6,124; the number of Croats had declined from 6,300 to 3,169; and the number of Yugoslavs and others had declined from 8,971 to 2,621. In the same period, the number of Serbs increased from 47,745 to 53,637. The "ethnic cleansing" continued in Prijedor, and when the war ended, in late 1995, fewer than a thousand Muslims survived.

"Ethnic cleansing" in Prijedor, as in many other communities in Bosnia, did not occur spontaneously. The groundwork was prepared months in advance by local Serb politicians acting in concert with various armed forces—local police, paramilitary organizations, and the JNA. The leader of the effort was Simo Drljaca, who was eventually shot and killed by British NATO troops on July 10, 1997, when he resisted arrest under a secret indictment handed down by the tribunal in The Hague. Members of Drljaca's paramilitary forces became guards at the camps, where, as elsewhere, the first to be marked for execution were those considered leaders of the Muslim community because of their prominence or their professional or educational attainments. Drljaca himself became police chief of Prijedor.

After the Dayton peace agreement ended the war, reports surfaced that thousands of Muslims from the Prijedor region—victims of Omarska and other camps like it—had been buried at an open-pit iron mine in a nearby town, Ljubija. *The New York Times* reported that the Bosnian Serbs were "exhuming the remains of victims from numerous mass graves in the area and transferring the bodies to this mine, where they are often mangled in old mining equipment, doused with chemicals and reburied under tons of debris in the open pits."[6] The evident intent was to prevent the bodies of those who died at the camps in the vicinity from being identified by the tribunal's investigators.

Vlatka Mihelic, Human Rights Watch's investigator, was not permitted to interview prisoners individually when she got into Omarska as *Washington Post* correspondent Peter Maass's translator, but a couple of inmates managed to speak to her out of earshot of the guards. One told her, "Until August 6, there were over two thousand of us here. Five hundred have been killed in this camp. They were beating us with sticks, rifle butts, and knives. We received food only once a day and were beaten while we were eating. It is a lot better now than it was a few days ago." While she was at the camp, some of the prisoners were taken to a cafeteria and fed meat, beans, and bread.

Later, after prisoners from Omarska were released through the International Committee of the Red Cross, I interviewed some at Karlovac and other refugee centers in Croatia. (Human rights colleagues interviewed many more at various locations.) They told me of beatings, torture, rape, sexual humiliation, and many deaths, some as a consequence of the terrible conditions or the beatings, others due to summary executions. Omarska was the camp where Dusko Tadic, who would become the first defendant tried and convicted by the tribunal, reportedly forced a prisoner to castrate a fellow prisoner with his teeth—an episode that figured prominently in the accounts by ex-inmates. Those I interviewed named other prisoners who died at Omarska; they also identified many of the guards, having recognized their torturers as Serbs who had lived in the vicinity—men they had known all their lives. The men they named were among the twenty-one commanders and guards from Omarska indicted by the tribunal in 1995.

At Keraterm, also in the Prijedor area, many prisoners were beaten to death. On July 24, 1992, ex-inmates subsequently told Human Rights Watch's investigators, the guards fired into a hall with automatic weapons, killing and wounding many; some said more than a hundred died that day. The shooting started when prisoners hallucinating from the summer heat, lack of water, and beatings panicked and started screaming. The camp commander at Keraterm raped at least one of the female inmates there. He and twelve other officials from Keraterm also were indicted by the tribunal. As at Omarska, most of the guards came from the vicinity of Prijedor and were identified by ex-inmates.

At Trnopolje, the other camp near Prijedor cited by *Newsday*'s Gutman, the inmates were mostly women, children, and the elderly. The UN War Crimes Commission found that "in Trnopolje, the regime was far better than in Omarska and Keraterm. Nonetheless, harassment and malnutrition were a problem for all the inmates. Rapes, beatings and other kinds of torture, and even killings, were not rare."[7] Some men who were held there disappeared and their whereabouts are unknown. At Manjaca, near Banja Luka, prisoners were routinely beaten and denied adequate food. At a camp known as Luka, near the town of Brcko, according to a submission by the U.S. government to the UN Security Council,[8] about three thousand men, women, and children were killed in May and June 1992. The report said the camp was controlled by the Serbian police, who continued the killing that had taken place when Serb paramilitary forces led by Zeljko Raznjatovic, a longtime criminal who used the *nom de guerre* "Arkan," and Vojislav Seselj, an extreme nationalist, attacked the town. (Arkan's followers referred to themselves as the "Tigers," and Seselj's adherents called themselves "White Eagles"; each formed a political party and both were elected to the parliament of Serbia after campaigns in which they boasted of their exploits. In 1997, Seselj was a candidate to succeed Milosevic as president of Serbia now that the latter had shifted to the federal presidency of Yugoslavia. In one round, Seselj got the most votes but the election was invalidated because the turnout was a shade under the 50 percent of eligible voters required. In March 1998, Seselj was appointed to be deputy president of Serbia.)

These forces killed between two thousand and three thousand people when they overran Brcko and surrounding villages. According to the U.S. government reports of one episode at Luka, detainees were ordered to sing Serbian Chetnik songs. Those who did not sing loudly enough were shot point-blank. Other detainees were made to carry out bodies—some still alive—to the camp garbage dump or to the nearby Sava River. Some of those who carried the bodies were themselves killed. Subsequently, bodies were transported by truck to be burned at factories in the area.

Another camp where killings reportedly took place on a similar scale was Susica, at Vlasenica, a town in eastern Bosnia from which the entire Muslim population of more than 18,000 was eliminated during 1992. Two years after *Newsday* published Roy Gutman's accounts of Omarska, *The New York Times* carried full-page reports on Susica,[9] a camp that was barely known to that point. Some of the information in the *Times* account, by Roger Cohen, came from survivors of Susica, but most was provided by a former guard, Pero Popovic, who told the reporter that he was troubled by what he saw and did at Susica. Popovic deserted the Bosnian Serb army on New Year's Day 1993 and subsequently provided evidence to the tribunal prosecutors.

According to Popovic and the camp survivors interviewed by the *Times,* three thousand people were killed at Susica. Every night there were executions of detainees selected more or less at random by the guards, who were often drunk. About three hundred were executed by firing squad after Bosnian government forces ambushed and killed a popular Serb from Vlasenica nicknamed "Kalimero." In another episode, more than half the surviving two hundred prisoners were executed when the camp was closed in September 1992, and the rest were put to work digging trenches. Many of the trench diggers—and perhaps all—ultimately were shot. Popovic named Dragan Nikolic as the man who ran Susica, and it was this testimony that made Nikolic the first person indicted by the tribunal on November 7, 1994.

In a different kind of conflict, focusing at the outset on someone as obscure as Nikolic would have sent the wrong message. But in Bosnia, where leaders like Karadzic and Mladic not only controlled the actions of subordinates but also rallied their fellow Bosnian Serbs who made conscious choices to join them in a murderous enterprise, it was a reasonable choice.

Nikolic was employed before the war at a bauxite mine near Vlasenica. He was not one of the architects of the "ethnic cleansing," and the crimes attributed to him by the tribunal's prosecutors—including the murder of eight prisoners and the torture of seven others—were no different in kind or severity than those of a hundred other potential defendants. Which was precisely the point: Here was an ordinary man of no significant accomplishment or history of evil deeds who took the first leadership position of his life and played an important part in the slaughter of innocent people. He was not an automaton following orders. And he did not try to put any distance between himself and the act of killing. The inmates of Susica were his schoolmates, his colleagues at work, his fellow villagers with whom he had lived peaceably all his life before the war. If prosecutors prove the charges against Nikolic, his responsibility for the criminal conduct of the war in Bosnia is no less than that of the leaders who inspired him.

Nikolic remains at large. At this writing, some two dozen of about eighty named defendants are in custody in The Hague. They include a Bosnian Croat who served in the Bosnian Serb army and who turned himself in for his role in the massacres at Srebrenica; two men who were handed over by the Bosnian government; three who were apprehended outside the former Yugoslavia; one who was seized by UN forces in Eastern Slavonia, near Vukovar; another captured by British NATO troops at Prijedor; two captured by Dutch NATO troops in Central Bosnia; nine of eleven men who purportedly turned themselves in but actually were forced to go to The Hague by the Cro-

Hermann Goering testifying at the first Nuremberg trial on May 13, 1946. In the dock are Goering's fellow defendants: (front row, left to right) Rudolf Hess, Joachim von Ribbentrop, Wilhelm Keitel, Ernst Kaltenbrunner, Alfred Rosenberg, Hans Frank, Wilhelm Frick, Julius Streicher, Walther Funk, and (to the right of the military policeman) Hjalmar Schacht. Behind them (left to right) are Karl Doenitz, Erich Raeder, Baldur von Schirach, Fritz Sauckel, Alfred Jodl, Franz von Papen, Arthur Seyss-Inquart, Albert Speer, Konstantin von Neurath, and Hans Fritzsche. *Corbis-Bettmann*

Mothers of the disappeared in the Plaza de Mayo, Buenos Aires, on June 28, 1982, hold white scarves bearing the names of their children and the dates they were abducted by security forces. Through weekly demonstrations, which began in 1977, the mothers demanded the truth about the fate of their children. When democracy was restored in 1983, their efforts led President Alfonsin to establish a body that became the model for "truth commissions" in many countries. *Reuters/Corbis-Bettmann*

Six priests, their housekeeper, and her daughter were assassinated on November 16, 1989. The murders led to the first conviction of an officer for a human rights abuse after nine years of civil war during which tens of thousands of murders were committed by El Salvador's armed forces. Military superiors named by a UN truth commission as having plotted the crime, and the officer, were freed under an amnesty adopted by the Salvadoran Parliament. *Reuters/Corbis-Bettmann*

Archbishop Desmond Tutu, chairman of South Africa's Truth and Reconciliation Commission, and Alex Boraine (at Tutu's left), deputy chairman, hear testimony on April 15, 1996. Witnesses before the commission included apartheid-era officials who, in exchange for amnesty, acknowledged crimes they committed. *AFP/Corbis-Bettmann*

Scenes from Vukovar, the Croatian city near the Serbian border bombarded by Serb paramilitary forces and the Yugoslav Army from August to November 1991, when they captured the city. *Photos this page courtesy Gilles Peress*

Skeletal remains and clothing of more than two hundred Croatian men summarily executed on November 20, 1991, at the Ovcara farm near Vukovar. The men had been patients at Vukovar's hospital. Three regular military officers in the Yugoslav Army are wanted by the International Criminal Tribunal for the crime.

Above: A woman in Sarajevo carting plastic bottles of water. During the siege from 1992 to 1995 many Sarajevans had to carry water up to high-rise apartments (elevators did not work for lack of electricity). Even worse, the route from the wells to their homes often exposed people to sniper fire. *Below:* Buildings such as these twin office towers in Sarajevo were easy targets for the Serb gunners in the surrounding hills. The city's economy came to an almost complete halt during the war, and though many buildings in the downtown area have been repaired since the Dayton peace agreement, little economic activity has resumed. *Photos this page courtesy Gilles Peress*

A destroyed mosque in Ahmici, central Bosnia, site of a 1993 massacre of Muslim villagers by Croat militiamen. These crimes led to indictments by the International Criminal Tribunal. Militiamen charged with those crimes turned themselves in to the tribunal in 1997 after the United States brought heavy pressure on Croatia. *Photos this page courtesy Gilles Peress*

In March 1993, more than two years before Srebrenica became the site of the largest massacre in Europe since World War II, Serb forces nearly overran the town. It was saved when the UN's General Philippe Morillon went there and promised its inhabitants: "I will never abandon you." Morillon negotiated the evacuation of five hundred wounded, including this woman. Shortly before the evacuation, the UN Security Council declared Srebrenica a "United Nations safe area."

After the massacre of an estimated eight thousand Muslim men from Srebrenica in July 1995, a team from Physicians for Human Rights, led by American forensic anthropologist William Haglund (foreground), exhumes one of the mass graves. *Photos this page courtesy Gilles Peress*

In 1997, many women and children who survived Srebrenica still lived in refugee centers such as this one near the industrial city of Tuzla.

During the 1994 genocide in Rwanda, many Tutsis fled to churches but were massacred there; these men, women, and children were killed at Rukara and Nyarube. *Photos this page courtesy Gilles Peress*

A wanted poster distributed by NATO to its troops in Bosnia-Herzegovina in early 1996 with photos of some of those indicted by the International Criminal Tribunal. For a year and a half after their arrival, NATO forces studiously avoided making arrests, but the policy changed in 1997. After a few indictees were seized, some other defendants turned themselves in, and those still wanted made themselves scarce.
AFP/Corbis-Bettmann

Dusko Tadic, the first man tried by an international tribunal for war crimes since Nuremberg and Tokyo, talks to his lawyer during his 1995 trial at The Hague.
AFP/Corbis-Bettmann

atian government, which acted under heavy international pressure (the other two were released for lack of evidence); three Bosnian Serbs who surrendered to American troops in the face of heightened activity by NATO troops threatening their arrest; and another Bosnian Serb who surrendered to French troops two weeks later. In late May 1998, NATO troops picked up a particularly noteworthy defendant: the former commander of Omarska.

That the first defendant brought to The Hague for trial was Dusko Tadic was fitting not only because of the character of his crimes but also because they took place at Omarska, so crucial to the establishment of the tribunal. Tadic, like Nikolic, was a Bosnian Serb Everyman who made a deliberate decision to take up the duties that led to his indictment. He had been a martial arts instructor, café operator, and reputed hoodlum in the small town of Kozarac. At Omarska, where he was a camp official, Tadic was accused of the sexual abuse, torture, and murder of his former Muslim neighbors in Kozarac and other nearby communities. He lost his job when Omarska was closed following Gutman's revelations in *Newsday,* and fearing he might be drafted by the Bosnian Serb army for actual combat, he fled to Germany. Tadic was recognized on the streets of Munich by survivors of Omarska, and eventually their complaints led to his arrest. The tribunal sought his extradition, and the German government obliged. He was tried, convicted, and sentenced to a twenty-year prison term, which he is now serving.

Tadic's case raised many legal issues for the first time. Among other things, his lawyers claimed that the circumstances in Prijedor when Omarska was established did not meet the definition of an armed conflict. The tribunal's Appeals Chamber disposed of that argument by pointing out that international humanitarian law applies to the whole territory of a conflict; it is not necessary for substantial armed clashes to have occurred at the one precise spot under consideration. Tadic was subject to the laws of war because "it is sufficient that the alleged crimes were closely related to the hostilities occurring in other parts of the territories controlled by the parties to the conflict."[10]

Tadic's alternate claim was more substantive: He argued that if the events at Prijedor were indeed part of an armed conflict, they were internal, not international, and thus beyond the specific charge of the tribunal. As a Bosnian Serb, he said, his alleged crimes were committed in the context of a civil war—a Bosnian Serb uprising against a predominantly Bosnian Muslim government. The applicable laws of war were those that govern internal armed conflicts. Since these lack provisions designating certain acts as grave breaches, he contended, violations cannot be prosecuted as war crimes.

The tribunal's Appeals Chamber could have disposed of this argument with a factual ruling that the entire conflict in ex-Yugoslavia was international because of the involvement of the internationally recognized states of Croatia and the Federal Republic of Yugoslavia, as well as Bosnia-Herzegovina. If it had done so, the laws of war for international conflicts would apply. It chose not to do so. Instead, the chamber held that the conflict had both international and internal aspects. This fact, the chamber said, was recognized at various times by the UN Security Council, which wished to bring to justice those responsible for serious violations of international humanitarian law "without reference to whether conflicts in the former Yugoslavia were internal or international."[11] Its instrument for this was the tribunal.

The Appeals Chamber then had to consider the long-disputed question of whether the international rules of war applicable to internal armed conflicts carry with them criminal sanctions. It was an issue the Security Council itself had addressed directly for the first time in the year after it created the tribunal for ex-Yugoslavia (but prior to the appellate decision in the Tadic case) because of the genocide in Rwanda. However one characterized the war in ex-Yugoslavia, there was no ambiguity about Rwanda. The conflict there was exclusively internal. Rwandans murdered other Rwandans. No external force took part. The laws applicable to international armed conflicts could not be invoked to prosecute the killers. The Security Council authorized the tribunal it established for Rwanda to prosecute those who committed genocide and crimes against humanity. Since these are subject to criminal sanctions under international law regardless of the nature of the conflict or even if committed in circumstances that do not constitute armed conflict, no legal innovation was required to endow the new court with such jurisdiction.

If the Rwanda tribunal had only been provided authority to judge these crimes, however, the prosecution would have had to prove that every crime was committed as part of a systematic or widespread attack. This might have proved too burdensome. The Security Council wished to make it possible to convict even when the Rwanda prosecutors could prove only a handful of murders or a single murder. It solved the problem by providing in the statute it adopted on November 8, 1994, "The International Tribunal for Rwanda shall have the power to prosecute persons committing or ordering to be committed serious violations of Article 3 common to the Geneva Conventions of 12 August 1949 for the Protection of War Victims, and of Additional Protocol II thereto of 8 June 1977." The statute enumerated the practices forbidden by these provisions of the laws of war that apply to internal armed conflicts, including murder, torture, mutilation, rape, enforced prostitution, and the taking of hostages.

In the Tadic case, the ex-Yugoslavia tribunal's Appeals Chamber analyzed international law and the domestic laws of many countries and arrived at the same conclusion. The trial court then upheld Tadic's argument that the Bosnian war was internal. But in accordance with the appellate ruling, it said that the international laws of war apply to internal armed conflicts as well as to wars between sovereign states, and therefore it convicted him for war crimes. In combination, the Rwanda statute and the Tadic decision make international legal precedent. The consequences could be far-reaching, even revolutionary.

Since the end of World War II, there have been more than a hundred internal armed conflicts all over the world. They are the pervasive form of warfare of our time. At this writing, such conflicts are under way in Afghanistan, India, Burma, Indonesia, Turkey, Iraq, Sri Lanka, Colombia, Peru, Congo, Uganda, Liberia, Somalia, Tajikistan, and Sudan. In theory, those committing abuses in these conflicts could be brought to trial before additional ad hoc tribunals or a permanent international criminal court, if one were established. Right now, however, war criminals could be prosecuted in any country that has legislation authorizing domestic courts to judge those responsible for war crimes wherever they were committed. Acting under such principles of universal jurisdiction, Belgium has prosecuted Rwandans accused of crimes against other Rwandans in Rwanda. If it had not turned Tadic over to The Hague, Germany would have tried him in its own courts. It subsequently convicted another man for crimes committed in Bosnia. Denmark has sentenced a man to eight years in prison for his crimes in a Croatian detention camp in Bosnia, and Britain launched a prosecution of an eighty-five-year-old immigrant from Belarus for crimes committed there more than a half century earlier during World War II. Although that case had to be dropped because of the incompetence of the defendant to stand trial, the fact that it was initiated suggests the long reach of universal jurisdiction. Another example: When reports from Cambodia in 1997 suggested that Pol Pot had been apprehended, some U.S. State Department officials proposed that he be sent to Canada, where he would stand trial in a country that has empowered its courts to exercise universal jurisdiction.

The notion that the conflicts in the former Yugoslavia were strictly internal, with all sides committing atrocities, worked nicely for many of those opposed to military or even legal intervention. In this convenient view, it would be pointless for outsiders to meddle in these civil wars; if anything, involvement in the Balkans would make matters worse. These were, after all, age-old antagonisms in a region primed for periodic warfare and attendant cruelty. A good example of this implied historic inevitability is an essay by Paul Johnson, a British author whose many published works include a disparaging book about intellectuals. The war in Bosnia inspired him to write:

> One of the great lessons of the 19th century is that the great powers should not waste too much time on the Balkans. The problems of the Balkans are infinitely complex and ultimately insoluble because they are rooted in the nature of the inhabitants themselves. . . . Short of exterminating them, there is really nothing to be done. . . . [T]he Balkans led to the first world war, thus ending a century of general peace, primarily because all the senseless fretting had convinced the powers that this miserable part of the world mattered.[12]

Anyone reading this must wonder what other peoples are so troublesome that there is nothing to be done about their problems short of exterminating them. Certainly, Jews and Gypsies, the objects of genocide during World War II, would rank high, but at various moments in history many other peoples would also have to be included. No doubt the ancient Romans and the Norse invaders several centuries later would have given Johnson's English forebears a prominent place on such a list.

An imagined version of history—one that achieves a greater reality in memory than the actual facts warrant—establishes the context in which such wars are fought. It provides the opportunity for ambitious leaders to present their aspirations in ways that resonate with potential followers and to manipulate the symbols of history to promote themselves or their cause. Grasping the history is essential to any understanding of wars such as those in Croatia and Bosnia and the ferocity with which they take place. Still, comprehension is a far cry from accepting historical inevitability. If governments outside the region and intergovernmental bodies such as the European Union, NATO, and the United Nations had acted in other ways at important moments, the events that unfolded in Croatia and Bosnia after 1991 could have been altogether different. It is also possible that a demonstration of international will to respond to genocide, first glimpsed by many people outside ex-Yugoslavia when they learned about Omarska, might have stayed the hands of those who launched the slaughter in Rwanda on April 6, 1994, two years to the day after the killing began in Bosnia.

This is not the place to replay history. It may be a place, however, to take note of the rueful comment by the eminent British historian Eric Hobsbawm, who has said that when he was younger, he believed that historians—unlike physicists—did not practice a profession that was dangerous, but he had come to know better. The idea that historical developments are impervious to external efforts to mitigate their brutality powerfully influenced key figures at various times during the Balkan wars. European Union mediator Lord David Owen and U.S. secretary of state Warren Christopher, for example, echoed the theme and said that all sides were to blame for atrocities. Neither Owen nor Christopher stated this consistently, and neither said in so many words that all sides were *equally* to blame. But as experienced spokesmen for governments and intergovernmental bodies, both should have been aware that statements they made at critical moments effectively excused those who committed abuses by making it seem that their transgressions were inevitable or that their abuses provoked and perhaps even justified those by the other side.[13] Former UN civilian administrator Yasushi Akashi and Lieutenant General Sir Michael Rose, who commanded UN forces in Bosnia in 1994, frequently made similar comments. All of them, if pressed, would deny they were excusing abuses by censuring everyone. Still, they shared an agenda: preventing the buildup of pressure for international military intervention. Each knew that blaming all sides would further that agenda. (Eventually, of course, when President Clinton decided, in 1995, that the United States should get involved forcefully, Christopher became an advocate of intervention and stopped suggesting that all sides were at fault.)

There is no denying that Croats and, to a considerably lesser extent, Bosnian government forces committed atrocities. Any attempt to suggest that all sides were equally to blame, however, is nonsense. Each party's abuses deserve condemnation in their own right, and those that constitute war crimes or crimes against humanity warrant prosecution before the United Nations tribunal. International humanitarian law is explicit in providing that violations of the rules of armed conflict by one side never justify abuses by the other side. Each side has an independent duty to respect those rules.

All sides maintained detention camps; the UN War Crimes Commission said it obtained information on some 715 such places. The abuses that were committed in detention camps by all sides reflected their general conduct of hostilities and their respect, or rather their lack of respect, for the rules of armed conflict.

Croatian forces ran a detention center at Pakracka Poljana, 60 miles southeast of Zagreb, during the 1991 war with Serbia. According to an ex-militiaman who came forward six years later to say that he tortured prisoners there, some of the detainees were doused with gasoline after they were tortured, then burned alive. Miro Bajramovic, the former militiaman, told his story to the Croatian Helsinki Committee, a human rights group that arranged for a Croatian newspaper, *Feral Tribune,* to interview him.[14] Bajramovic also told of many killings of noncombatants by Croatian paramilitary forces at Gospic, a town that became infamous during the 1991 war for the many abuses committed there.

Perhaps the most extensive use of detention by Croatian forces in Bosnia took place in Mostar, the former capital of Herzegovina— an old town of great beauty named for its famous old bridge *(Stari most)*. In *Black Lamb and Grey Falcon,* Rebecca West's classic account of her travels, in 1937, in what was then Yugoslavia, Mostar is described as a Muslim town and the feature for which it is named is portrayed idyllically as

> one of the most beautiful bridges in the world. A slender arch lies between two round towers, its parapet bent in a shallow angle in the center.
>
> To look at it is good; to stand on it is as good. Over the gray-green river swoop hundreds of swallows and on the banks mosques and white houses stand among glades of trees and bushes.[15]

The bridge was demolished by Croat forces in November 1993. Although Mostar was a predominantly Muslim town at the start of the war in Bosnia, it had a substantial Croat minority. Many of the surrounding communities were populated primarily by Croats, and they sought the town as the capital of the state they wished to carve out of Bosnia and ultimately annex to the new nation of Croatia. In addition, there was a Serb minority that claimed part of the town.

Mostar became the scene of intense fighting between Bosnian government forces and Bosnian Croat (HVO) forces. As elsewhere, the Bosnian government's forces were badly outgunned, and despite the numerical superiority of Muslims in the town, the Croats gained the upper hand. In mid-1993, they blocked the delivery of relief supplies to Muslims on the eastern bank of the river that divides the city, creating severe shortages of food and medicine. They also shelled that section of the city relentlessly, obliterating entire neighborhoods.[16] And they held 15,000 Muslims, the majority draft-age men, in detention centers near Mostar, limiting them to a near-starvation diet, subjecting them to severe beatings, and forcing them to dig trenches at night on the front lines. Many died because of the conditions in these camps or because they came under fire while digging trenches.

In September 1993, I met with Croatia's defense minister, Gojko Susak, known as a leading hard-liner in President Tudjman's cabinet, to ask him to denounce the Mostar abuses publicly or to take other effective action against those responsible. I pointed out that the Croatian government's silence implied support for the HVO, the Bosnian Croat forces who committed these crimes. Susak, a native of Herzegovina, was an émigré to Canada, where he owned a chain of pizza parlors and had raised funds for Croatian nationalists before Croatia became independent. Regarded by many as the power behind the Bosnian Croat forces, he did not deny the abuses. Instead, Susak argued that the commanders responsible were beyond his government's control and that it would be futile for Croatia to take measures against them. In January 1994, however, when HVO forces were faring badly against Bosnian government troops in central Bosnia, Susak threatened direct Croatian government intervention to assist them, and Croatian military jets defied NATO prohibitions on aerial attacks in Bosnia to assist the beleaguered HVO.

The most severe abuses of detainees known to have been committed by Bosnian government forces occurred at Celebici, a village near Mostar, between May and early August 1992, when Roy Gutman's articles on Serb detention camps started to appear. Gutman's stories and the furor they aroused had the effect throughout Bosnia of enabling the International Committee of the Red Cross to get into camps from which they were previously excluded. Bosnian government camps were no exception.

Ex-inmates of Celebici interviewed by Human Rights Watch testified that they were beaten as they were transported to the camp and beaten again in camp. Seven men were held in an underground storage pit for two days without food, water, or toilet facilities, and as many as two hundred were confined for weeks in a warehouse, where they were fed inadequately and permitted no outdoor exercise. All the prisoners were Serb men from villages in the area. Beatings at the camp, from which a number of men died, continued until Red Cross inspection visits began in August 1992.[17]

In March 1996, the tribunal indicted three Bosnian Muslims and a Bosnian Croat for crimes committed in Celebici and, in short order, obtained custody of all four. The Muslim commander of Bosnian government forces in the area was captured in Munich, and the Croat camp commander was apprehended in Vienna. The two other camp officials named in the indictment were taken into custody by the Bosnian government and handed over to the tribunal.

The practices of the three sides in detention camps are representative of their conduct generally. In the case of the Serbs, the abuses followed a clear pattern and practice and were so widespread that it is clear they were part of a policy made at the highest level. The objective was to further "ethnic cleansing" by terrorizing non-Serbs to flee and, in camps such as Omarska and Susica, by exterminating a portion of the Muslim population, especially those deemed capable of leadership. In the case of the Croats, the abuses reflect, at least, tolerance of atrocities by the principal authorities. Those authorities shared direct culpability for such crimes as the sustained indiscriminate bombing of east Mostar, and the burning of houses and the killing of 230 Serb civilians, most of them elderly, following the military success of the Croatian Army in the Krajina in the summer of 1995.[18] In the case of the Bosnians, the atrocities are an ugly stain on the government's record. It's unclear to what extent these abuses were directed by top government officials or known and tolerated by them. But the fact that the Bosnian government promptly arrested camp officials following their indictment and sent them to The Hague suggests that top civilian officials were not fearful that testimony would implicate higher-level authorities.

It is possible that Bosnian government forces committed fewer abuses because they had fewer opportunities. When I visited Mostar after the fighting there ended and noted the contrast between the destruction on the Muslim side and the almost complete lack of damage on the Croat side, I was told a story about another American who had publicly commented on the same thing—clear evidence, she said to an audience, that there was less hate on the Muslim side. One listener, a Bosnian government soldier who fought at Mostar, demurred. The Muslim side wanted to retaliate, he said, but they had no ammunition. Later on in the war, Bosnian government forces were better armed—but were not more inclined to greater abusiveness.

Regardless of the reasons for their disparate conduct, each side should be held accountable for its own abuses. Aristotle pointed out long ago that the just is the proportionate and the unjust is the disproportionate.[19] To do justice, the prosecution must strive for proportionality in its indictments. At the same time, however, justice requires that no one should be indicted solely for purposes of seeing to it that all sides are represented, or represented equally, among the defendants. The task of the prosecutor, therefore, is to ensure both that individual culpability is the basis for indictments and that the indictments fairly reflect the extent and severity of the crimes committed by the three sides. Similarly, public officials and others who speak out about abuses have a responsibility neither to spare any of the parties that committed abuses from criticism nor to liken them to one another in a manner that seems to excuse those most culpable. Blame, quite simply, should be apportioned as fairly as possible.

The discovery of Omarska and other detention centers in Bosnia invited comparisons to Nazi death camps—comparisons that proved crucial in mustering the international will to do something about them. But there were important differences, first and foremost the scale of killing. Tens of thousands died in the camps in Bosnia, where most of the killing ended a few months after it began, when press coverage made the camps an international cause célèbre. In contrast, the Nazis killed millions over a period of years in the camps they established in Poland; although these operations were known during the war, they inspired only a muted reaction, particularly in the American press.[20]

Another difference was the manner in which the killing took place. The Nazis bureaucratized murder. One objective was to kill as efficiently as possible, which was critical to their self-assigned mission: to rid Europe of its Jewish population of several million people. At this, the Nazis succeeded all too well. A subsidiary purpose was to sanitize the process, not out of solicitude for the victims but rather out of concern for their own personnel. Thus, Ukrainian guards were employed to do the dirty work at three of the six major killing centers: Belzec, Sobibor, and Treblinka. As for the German personnel at Auschwitz and other camps, they were not elite units such as the Waffen SS. It would have been beneath their dignity to take on such a task.

Raul Hilberg has discussed the concerns of the Nazis about the effects of service in the death camps on their forces:

> The personnel problem arose in two different forms—sadism and corruption. . . . With regard to sadism, it must be kept in mind that the bureaucracy was not so much concerned with the suffering of the victims as with contamination of the perpetrators. Thus the SS paid no attention whatsoever to the host of indirect tortures which it had built into the camp routine: hunger, exposure to freezing weather, overwork, filth, and utter lack of privacy. All this suffering was a consequence of the very nature of SS camp maintenance and operations. It was simply no problem.[21]

The Nazis did inflict pain on those who violated rules, and there were cases in which German camp personnel engaged in patterns of sadistic behavior that were not related directly to the efficient operation of a killing center. But these were the exception, not the rule: It was the Nazis' vision that they were pursuing an ideal and that they would degrade themselves by indulging in "excess." Memoirs by survivors of Auschwitz, such as Primo Levi, describe the extreme deprivation suffered by those not immediately sent to the gas chambers, but they are not chronicles of beatings and sexual torture.[22] Corruption also was considered degrading, and as Hilberg has reported, a number of investigations were launched to try to root this out from the administration of the camps.[23]

The Serbs who established Omarska and the other camps had no such vision. As accounts by survivors make clear, sadism and corruption were the modus operandi.[24] While it is the beatings, torture, and rapes that are rightly the focus of attention, accounts by survivors make clear that the camps also were used to extort money from detainees and their families. As Bosnian Muslims were taken into custody, their homes were looted. Inmates and their families were forced to pay to avoid specific tortures, or to get a meal, or to buy their freedom.

The most striking difference, however, was that many of the guards at the camps in Bosnia—indeed, the great majority in all likelihood—previously knew or were known to the inmates they guarded. They were their neighbors, fellow employees, schoolmates, teachers, taxi drivers, and policemen. As Ed Vulliamy has written, "the most extraordinary hallmark [of Omarska] was its grotesque intimacy."[25] This was a far cry from the intentional depersonalization of killing by the Nazis. In fact, there may be no precedent for camps such as Omarska, where people who had lived next door to each other all their lives were suddenly separated into two groups: one of guards practicing every means of torture and murder, the other of prisoners forced to submit to every form of degradation and pain and, at any moment, in imminent danger of being killed. But Omarska may have foretold horrors to come: The genocide in Rwanda also saw atrocities committed by neighbor against neighbor.

The differences between the camps in ex-Yugoslavia and those operated by the Nazis complicate the prosecution and punishment of war criminals. In the case of the Nazi death camps, it seemed appropriate to focus on those who had established and administered them and on those guards who had indulged in cruelties that went beyond assisting in their efficient operation. Among the bureaucrats, as Hilberg has written, most "composed memoranda, drew up blueprints, signed correspondence, talked on the telephone and participated in conferences. They could destroy a whole people while sitting at their desks" but were not obliged ever to see the corpses of those killed as a consequence of their desk work.[26]

As for intentional cruelties, it's useful to examine briefly the case of John Demjanjuk, a Ukrainian-born immigrant to the United States. Demjanjuk was alleged to be "Ivan the Terrible," a guard at Treblinka notorious for his cruelty, and was extradited to Israel to stand trial. He eventually was freed in July 1993 by Israel's Supreme Court on grounds of reasonable doubt. The court was persuaded that Demjanjuk had been a concentration camp guard, but there was evidence that the actual "Ivan the Terrible" had been another Ukrainian named Ivan Marchenko. Despite its belief that Demjanjuk had been a guard at a death camp, and therefore an active participant in a depersonalized killing process if not a practitioner of extra cruelties, the Israeli Supreme Court declined to permit his retrial on other charges.

At camps such as Omarska, it is difficult to draw the line between the guards who conducted themselves like "Ivan the Terrible" and those who performed routine duties. Where most guards and inmates knew one another, as Dusko Tadic knew the men he murdered and tortured, gratuitous cruelties were the norm. Nothing was routine.

10

Sarajevo
and Siege
Warfare

On April 6, 1993, the first anniversary of the war in Bosnia and the assault on its capital, Sarajevo, I joined about 150 residents of the besieged city at a Passover seder celebrated at the local Jewish community center. The seder was conducted mostly in Ladino, a dialect preserved in the city for five centuries, ever since Jews had found a safe haven in Sarajevo following their expulsion from Spain, and it included songs intoned by a teenage boy in the manner of Gregorian chants. Its list of distinguished guests was unusual, to say the least. Among them were the chief Muslim cleric of ex-Yugoslavia, the Catholic archbishop of Bosnia-Herzegovina, the leader of Sarajevo's Orthodox community, and a representative of the Seventh-Day Adventists. Their intent was plain: By attending, they were making a statement about the city's diverse religious, ethnic, and cultural character. Those qualities, under brutal attack, now mattered more to Sarajevans than ever before.

For a year, they had been shelled, sniped at, denied adequate food, and most of the time, cut off from running water, electricity, and gas. In that year, relentless firepower had killed several thousand city residents and wounded tens of thousands more. Homes and possessions had been destroyed and almost every building in the city had suffered some damage. Waterborne diseases were just beginning to take their toll; the spring thaw was under way and sewage that had been frozen all winter was starting to leach into the underground water that had kept the city alive. The citizens had frozen during the winter, as I well remembered from an earlier visit at New Year's, when I had been colder than ever before in my life. Indoors. Diet? A nattily attired eighty-three-year-old man who sat across the table from me at the seder summed it up nicely. Looking down at one of the small chicken legs the Jewish community had managed to bring into the city for the Passover meal, he told me it would be the first meat he had tasted in a year.

It was not only at such ritual occasions that Sarajevans under siege showed what they stood for. On that visit, I was struck by the word that the city's residents used to label the forces attacking them. When I had interviewed refugees from provincial towns or rural communities, they almost invariably spoke of "Chetniks." Sarajevans, in contrast, did not use "Chetnik" or even "Serb" to refer to the besieging forces. The word of choice in the city that first year of siege was "aggressors." It connoted culpability, but that did not seem to me the principal reason for its use. Far more important was that it avoided an ethnic label. The Sarajevans with whom I came in contact resented it when foreign officials or journalists referred to them as Muslims. Labeling them by religion denigrated the government side as one of three ethnic factions and inaccurately identified them as a group. It was a point of considerable pride to them that Orthodox Serbs, Catholic Croats, Jews, and others—including many of mixed descent—remained in the city and tried to survive the siege collectively. Unlike some of their compatriots in rural areas and small towns, they were not comfortable with an ethnic or religious label. They were Bosnians and Sarajevans. Those were the identities that mattered.

It also mattered to the aggressors. The Serb forces assaulting Sarajevo were made up largely of fighters from provincial areas. In attacking the city, they were killing not only Muslims but Serbs as well—Serbs who made up more than a quarter of the city's population before the siege and still accounted for roughly that proportion of the much reduced number who remained in the city a year later. It was the city's cosmopolitan aspect and ethnic and religious diversity that seemed to be the primary targets of the aggressors. Over time, they substantially succeeded in destroying these characteristics. Sarajevo's ethnic mix began to shift and its urbanity began to diminish as more and more provincial Muslims, "ethnically cleansed" from villages and rural areas, sought refuge in the city, even as an increasing number of its cosmopolitan residents gave up hope and fled the country. Unhappily, Sarajevo today has lost some of the character that allowed many of its citizens to take pride in withstanding the hardships of that first year of the siege.

Early in the siege,[1] the Bosnian government recorded an exchange on Serb radio frequencies between the commander of the Bosnian Serb forces, General Ratko Mladic, and two subordinates. Mladic, apparently at the Lukavica barracks in the southwest suburbs of Sarajevo, was speaking to a colonel, identified only by a code name, who was located in Vraca, a hilltop suburb south of the city; also on the line was another code-named colonel, located southeast of the city, on Borije Mountain. The colonel in Vraca questioned Mladic's instructions about artillery attacks because the areas being shelled had many Serb residents. Mladic overruled his subordinate and ordered the bombardment. "Burn it all," Mladic demanded, and instructed his forces to use the heaviest weapon in their arsenal, 155-millimeter howitzers, to destroy an area with a large Serb population. Serbs who cast their lot with their fellow Sarajevans were also his enemy.

The cultural war against Sarajevo was clear from the deliberate destruction of the city's historic treasures. The hit list included its beautiful sixteenth-century mosques, with their slender stone minarets, and churches regardless of denomination. It also included the Basck Carsija, or medieval quarter of the city, and the building the city's residents seemed to mourn most—the national library, which had previously been the town hall. The building was a large, ornate Austro-Hungarian affair on the banks of the Milijacka River, which runs through the heart of the city and creates the narrow valley in which Sarajevo is nestled and is easily shelled from the mountains that rise steeply on all sides. It was from this building that Archduke Franz Ferdinand and Countess Sophie set out on June 28, 1914, the anniversary of the battle of Kosovo, moments before Gavrilo Princip, a Bosnian Serb, fired the shots that killed them and triggered World War I. The intensive shelling of the library by Serb forces at the outset of the siege set it ablaze and destroyed most of its priceless collection of old books, manuscripts, and historic documents. (Like many residents of Sarajevo, I carried away a fragment of carved stone from the ruins as a memento.)[2]

There is, of course, nothing new about siege warfare. It has been a means throughout history for forcing the submission of an opponent. The Bible tells us that the Israelites besieged Jericho. Homer's *Iliad* records the events of the tenth and final year of the siege of Troy. The siege of Carthage by Rome's legions lasted three years before the city was overrun and destroyed, and Josephus wrote movingly about the Roman siege of Jerusalem in A.D. 72. Among the most stirring and terrifying passages in Shakespeare is Henry V's address to the delegates from Harfleur about the consequences that will befall them should they refuse to surrender to his forces besieging the city. One of the great turning points in the history of Western civilization was the Ottoman Turk siege of Greek Constantinople in 1453. The French acquired their taste for horse meat during the siege of Paris in the Franco-Prussian War, and in the latter weeks of the siege, many Parisians also dined on cats and rats. In our century, the greatest loss of life in any city due to warfare— several times the combined death toll of Hiroshima and Nagasaki— was in Leningrad during the siege by German and Finnish forces; it lasted nearly 900 days, from September 8, 1941, until January 27, 1944. Shelling, starvation, cold, and disease reportedly resulted in 650,000 deaths in 1942 alone.

Michael Walzer discussed the siege of Leningrad and whether it constituted a war crime in his classic 1977 work, *Just and Unjust Wars*.[3] The date of publication is important because it was the year the Additional Protocols to the Geneva Conventions of 1949 were promulgated. Accordingly, given the lapse of time from the completion of Walzer's book until publication, he was writing before the First Protocol added substantially to the list of "grave breaches" specified in the Geneva Conventions. Several of the additions deal with siege warfare.

According to Walzer, "Civilians have been attacked along with soldiers, or in order to get at soldiers, as often in ancient as in modern times. Such attacks are likely whenever an army seeks what might be called civilian shelter and fights from behind the battlements or from within the buildings of a city, or whenever the inhabitants of a threatened city seek the most immediate form of military protection and agree to be garrisoned. Then, locked into the narrow circle of the walls, civilians and soldiers are exposed to the same risks."

In this scenario, the defending forces bear at least part of the responsibility for the devastation caused by a siege. By using the civilian population as cover, or by shielding themselves in and among civilian structures, the troops expose noncombatants to risk. Since it is legitimate in warfare to attack the opposing armed forces, and since it may not be possible to do so except by also attacking the civilians now proximate to those forces, siege warfare cannot be ruled out entirely. There might still be questions of proportionality—an attack on an entire city would not be legitimate if a small force with little or no offensive capacity takes refuge there—but a siege is not impermissible per se.

Walzer's scenario applied to Leningrad. The Red Army had 200,000 men in the city, and because they got first crack at food supplies, they did not starve. Leningrad also continued to manufacture munitions throughout the siege. Even with such a large force and such industrial capacity, the civilian death toll makes proportionality an important issue. But it is not possible to argue that the besieging forces lacked an important military objective. (In more recent times, the Walzer scenario also applied to Grozny, where Chechen fighters deliberately made the presidential palace and other buildings in the center of the city into strongholds that symbolized their resistance to Russian power. Pointing this out does not excuse the assault on Grozny; the real issue was the disproportionate and indiscriminate character of the Russian bombardment and the disregard for civilian casualties.)

Walzer contended there should be a right of civilians to leave a besieged city. He pointed out that the Talmud's rules on sieges, espoused by Maimonides in the twelfth century and picked up from his writings by Grotius in the seventeenth century, required that a siege not surround a city completely. A path should be left for those who want to flee. When an attempt was made to prosecute a German military officer at Nuremberg for the siege of Leningrad, this principle was invoked.

The charges against Field Marshal von Leeb at Nuremberg were based on an order he issued at the outset of the siege that civilians attempting to leave Leningrad should be shelled. The purpose of forcing them to remain in the city was to maintain the pressure created by shortages of food and other necessities. Von Leeb defended himself on these grounds, claiming that his order was consistent with military practice. The argument prevailed. Since the surrender of the city—with its 200,000 troops and its munitions plants—could have been hastened by maintaining the pressure, the judges concluded that von Leeb had not committed a war crime under the laws of war in effect during World War II.

The siege of Sarajevo differs from the siege of Leningrad not only because the laws of war have evolved. Unlike Leningrad and other sieges described by Walzer, and unlike Grozny, Sarajevo and several other Bosnian towns that came under such attack lacked legitimate military targets. There never was a Bosnian Army before the start of the war, nor had there been Bosnian militias. The Yugoslav Army had barracks in Sarajevo, but most of the troops stationed there maintained their loyalty to the JNA and, two months after the siege began,[4] were permitted by the Bosnian government to evacuate in an eighty-vehicle convoy to join the forces attacking the city. Neither Sarajevo nor the besieged communities in eastern Bosnia were armaments-production centers, and any industrial capacity they had did not contribute materially to the war effort.

The purpose of the war in Bosnia was "ethnic cleansing." The purposes of the sieges of Sarajevo and the eastern side of Mostar were killing Muslims and attempting to destroy the symbols of cosmopolitanism and of ethnic, religious, and cultural pluralism. Civilians and civilian structures in these communities were not collateral casualties of an assault on legitimate military targets. Removing or destroying the civilians and their cultural monuments was the whole point.

At various times, the Serbs surrounding Cerska and Srebrenica offered guarantees of safe passage to civilians wishing to leave. Had it wished to do so, the Bosnian government probably would have been able to negotiate the wholesale departure of the civilian population from Sarajevo. In February 1993, the United Nations high commissioner for refugees transported women and children from Cerska to the Bosnian government–held city of Tuzla, an industrial center that was relatively defensible against Serb attacks. Along the way, a couple of children died, apparently crushed to death on the overloaded trucks. This provided the Bosnian government the pretext it sought to halt the evacuations.

Serb forces allowed civilians to leave besieged towns because it furthered the goal of "ethnic cleansing." The Bosnian government resisted such departures for the same reason. In addition, the Bosnians knew that the flight of the women and children would hasten the fall of those towns, since most of the defenders were husbands and fathers, frequently armed with old hunting rifles, whose main motivation was saving the lives of family members. If the women and children left, the Bosnian government was aware, these men quickly would find a way to follow them, permitting Serb forces easy entry into towns they had kept under siege for many months. That, in fact, is what happened in Cerska, which fell in March 1993. Field Marshal von Leeb had forced civilians to remain in Leningrad to further his goal—the defeat of the Red Army. In Bosnia, where the goal was driving away those who would sully the ethnic purity of Greater Serbia, the considerations were reversed.

According to Walzer, writing two decades ago, "siege warfare is not ruled out by the laws of war." Even then, this assertion required qualification. Under the Fourth Hague Convention, adopted in 1907, and a similar provision in the Second Hague Convention of 1899, attacks or bombardment "by any means whatever of towns, villages, habitations or buildings which are not defended" are impermissible. The Conventions also require "all necessary steps . . . to spare" buildings devoted to religion, art, science or charity, historic monuments, hospitals, and other places where the sick and wounded are collected. They were adopted before the age of aerial attack but at a time when the drafters thought new methods of bombardment might be devised. Specifically, these might include the use of balloons as weapons of war—hence the reference to attacks "by any means."

In the early days of World War II, before the United States became a party to the conflict, Franklin D. Roosevelt cited these provisions of the Hague Conventions in condemning German bombing raids. Subsequently, when the Allies retaliated in kind, Roosevelt fell silent. Charges of terror bombing for the destruction of Warsaw, Rotterdam, and Coventry were brought against Field Marshal Hermann Goering, the top Nazi defendant at Nuremberg (who cheated the gallows by taking poison). But Goering was exonerated on those counts by persuading the judges that Warsaw was a legitimate military target as a railroad center, that Coventry was an important armaments-manufacturing site, and that the obliteration of Rotterdam was a mistake resulting from faulty communications with a German force on the ground.

That there were ample grounds for sentencing Goering to death on other charges may have contributed to the decision by the judges. But a bigger factor probably was the difficulty distinguishing what the Germans had done from aerial raids by the Allies. The destruction of such cities as Hamburg, Dresden, Berlin, and Tokyo and, of course, the nuclear annihilation of Hiroshima and Nagasaki left the Allies—and the United States in particular—vulnerable to charges similar to those brought against Goering. Indeed, the Allies seem to have determined early in the war that they were free to pattern their own aerial attacks on those of the Germans.

On the eve of World War II, at the time of the Spanish Civil War (1936–39), Britain outspokenly denounced the bombing of civilian population centers. The Italian dictator Benito Mussolini had assisted the Nationalist forces of Generalissimo Francisco Franco by providing hundreds of aircraft that engaged in indiscriminate attacks on Barcelona in early 1938 in a deliberate attempt to destroy civilian morale. More than 1,000 residents were killed. Even Prime Minister Neville Chamberlain, who was sympathetic to Franco, felt obliged to condemn the bombings, telling Parliament, "The one definite rule of international law . . . is that the direct and deliberate bombing of non-combatants is in all circumstances illegal."[5] Chamberlain subsequently elaborated on this statement, setting forth rules that, in essence, are those that are accepted today:

> In the first place, it is against international law to bomb civilians as such and to make deliberate attacks upon civilian populations. That is undoubtedly a violation of international law. In the second place, targets which are aimed at from the air must be legitimate military objectives and must be capable of identification. In the third place, reasonable care must be taken in attacking those military objectives so that by carelessness a civilian population in the neighborhood is not bombed.[6]

Revulsion against the bombing of civilians in Spain and against Japan's bombing campaign in China prompted the adoption on September 30, 1938, by unanimous vote, of a League of Nations resolution asserting that "the intentional bombing of civilian populations is illegal" and that "any attack on legitimate objectives must be carried out in such a way that civilian populations in the neighborhood are not bombed through negligence."[7]

Although British leaders had condemned indiscriminate bombing when their own cities came under such attack, they were not willing to follow the course of the Persian King Xerxes in Herodotus's account. Instead they took reprisals against German civilians and civilian structures. A communication to the State Department from the U.S. ambassador in London, dated May 10, 1940, conveyed the new attitude following German bombing raids of British cities. The British, cabled Joseph P. Kennedy, would now abandon any restraint exercised up to that time and would reserve to themselves the right "to take any action they consider appropriate in the event of bombing by the enemy of civil populations." Even before the United States entered the war following the Japanese attack on Pearl Harbor in December 1941, Franklin Roosevelt had refrained from citing the Fourth Hague Convention's proscription on bombardment of undefended localities when it became clear that doing so also would imply condemnation of RAF raids then being launched on German population centers and towns in German-occupied Europe. Indiscriminate raids became official British policy on February 14, 1942, when Directive No. 22 instructed that bombing was to be "focused on the morale of the enemy civil population and in particular of the industrial workers."[8] A few days later, on February 23, Sir Arthur ("Bomber") Harris was appointed head of Bomber Command and carried out that directive in a manner that made his name synonymous with attacks on civilians.

Historian and literary critic Paul Fussell has offered a different view of the bombing of civilian populations during World War II. Fussell has argued that the general public was grossly misled during the war years by a military claiming it was capable of "precision bombing." The technology available at that time and the actual conditions of warfare, he said, made such claims ludicrous. "It was the grave inaccuracy of the bombers that led finally to the practice of 'area bombing,' whose effect was in Churchill's memorable euphemism, to 'dehouse' the enemy population. And area bombing led inevitably, as intensification overrode scruples, to Hiroshima and Nagasaki."[9] This argument strains credulity as an explanation of how Britain and the United States came to firebomb Dresden, Hamburg, and Tokyo and to drop atomic bombs on civilian population centers. But Fussell has a point in suggesting that aerial bombardments were far less accurate than was widely portrayed, especially when the bombers were trying to dodge anti-aircraft fire or enemy fighter planes. Half a century later, after enormous technological advances, the aerial bom-

bardment of Iraqi cities during the Gulf War was sometimes spectac-
ularly accurate when laser-guided smart bombs were used; when
they were not, as many journalists reported at the time, bombs frequently fell far off the mark. Many hundreds and perhaps thousands
of Iraqi civilians died because bombs went astray and landed on civilian homes or in civilian neighborhoods.[10]

Although inaccuracy on both sides caused countless civilian casualties during World War II, the failure to prosecute the top Nazi war
criminals for the deliberate bombardment of civilians or for grossly
indiscriminate bombardments had a more fundamental basis: The Allies did not have clean hands. Indeed, with respect to indiscriminate
bombing, their hands were as dirty as those of the Germans and the
Japanese. The most that can be said for the Allies is that the Japanese (Chongqing, 1938) and Germans (Warsaw, 1939) did it first, although this is no justification for similar practices by Britain and the
United States that caused an even larger number of civilian casualties.
The laws of war were and are clear that the abuses of one side do
not legitimate abuses by the other side; each party is independently
responsible for its own conduct and has an obligation to respect the
prohibitions on certain practices. Yet the possibility of a *tu quoque*
(you also) defense ensured that it was not in the interest of the Allies
to press such charges.

Given the failure at Nuremberg and Tokyo to apply the terms of
the Hague Convention meaningfully, it's understandable why Walzer
asserted that sieges are not necessarily outside the bounds of legitimate warfare. Moreover, by prohibiting attacks only on sites "which
are not defended," the Fourth Hague Convention did not fit exactly
even the towns of eastern Bosnia or Sarajevo. In fact, these places
were defended pitifully, given the paucity of arms available to the pu-
tative defenders. Still, many of the buildings or neighborhoods deliberately bombed by Serb forces—for example, the national library
in Sarajevo—did fit the proscription of the Hague Convention on attacks on "habitations or buildings which are not defended." (During
World War II, many bombing targets of both sides were undefended
buildings, and therefore, those attacks also violated the Hague Convention.) What's more, the Hague Convention's language makes it
clear that international law has recognized throughout the twentieth
century that attacking a city or a residential neighborhood where
there is no legitimate military target is impermissible.

The thrust of Walzer's analysis was based on his concept of a siege as warfare aimed at the defeat of a military opponent who has made use of a city's structures and inhabitants to enhance his own capacity to resist an attacker. In this view, a siege meets the test of military necessity. But the forces defending Sarajevo, or the towns of eastern Bosnia eventually overrun by the Serbs, were like householders picking up whatever weapons came to hand to defend their families and themselves against marauders attempting to kill them. Certainly during the first two years of the war, they did not constitute military forces that could be deployed on other battlefields if their own communities were spared attack. (Later on, as they acquired combat experience and weapons, the Bosnian government's troops became a credible military force.)

It is always possible, of course, to come up with military argu-ments to justify attacks even on undefended or poorly defended towns like Sarajevo and Gorazde. Consider, for instance, the case for dropping atomic bombs on Hiroshima and Nagasaki: that the awe-some destruction created by these demonstrations of nuclear weapons hastened the end of the war and, in the process, spared as many as a million lives—both Americans and Japanese—that would have been lost in an invasion of Japan.

There are difficulties with this argument. First, it does not follow that it was necessary to drop the atomic bombs on civilian popula-tion centers to demonstrate the weapon's unprecedented might. Japan might have been persuaded to surrender if an atomic bomb had been dropped on an unpopulated location, where its destructive power still would be evident. If that were not effective, a second bomb could have been dropped on a military target—an ammunition or armaments storage area, an airfield, a naval base, an industrial site, even a troop center. In any event, more than one bomb was avail-able, and a predominantly civilian city such as Hiroshima should have been the last target, not the first. The bombing of its residents was not justifiable on grounds of military necessity.

Another problem is more fundamental. If the killing of great num-bers of noncombatants is warranted because the effect is to hasten the submission of the enemy and reduce your own future losses, no form of combat—or cruelty—is out of bounds. Every form of bar-barity *could* produce the desired result. Not only is the effect to nul-lify every rule ever devised to circumscribe armed conflict; acceptance of the principle also legitimizes such practices as pre-emptive nuclear strikes (as some Cold Warriors advocated in the

1950s) and cruelties practiced outside the context of actual combat, such as torture, rape, and summary executions, on the ground that the end justifies the means.

An argument that the siege of Sarajevo would accelerate the submission of the Bosnian government and thus could be justified as a military measure is even more vulnerable to criticism than the claim that dropping atomic bombs on Hiroshima and Nagasaki saved lives. After all, the submission of Japan quickly followed the nuclear attacks and did end the slaughter. In the Bosnian war, however, the only prospect was more "ethnic cleansing"—that is, the submission of Sarajevo would have meant that the survivors would be detained, killed, or expelled, and those detained would ultimately be killed or expelled. The fate of another city, Srebrenica, makes the point: When it fell in 1995, the women and children were driven away while the men and boys were slaughtered. Furthermore, the fall of Sarajevo would not have spared other towns; it would have freed the Serb forces terrorizing the city to turn their firepower on other Bosnians until they too were driven away or killed.

The Geneva Conventions of 1949, drafted in the wake of Nuremberg and Tokyo, criminalize "wilful killing of civilians"—that is, the deliberate killing of a civilian. But the Fourth Convention, which deals with the protection of the civilian population, does not provide that indiscriminate attacks or attacks that cause disproportionate numbers of civilian deaths constitute grave breaches, or war crimes. If prosecutions had been brought at Nuremberg for such attacks, the Allies would have opened themselves up to the argument made by Robert Servatius, defense counsel for the Nazi Party leadership and, a decade and a half later, the attorney for Adolf Eichmann at his trial in Jerusalem—that the Hague Conventions were obsolete because the Russians had systematically violated them. If they did not apply to the Russians, Servatius told the Nuremberg judges, they could not apply to the Germans.[11]

By 1977, a generation had passed since World War II. The authors of the Additional Protocols to the Geneva Conventions were no longer concerned with the potential culpability of the victors in the great struggle against Nazism and Japanese imperialism. Indeed, their context was the conflicts of the post–World War II era. There was, for example, the Biafran War from 1967 to 1970, in which a million or more civilians died in indiscriminate attacks and from starvation and

disease caused by sieges and blockades. According to an American
participant in the drafting of the protocols, the authors also had their
eyes on television coverage of the Vietnam War. As George Aldrich
has written, "Every evening for years the horrors of war were displayed graphically in every living room and the suffering of the civilian population in a war of guerrillas and high technology was also
emphasized. A free press also gave a platform to propagandists of all
persuasions, and the Government of the United States became sensitive to charges of indiscriminate bombardment, attacks on civilians,
attacks on dikes and the environment and similar charges."[12] Prohibiting such conduct became a driving purpose for the authors of
the protocols, which have acquired the status of customary international law and are universally binding. (In ex-Yugoslavia, they are
also binding as treaty law.)

Article 85 of the First Additional Protocol of 1977 specifies that
grave breaches in international armed conflicts include:

> 3a) making the civilian population or individual civilians the object of
> attack;
> b) launching an indiscriminate attack affecting the civilian population or
> civilian objects in the knowledge that such attack will cause excessive
> loss of life, injury to civilians or damage to civilian objects. . . .
> 4d) making the clearly recognized historic monuments, works of art or
> places of worship which constitute the cultural or spiritual heritage of
> people . . . the object of attack. . . .

In addition to these provisions enumerating war crimes, the Protocol sets forth detailed rules that must be followed by combatants to
avoid indiscriminate attacks. Article 51 (5) prohibits "an attack by
bombardment by any methods or means which treats as a single military objective a number of clearly separated and distinct military objectives located in a city, town, village or other area." In other words,
under the terms of the Protocol, it is not legitimate to bombard the
markets, apartment houses, hospitals, schools, historic monuments,
and breadlines of a city like Sarajevo just because it may have a military barracks, an ammunition storage area, and a number of ma-
chine-gun emplacements. The forces besieging the city may attack
the military targets as such, which is not what happened in Sarajevo.
As John Burns reported in *The New York Times* after he visited Serb
gunners in the hills surrounding Sarajevo: "Anybody who stops and

climbs atop the mud walls can see what the Serbian gunners see, and it is an astonishing sight. Many of the guns are less than one thousand yards from the high-rise buildings in the center of the city, and perhaps 500–1,000 feet above them. . . . It is plain, numbingly so, that the men firing the guns can see exactly what they are hitting. What this means is that the Serbian gun crews cannot have any doubt when their shells strike hospitals, schools, hotels and orphanages and cemeteries where families are burying their dead."[13]

Article 51 (5) of the First Protocol goes on to prohibit "an attack which may be expected to cause incidental loss of civilian life, injury to civilians, damage to civilian objects, or a combination thereof, which would be excessive in relation to the concrete and direct military advantage anticipated." Under this rule, if a Bosnian militiaman with a rifle takes up a post in the middle of a hospital complex and shoots back at the Serb gunners in the hills, the gunners are required to consider the loss of civilian life that would result from attacking the militiaman with howitzer shells even though he himself is a legitimate target. The militiaman, on the other hand, may not take advantage of his position to make himself invulnerable: According to the Protocol, "The presence or movements of the civilian population or individual civilians shall not be used to render certain points or areas immune from military operations, in particular in attempts to shield military objectives from attack, or to shield, favor or impede military operations." In other words, it is perfectly legitimate for snipers to try to kill the militiaman. Although civilians might be killed in a crossfire, the blame falls on the militiaman who takes up a post in a hospital, or with the hospital that allows him to do so. Military necessity justifies shooting him. In contrast, if heavy artillery is used in such circumstances, the harm to civilians certainly "would be excessive in relation to the concrete and direct military advantage anticipated."

Whether attacks on civilians in Sarajevo were "excessive" was not the issue, according to the UN War Crimes Commission. It found that "irrespective of the rule of proportionality, it is reasonable to presume that civilian casualties caused by sniper fire are the result of deliberate attacks on civilians and not the result of indiscriminate attacks." That is, the sniper who sighted, shot, and killed a seven-year-old boy a few yards from the Holiday Inn in the Bosnian capital while I was there in November 1994 knew that he was shooting someone who was not a combatant; his act, "wilful killing," was a

war crime. The Commission also thought that the rule of proportionality "is of questionable relevance to many of the artillery bombardments." "Attacking the civilian population is a war crime," the
Commission asserted, adding that "it would be possible to develop a
prima facie case against the commander of the Bosnian-Serb forces
surrounding Sarajevo for deliberately attacking the civilian population."[14] The tribunal's prosecutors agreed, and indicted Karadzic and
Mladic for their conduct of the siege of Sarajevo.

The detailed provisions of the First Protocol also cover such matters as attacks on civilian structures—for example, houses, schools,
cultural objects, places of worship, and water installations and the
like that are indispensable to the survival of the civilian population—
as well as starvation as a method of warfare. All these were flagrantly
violated during the sieges of the towns of Bosnia.

Further, the First Protocol addresses siege warfare in several articles that discuss humanitarian relief. The Fourth Geneva Convention,
promulgated twenty-eight years earlier, deals with the distribution of
relief, but only insofar as occupied territories are concerned. By 1977,
the international community was ready to outlaw the practice central
to the very idea of a siege: obstruction of the delivery of food and
other supplies to territory held by the other side so as to starve,
freeze, or otherwise coerce the submission of the population under
assault. The most important provisions are in Article 70, which requires that if civilians are not adequately supplied, "relief actions
which are humanitarian and impartial in character and conducted
without any adverse distinction shall be undertaken." The parties to
the conflict "shall allow and facilitate rapid and unimpeded passage
of all relief consignments." No diversion or delay is permitted.

Relief supplies to some towns in Bosnia were obstructed by Serb
forces for several months at a time. The United Nations High Commissioner for Refugees was barred for nine months from bringing
supplies to Zepa, a village with a population swollen to 30,000 because residents of nearby communities took refuge there until it was
overrun by Serb forces in July 1995. In Gorazde, with 80,000 residents
during the siege, amputations were done at the local hospital with
wood saws and without anesthetics because the Serbs prevented
medical supplies from getting in.

In some ways, besieged provincial communities suffered far
more from this form of warfare than Sarajevo did. The absence of
medical supplies was most critical in the enclaves. Food shortages

also caused great misery. At first, the residents survived because peasants from surrounding villages came in with their farm animals; it got much worse when the meat from slaughtered livestock, much of which they smoked, ran out. Then the obstruction of relief convoys for months at a time took a heavy toll. Residents of the enclaves coped with the icy cold of the Bosnian winter by cutting down trees for firewood in the rural areas of the besieged zones. Drinking water was somewhat more available from wells in these provincial towns than in the city.

Frequently interrupted for several days or even weeks at a time, relief supplies still managed to get into Sarajevo throughout the siege. As a consequence, crucial medical supplies did not run out, although the lack of electricity sometimes forced surgeons to conduct operations by flashlight and the lack of running water caused severe privations and made maintenance of the hospital particularly difficult. Enough food entered Sarajevo to prevent starvation, just barely. During the siege, residents of the city typically lost 20 or 30 pounds. Virtually every tree in the city was cut down in the first winter of the assault; many people used chopped-up furniture for firewood as well. In some apartments I visited, books were burned by families desperately trying to stay warm, the balls of crumpled paper from their pages becoming a familiar sight. Refugees from outlying communities and residents of the city forced to leave their homes because of the shelling ripped up the floorboards of the schoolrooms where they were housed for firewood. In such fashion, and by bundling themselves up as best they could and stretching sheets of plastic supplied by UNHCR over window frames shattered by the shelling, the citizens of Sarajevo kept from freezing to death.

Everywhere, the greatest misery was caused by the constant shelling and sniping. In Sarajevo, more than 10,000 men, women, and children were killed during the siege and several times that number were wounded. The casualty rate in the city may have been as high as 25 percent, given the reduction in Sarajevo's population as those able to do so braved the sniper fire to get out. The elderly and the infirm paid an especially high price. No electricity meant no elevators, which meant long journeys up and down staircases of high-rise apartment buildings—and sometimes miles outside—to get food and water.

Identifying those principally responsible for these sieges did not pose great difficulty for the prosecution in bringing indictments before the tribunal. The overall responsibility of a civilian leader such as Radovan Karadzic or that of a military leader such as General Ratko ("Burn it all") Mladic was relatively easy to establish. The July 25, 1995, indictments of Karadzic and Mladic for war crimes, crimes against humanity, and genocide included twelve specific crimes in which multiple casualties were caused by the shelling of civilian gatherings (ten in Sarajevo and one each in Tuzla and Srebrenica) and fifty-three cases in which snipers killed and wounded civilians in Sarajevo, including nineteen in which the victims were as young as two years old.

"If there is a general rule that civilian deaths must not be aimed at," Michael Walzer wrote in *Just and Unjust Wars,* "the siege is a great exception—and the sort of exception, if it is morally warranted, to shatter the rule itself." Whatever moral justification there may have been in the past for making a siege an exception was based on the presence of legitimate military targets and on the effort by defending military forces to shelter themselves within a city. Even with that justification, it was impermissible to attack indiscriminately or disproportionately, as British and American leaders clearly recognized on the eve of World War II before they abandoned such principles to take reprisals. The principle of proportionality is central to the concept of justice generally and has been applied explicitly to the conduct of war by the First Additional Protocol of 1977. Indiscriminate attacks or attacks that cause disproportionate harm to civilians are prohibited. They are not only impermissible but are now plainly designated as grave breaches, or war crimes. Successful prosecutions for siege warfare are unprecedented. A good place to begin is with Karadzic, Mladic, and the others who directed their forces to lob mortar shells into crowded parts of a large city and take deadly aim at children.

11

Rape

AMONG THE CRIMES for which the wars in Croatia and in Bosnia-Herzegovina became notorious is rape. Much of the public outcry for a war crimes tribunal arose from the outrage generated by the rapes committed during these conflicts. For a time, the war in Bosnia became virtually synonymous with rape, acquiring a reputation for uncommon ugliness in the process and helping to create unprecedented awareness of rape as a common method of warfare and political repression worldwide.

In the course of my own visits to Croatia and Bosnia, I got an inkling of the crime's dimensions. I did not specifically seek testimony on rape, and relied on others to gather this data, in the belief that the female victims would disclose their personal experiences more readily to female human rights investigators than to a male interviewer. But I discovered that questions about other abuses inevitably produced information on rape as well.

In February 1993, I visited a refugee camp in Croatia where I had reason to believe I might find witnesses to corroborate accounts of a gruesome incident that had been reported to Human Rights Watch.

We had heard that a group of Muslim women who had been confined in detention camps were marched across a bridge to be released and expelled from Serb-controlled territory; as they moved
across the bridge, they were told to throw their belongings over the
side. A soldier had approached one woman and demanded that she
toss a bag she was carrying into the water. When she protested that
there was a baby in the bag, according to the reports, the soldier
seized it and threw the bag, baby and all, into the river. To stop her
screaming, he then shot the woman.

In the refugee camp, two women I interviewed said they were in
the same line of march, had heard about the incident, but had been
too far away to see or hear the mother's confrontation with the soldier. Another woman said that she had been a few paces away when
the incident happened, however, and that she had seen and heard
everything. Her testimony seemed credible, since the details matched
the accounts that other witnesses had provided independently.

In interviewing these women, I asked about their own experiences. They had been confined at a detention camp in the predominantly Muslim village of Trnopolje. The main building of the camp
was a school before the war in Bosnia began, in April 1992. A large
hall at the school was used by Serb troops to hold the women from
the surrounding villages after the war came to that area on May 23,
1992.

Aida, a small, pretty eighteen-year-old, told me that at night,
when the hall was dark, Serb soldiers would arrive, shining flash-
lights into the faces of the women lying on the floor, choosing those
they fancied and taking them out, presumably to be raped. The older
women tried to hide their daughters and daughters-in-law under their
skirts or under blankets to protect them, but the soldiers would pull
these away. Women who resisted were beaten and taken away anyway. The soldiers reeked of liquor, according to Aida. I asked
whether she recognized any of the soldiers. She told me that two of
them had been her high school teachers. One, Ljubomir Zjelar, taught
her physics. She said she had been his student for four years and always thought that she was his favorite. In Trnopolje, she told me, he
pretended not to recognize the girls who had been his students. She
described the other, crafts teacher Miso Radulovic, as one of the most
brutal of the guards. (Radulovic has been accused of taking part in
the castration of a male inmate at Omarska.)

I did not ask Aida whether she herself had been raped, because

I was looking for other information and because it was evident that she was embarrassed discussing these things. She implied that she had escaped rape because her mother had found a good place in the corner of the hall, where she was able to hide Aida well. Some women who were taken away never returned, Aida said. Others came back many hours later or after a couple of days, often crying, but did not want to talk about what happened to them.

Other women who were confined at Trnopolje told me and my colleagues similar stories. Some said they had been raped. Most of those said they had been gang-raped.

The experiences of Muslim women at other detention camps were similar. One woman confined in the Keraterm camp, at the site of what had been a ceramics factory, told my colleagues that one of the two men who raped her at that camp was Dusko Sikirica, the camp commander. This woman, who was in her forties, identified him because, like Aida's high school teachers, he was someone from her own community whom she had known previously. Other women held at Keraterm also identified Sikirica. On July 25, 1995, Sikirica and twelve of the shift commanders, guards, and interrogators who worked under his direction at Keraterm were named by the tribunal in a 20-page indictment that enumerated a long list of crimes they were accused of committing at the camp.

It was much the same when I visited Kosevo Hospital in Sarajevo in April 1993. I went to find out about attacks on the hospital, one of the largest and best-equipped in Yugoslavia before the breakup. It was located near the front lines, which made it an easy target for Serb forces, who shelled it repeatedly, killing patients and staff, but most of its three thousand employees stayed at their jobs. Kosevo won admiration from the city's residents, journalists, relief workers, and United Nations troops alike for the professionalism and heroism with which its personnel coped with every imaginable disaster—and some beyond imagining.

Rape inevitably came up, even though there were not many of them in Sarajevo itself: the siege kept the opposing sides apart, providing few opportunities. Nevertheless, doctors at Kosevo told me that a year after the outbreak of the war, they already had treated twenty-five women who had been raped in connection with the conflict. Most of these women had lived in suburbs of Sarajevo and were raped when Serb forces overran their communities; they had subsequently made their way into the city. Three were girls, aged fourteen and younger, who had only just come to the hospital in a prisoner exchange. They had been detained for up to ten months in Foca, a town the Serb forces had taken at the beginning of the conflict, and had been raped often during that period. Not long after my visit to Kosevo Hospital, journalist Roy Gutman published an account of a "rape camp" at Foca in *Newsday*.[1] On June 27, 1996, eight Bosnian Serbs were indicted by the tribunal for mass rape at Foca, becoming the first defendants in an international criminal proceeding ever to be indicted solely for that crime. One of them, who surrendered to French troops in 1998, pleaded guilty to the rape charges.

The doctors at Kosevo said that four of the victims they treated had been detained for long periods and came to them pregnant from rape when it was too late for abortions. They subsequently gave birth. The director of obstetrics told me he had been practicing for thirty years but had never previously encountered a woman who refused to see her child after it was born. Three of these four women would not look at their babies, he said. The hospital was caring for the infants.

(Sexual abuse in the Bosnian conflict was primarily, but not exclusively, directed against women. As in other wars, some male prisoners were also sexually abused and humiliated by their captors. The victims seemed at least as reluctant as the women who were molested to discuss such experiences. Most notorious, of course, was the case in which a prisoner at Omarska was reportedly castrated. The United Nations War Crimes Commission also reported one case in which a Bosnian prisoner's penis was cut off; another in which a prisoner was given electric shocks to his scrotum; and a third in which guards forced a father and a son to perform a sex act with each other.)[2]

Although I obtained evidence about rape without seeking it during five visits to the war zone in 1993, and although female colleagues at Human Rights Watch who sought such testimony obtained much more, we never had any idea how many rapes were committed and never provided estimates. Others were not similarly encumbered. For a period, statistics were bandied about with considerable freedom.

In October 1992, after the war in Bosnia-Herzegovina had been under way for six months, the Bosnian government issued a claim that 50,000 Muslim women had been raped. This sparked concern within the European Community, which appointed an investigative commission headed by Dame Anne Warburton of Britain. In January 1993, that commission issued its report. Apparently intent on being more conservative than the Bosnian government, the commission estimated—or gave credence to an estimate—that 20,000 Muslim women had been raped, although it failed to cite evidence to support this figure or to indicate in its 7-page report how it was determined. Nevertheless, a report by a group operating under the auspices of the European Community was an important matter, and it attracted headlines worldwide. *The New York Times,* which a few weeks earlier had published John Burns's riveting account of the atrocities committed by Borislav Herak, including many rapes, featured the report prominently on its front page, and cited in its headline the statistic that 20,000 women had been raped.[3] The commission's investigation, the basis for the EC report, had lasted a week, from December 18 to 24, 1992. Investigators spent a day and a half of this period in Geneva, the remaining time in Zagreb. In all, they interviewed eight witnesses. The commission's figure on the number of rapes was contained in a single, qualified sentence: "The most reasoned estimate suggested to the delegation indicated a figure in the region of 20,000 victims."

Others rushed to top that figure. Within days, *Washington Post* columnist Judy Mann reported a finding by prominent feminist law professor Catharine A. MacKinnon that 50,000 Muslim women had been raped in the Bosnian conflict and, for good measure, that another 100,000 Muslim women had been killed.[4] (Actually, 100,000 was at the high end of estimates for the total number killed to that point in the war; as in most wars, it appeared that most of the dead were males, and not all were Muslims.) Again, no information was provided to back up these figures. Several weeks later, MacKinnon appeared on a panel with me at a forum sponsored by the Association of the Bar of the City of New York and spoke of 30,000 women who had become pregnant as a consequence of rape in Bosnia,[5] an astonishing figure in light of what is known about how frequently, or infrequently, rape leads to pregnancy. (During a question period, when MacKinnon was taken to task for using a number that implied that there had been several hundred thousand rapes, she disclaimed personal responsibility for the statistic, saying it was merely one she had obtained from a source in Bosnia, whom she did not identify.)

The EC report and other number-filled accounts inspired a flood of press stories. Journalists rushed to Croatia to find and interview

Bosnian refugees who had been raped. Some reporters were cynical about what they were doing, and I repeatedly heard from them the well-worn story of the journalist who flies into a town just after a military raid and walks the streets shouting, "Anyone here been raped and speaks English?" Yet journalists who told the tale found themselves doing just that. Some had difficulty finding anyone to speak to them, probably because many victims had no desire to talk about the horrific experience to journalists, especially not in front of television cameras. The press did find a few women willing to talk about being raped, and as elsewhere, the same victims were interviewed over and over.

One chilling detail that emerged from accounts by victims was that some rapists told them that they would give birth to "little Chetniks." Such boasts by Serb soldiers were gratuitous acts of cruelty, intended to cause additional suffering. But the press stories aroused suspicion among some feminists and others that more was involved—that there was a conspiracy by Serb forces to impregnate Muslim women and make them bear Serb children. The speculation was that detentions were deliberately prolonged to prevent timely abortions. It was reminiscent of events more than twenty years earlier, when forced impregnation was widely reported during the war for Bangladesh's independence from Pakistan. According to accounts then, the number of Bangladeshi women raped by Pakistani soldiers ranged into the hundreds of thousands, and thousands of children were born as a consequence. (The population of Bangladesh was more than 20 times that of Bosnia and more than 50 times that of its Muslims.) The number of births reflected both the confinement of some of these women in detention camps until it was too late to terminate their pregnancies and a lack of access to abortions. According to reports at the time, some rapists then told their victims that they would give birth to "true Muslims."

The possibility that rapes were committed for the purpose of impregnating the victims provided grounds for an argument by some feminists that these crimes should be labeled genocide. Again, MacKinnon was in the legal forefront. Under the Alien Tort Claims Act, a federal law of uncertain provenance dating back to the end of the eighteenth century, victims of gross abuses of human rights who are in the United States but who suffered such abuses in another country may bring suit in American federal courts against those who abused them, provided that the abusers also are in the United States. An important precedent was set in 1980, when a U.S. appellate court permitted such a suit after a woman recognized on the streets of Brooklyn the Paraguayan military man who had tortured her brother to death in Paraguay.[6] Attempting to build on that precedent, Mac-Kinnon, joined by the National Organization for Women Legal Defense Fund, took advantage of a visit to the United States by Radovan Karadzic to sue him for "genocidal acts of rape, forced pregnancy, enforced prostitution" on behalf of Bosnian and Croatian refugees in the United States. It was one of two such lawsuits against Karadzic; the other, brought by several groups, including the Center for Constitutional Rights, which had litigated the precedent-setting Paraguayan case, charged "genocide, war crimes and crimes against humanity" for "rape and other gross human rights abuses." These lawsuits did not achieve any material results, in part because after the tribunal was established Karadzic stayed away from the United States for fear of arrest. Nevertheless, they served a political purpose for the groups sponsoring them: They announced loud and clear the views of a segment of the feminist movement on how rape should be regarded.

Although rape is bad enough without being labeled genocide, and although some statistics were used irresponsibly, the labels and the numbers helped to build a constituency committed to prosecuting those responsible for war crimes in ex-Yugoslavia. Violence against women, the failure of the machinery of justice to respond adequately, and the related issue of sexual harassment had become the predominant concerns of American feminists. In the 1990s, these questions vaulted ahead of equality of opportunity in employment, day care, or even the right of a woman to control her own reproduction among the issues on the agenda of most outspoken advocates of women's rights. Prior to Bosnia, there was never an issue involving women in other countries that preoccupied American women. Overnight, however, it seemed that the plight of Bosnian women had become a domestic political issue to American feminists. For a time, it was possible to hear conversations that would slide directly from a discussion of the Tailhook episode or Senator Robert Packwood's harassment of his female staff to whether Serbian troops would be tried as war criminals for raping Bosnian women.

This phenomenon was not confined to the United States. At the United Nations World Conference on Human Rights in Vienna in June 1993, more than eight hundred women's groups from around the world lobbied strenuously, and successfully, for incorporation of women's rights in the United Nations' human rights agenda for the first time. They seemed almost single-mindedly focused on violence against women, and the issue that epitomized their concern was rape in Bosnia. The formal rules of the World Conference prohibited criticism of particular countries, but an exception was made for denunciation of Serb atrocities in Bosnia, particularly rape. Two years later, 30,000 women assembled outside Beijing for a nongovernmental world conference on women that took place during an official meeting on the same subject sponsored by the UN. Bosnia no longer dominated the agenda, but violence against women remained the central issue.

Catharine MacKinnon was front and center at the 1993 Vienna conference, this time arguing that the rapes in Bosnia and Croatia were inextricably linked to what had long been the main target of her crusading—pornography. The connection was twofold, she claimed: The rapes were provoked by pornography and also served the purpose of producing pornography. As an example of provocation, she cited "Serbian tanks plastered with pornography." As for production, she told her listeners that Serb forces videotaped their rapes for future viewing.[7]

MacKinnon developed her thesis in a *Ms.* magazine cover story, "Turning Rape into Pornography: Postmodern Genocide."[8] Her article was filled with so many images of violent sex that some might have mistaken MacKinnon's own writing for pornography. "Pornography saturated Yugoslavia before the war," she wrote, implying that this explained the incidence of rape. She pointed out that "the propagandist Julius Streicher—editor of the anti-Semitic newspaper *Der Stürmer,* which contained pornographic anti-Semitic hate propaganda"—was hanged at Nuremberg. MacKinnon asked, "In the war crimes trials for the genocidal war against Bosnia-Herzegovina and Croatia, will those who incited to genocide through rape, sexual torture, and murder—the Serbian pornographers as well as the high policy makers and the underlings—get what they deserve?"[9]

What also made rape in Bosnia an urgent concern to feminists was confusion about whether it qualified as a war crime. Somehow, word got around that it is not covered by the Geneva Conventions, and many newspapers published editorials calling for amendment of the conventions to redress the error.[10]

It's true that the word "rape" does not appear in the war crimes provisions of the Geneva Conventions. But international law generally recognizes that rape is covered by the language of the Fourth Geneva Convention, which designates "wilfully causing great suffering or serious injury to body or health" and "inhuman treatment" of civilians as grave breaches of the convention.[11] When used to coerce detainees to furnish information, rape also may be a grave breach under other provisions, such as the prohibition of torture. In Bosnia, where the purpose was "ethnic cleansing," rape could be covered as well by Additional Protocol 1 of 1977, which provides that grave breaches include "inhuman and degrading practices involving outrages upon personal dignity, based on racial discrimination." The word actually does appear elsewhere in the conventions. Article 27 of the Fourth Geneva Convention provides that "women shall be protected in particular against rape, enforced prostitution, or any form of indecent assault." This language is repeated in Article 76 of the First Additional Protocol. By explicitly prohibiting such practices, the conventions help to make it clear that the general language designating "willfully causing great suffering or serious injury to body or health" in the section listing grave breaches is intended to cover rape.

Even though contentions that the Geneva Conventions do not make rape a war crime are mistaken, there is merit to the call for an amendment. Indictments for the rapes at Foca issued by the tribunal for ex-Yugoslavia might seem to remove any shred of doubt. Still, given how frequently this crime is committed during armed conflict, it should be explicitly named a war crime and not covered only by more general language such as "great suffering," "serious injury," "inhuman treatment," "torture," "degrading practices," and "outrages upon personal dignity."

If rape is not explicitly cited as a war crime in the Fourth Geneva Convention, it may be in part because its authors were focused on a less common atrocity, "biological experiments." The conventions were adopted in 1949, not long after the world learned of the revolting biological experiments the Nazis had conducted on concentration camp inmates. (Such experiments also were carried out by the Japanese during World War II. Unit 731 in Manchuria conducted a wide variety of painful experiments on human guinea pigs; and Kyushu Imperial University did vivisection experiments on downed American fliers, but these were not dealt with by the Tokyo Tribunal and only became known publicly much later.)

Rape, in fact, did not figure prominently in the Nuremberg trials of the top Nazi war criminals. It was explicitly cited as a crime against humanity in the statute under which prosecutions took place,[12] and German troops and security forces such as the SS did engage in rape and forced prostitution. But rape was not a crime particularly associated with those forces. Nazi theories and laws forbade sexual relations with inferior races, and given the disciplinary authority exercised by German officers, these prohibitions were generally obeyed. Among those Nazi racism did not protect against rape were Frenchwomen, and their victimization was dealt with briefly at Nuremberg. But the French prosecutor who raised the issue apparently thought that summary consideration would spare his countrywomen further humiliation, saying, "The tribunal will forgive me if I avoid citing the atrocious details." Nazi allies like the Iron Guard in Romania and pro-Nazi militias in the Ukraine committed a great many rapes, and were less discriminating in their choice of victims, but their leaders were not tried at Nuremberg.

Another reason for downplaying rape at Nuremberg is that the victorious allies may have been more guilty of the crime than the Nazis. Russian troops raped countless women as they swept through the countries of Eastern and Central Europe and, finally, Germany. (The memory of what Russian soldiers did as they moved west—like memories of Japanese atrocities in Asia during the war—has lingered in the affected countries to this day.) And the Russians weren't alone. Notoriously, the French let it be known to the Moroccan troops they deployed in Italy that rape was one of the bounties of war—behavior fictionalized by Alberto Moravia in *Two Women* and put on film by Vittorio De Sica in his treatment of the novel starring Sophia Loren. But since the Russians and French joined the Americans and British as the prosecutors and judges at Nuremberg, it was hardly in their interest to call attention to the sins of their own forces. At Nuremberg, rape was a victim of victor's justice.

Rape did play a part in the trial of top Japanese war criminals at Tokyo. One of the great crimes for which they were responsible, the prosecution charged, was the "rape of Nanking"—so named because Japanese commanders gave their troops license to rape at will after they conquered the Chinese city in 1937. Thousands and thousands of Chinese women were raped, then murdered by their rapists. Prosecutors presented extensive evidence about what happened at Nanking, and the judgment at Tokyo reviews it in horrifying detail. But the Tokyo tribunal did not attract as much attention worldwide as Nuremberg, and it was the crimes associated with the Nazis that were specified when the provisions of the 1949 Geneva Conventions dealing with grave breaches were drafted.

To make it absolutely clear that rape would be subject to prosecution before the international tribunal for ex-Yugoslavia, the Security Council of the United Nations said so explicitly in the tribunal's charter. Paragraph 48 states: "Crimes against humanity refer to inhumane acts of a very serious nature, such as wilful killing, torture or rape, committed as part of a widespread or systematic attack against any civilian population on national, political, ethnic, racial or religious grounds. In the conflict in the territory of the former Yugoslavia, such acts have taken the form of so-called 'ethnic cleansing' and widespread and systematic rape and other forms of sexual assault, including enforced prostitution." Paragraph 49 provides that "the International Tribunal shall have the power to prosecute persons responsible for the following crimes when committed in armed conflict, whether international or internal in character, and directed against any civilian population . . . rape. . . ."

In adopting "Rules on Procedure and Evidence," the judges of the UN war crimes tribunal provided that in cases of sexual assault, "no corroboration of the victim's testimony shall be required." In addition, the rules state that "consent shall not be allowed as a defense if the victim (a) has been subjected to or threatened with or has had reason to fear violence, duress, detention, or psychological oppression, or (b) reasonably believed that if she did not submit, another might be so subjected, threatened or put in fear" (a provision that addresses the situation of women in Croatia and Bosnia whose families are subject to reprisals), and that "prior sexual conduct of the victim shall not be admitted in evidence."[13] Subsequently, the rules were amended to provide that "before evidence of the victim's consent is admitted, the accused shall satisfy the Trial Chamber *in camera* that the evidence is relevant and credible."[14]

The first indictments solely for rape—in June 1996, covering the rape camp at Foca—discussed the ordeal of fourteen Muslim women and girls, some as young as twelve, held at the camp between April 1992 and February 1993. According to the indictments, the defendants, including Foca chief of police Dragan Gogovic, had committed war crimes. The defendants were not charged with other offenses, which was important: Indictments specifying rape and only rape seemed to resolve once and for all the question of whether the crime is covered by the provisions of the Geneva Conventions enumerating grave breaches. On March 9, 1998, one of the Foca defendants, Dragoljub Kunarac, who had turned himself in to French troops a few days earlier, admitted to the tribunal in The Hague that he had raped Muslim women detained in 1992.

Some feminists argue that rape, almost always a party to armed conflict, was never taken seriously in the context of war until the emergence of the contemporary women's rights movement. This perspective ignores or misreads much history. Even in ancient times, the connection between rape and warfare was widely recognized. The opening paragraphs of *The Histories* by Herodotus discuss the abduction and rape of Io, daughter of Inachus, and other women by the Phoenicians; the reprisal abduction and rape of Europa by the Greeks, who also abducted and raped Medea; and the episode fifty years later that launched the Trojan wars—the abduction and rape of Helen by Paris, son of Priam.

In medieval Britain, rape was a capital crime in military codes promulgated by Richard II (1385) and Henry V (1419).[15] In English literature, when Shakespeare's King Henry V threatens officials of the French town of Harfleur with the consequences for its citizens if they do not surrender, he asks:

What is't to me, when yourselves are cause,
If your pure maidens fall into the hand
Of hot and forcing violation?

The Dutch jurist Hugo Grotius, citing Greek and Roman authorities who condemned rape in times of war, as well as the Christian view, wrote in the early seventeenth century that "whoever forcibly violates chastity, even in war, should everywhere be subject to punishment."[16] In more recent times, rape was a capital crime in the Lieber Code of 1863, drawn up to regulate the conduct of the U.S. Army during the Civil War, one of the building blocks on which contemporary laws of war are based.

More than three decades later, as the century was drawing to a close, rape again became a focus of attention during an armed conflict. Reports of rapes of Cuban women by Spanish troops got major play in Hearst newspapers and helped to generate the public outcry that eventually brought the United States into what became the Spanish-American War.

The feminists of the early 1900s—antecedents of the modern women's movement—focused on other issues and did not take up the cause of the rape victims, but the crime was not ignored by those who documented the atrocities of war. In fact, the leading account of the wars that devastated the Balkans in the early twentieth century pays plenty of attention to the crime and, in a chilling portent, to its frequency as well.

In 1913, the Carnegie Endowment for International Peace, then just three years old, established the International Commission to Inquire into the Causes and Conduct of the Balkan Wars, and the following year published the commission's 420-page report.[17] The report devotes about 100 pages to detailed accounts of atrocities: Rapes—or "violations of women," in the usage of the time—are discussed on almost every page. This does not reflect a particular gender sensitivity to the crime, since all eight commissioners were male—standard operating procedure for the time. Rather, the report apparently was a good-faith effort to paint an accurate picture of what happened during wars that involved not only the territories that eventually would become Yugoslavia but also those that had engulfed Bulgaria, Romania, Greece, Albania, and Turkey. (If pornography saturated Yugoslavia before the wars in Croatia and Bosnia, as Catharine MacKinnon asserts, there is no record that it was also a precursor of the Balkan wars eight decades earlier, even though rape was pervasive during the conflicts.)

The Balkan wars of 1912 and 1913 were followed almost immediately by World War I. During the Great War, rapes were widely reported. Whenever the "Belgian atrocities" were discussed, the reference was to allegations that German soldiers had committed systematic rapes during their conquest of Belgium. In fact, many stories of atrocities were unfounded, or so a Belgian government commission determined at the close of the war. Its report was so damning that for years afterward, "atrocities" was considered almost synonymous with lies. The lasting consequences helped to fuel public skepticism about early reports of Nazi death camps a quarter century later—reports that turned out to be all too true.

Although heightened awareness of rape as an instrument of warfare, and its role in humiliating and demoralizing communities under attack, serves a valuable purpose, it also may lead to the assumption that such practices are inevitable. They are not. Military forces disciplined not to engage in rape or other forms of sexual harassment refrain from such conduct. One example not long ago was the Eritrean Popular Liberation Front (EPLF), which finally won a thirty-year war against Ethiopian rule in 1991 and became the only separatist movement in postcolonial Africa to establish an internationally recognized independent state. The EPLF made it known early in its long campaign that sexual attacks would be punished severely; as a result, its record on the treatment of women was exemplary.

If such crimes can be prevented by instilling awareness that they are condemned and that punishment will follow, it greatly strengthens the argument for war crimes prosecutions of those committing, encouraging, and tolerating rape in the wars in Croatia and Bosnia. Indeed, the impact of prosecutions—against the Foca camp rapists, for example—could be profound. Not only does it send a signal to others who might engage in such conduct; it also signals victims that the international community acknowledges and cares about their suffering. Furthermore, the prosecution and punishment of political leaders and military commanders who tolerated or directed rapes could turn the tables by humiliating and degrading *them*. They deserve to be stigmatized as rapists.

Some human rights researchers and others who gathered evidence on rape in the former Yugoslavia expressed reservations about the focus on this particular crime, at least in conversations with professional colleagues, because they thought it presented a distorted picture of the suffering. The women they interviewed often saw their husbands, parents, or children killed, had spent months in detention camps under conditions of extreme deprivation and cruelty, had lost their homes and all their possessions, and were left completely destitute. To these women, the researchers said, rape was one of many afflictions, but not necessarily the most grievous. Charging genocide because of rape, in this view, depreciates the multiple harms done to them.

The irresponsible use of numbers only made matters worse. Human rights groups abhor unsubstantiated or unsupported statistics. The arousal of international public opinion—the principal means of protecting rights—depends on the reliability and credibility of information. Flabby numbers cheapen the currency of human rights reporting and undermine its effectiveness. Moreover, human rights groups fear a backlash if abuses are exaggerated. Examples abound, such as the long-lasting, harmful consequences of the false reports of atrocities by German soldiers during World War I. A more recent case was a report that Iraqi troops had thrown scores of premature babies out of incubators in occupied Kuwait. President Bush and other advocates of U.S. military intervention seized upon the report as one of the justifications for launching the Gulf War. Amnesty International, ordinarily meticulous in its work, helped to disseminate the false report about the premature babies. Its leaders were mortified by the discovery that they were misled, and eventually issued a retraction. The debunking of the story created an impression in some circles that the portrayal of Saddam Hussein as "another Hitler" was a gross exaggeration promulgated by war hawks, and that reports of Iraqi atrocities generally were unfounded. In fact, although the incubator story was false, the Iraqi leader's crimes against the Kurds in the north, the Shi'ites in the south, and the Marsh Arabs in the southeast, against dissenters anywhere in Iraq, and the genuine crimes committed in occupied Kuwait were grotesque enough to make comparisons with the Nazis more or less appropriate.

Labeling rape as genocide raised particular concern about hyperbole. "Ethnic cleansing," as carried out by Serb forces in Bosnia, fit the definition, since they tried to destroy a distinctive ethnic/religious group, the Bosnian Muslims, by deportations, bombardment of civilian towns, internment of civilians in detention camps, destruction of cultural monuments, pillage, torture, summary executions—and rape. These were related elements of a genocidal strategic campaign. But it was inappropriate to single out one element, rape, and assert that it, by itself, constituted genocide. Equating rape with genocide promoted a cause with militant adherents in the United States and other countries, but it distorted the reality of the harm done to women and men in Bosnia and Croatia.

It also made too much of the cruelty of Serb soldiers who told Muslim women that they would give birth to little Chetniks. Those soldiers deserve condemnation, prosecution, and punishment for their vile behavior—first and foremost for committing rape, second for attempting to aggravate the injury. But it is hard to imagine that many rapists believed that they could keep their victims in captivity for nine months, then take the children of rape and give them to Serb families to raise as Serbs. And of course unless they did precisely that, they could be certain pregnant women either would secure abortions or, if they gave birth, would not raise the children as Serbs. It is more likely that the talk of little Chetniks was a boast of their masculine triumph over their victims by claiming the potency to impregnate them.

Beverly Allen, one of the writers who has equated rape with genocide, argues that there is a logic behind the illogical reasoning of the Serb soldiers who talked of little Chetniks. "In the case of enforced pregnancy," Allen argues, "its illogical reasoning is founded on the negation of all cultural identities of its victims, reducing those victims to mere sexual containers."[18] The genocidal element, in this formulation, is the negation of cultural identity, with the intent to destroy Bosnian Muslims as a people.

The most persuasive argument for equating rape with genocide depends on the premise that the purpose or effect was forced impregnation. This would implicate Article II(d) of the Genocide Convention, which provides that one of the practices that constitute genocide when "committed with intent to destroy, in whole or in part, a national, ethnical, racial or religious group, as such" is "imposing measures intended to prevent births within the group." Anne Tierney Goldstein has maintained that forced impregnation prevented Bosnian births "at least temporarily and in many cases permanently. For at least the nine months it takes to carry the rapist's child to term, a woman is incapable of conceiving and bearing a child of her own ethnicity. If she is nearing the end of her child-bearing years, if she encounters complications in pregnancy that impair her future fertility, or if as a result of her pregnancy she is rendered unmarriageable within her community, the enforced pregnancy may preclude her permanently from having a child of her own ethnicity or genetic heritage."

Cherif Bassiouni, former chairman of the UN War Crimes Commission, who is a leading authority on international criminal law and a Muslim, and coauthor Peter Manikas have written: "According to Islamic law, women who have sexual relations outside marriage are not marriageable. Despite the fact that women do not consent to the acts in cases of rape and sexual assault, they are still often considered unmarriageable under this precept. This same dynamic may occur in other groups as well; that is women of any ethnic, religious or national group may be less likely to marry or re-marry and to procreate after being raped."[19]

Ultimately, however, to demonstrate that the purpose was to commit genocide by preventing births within the group, a quantitative test is required. It is not enough to show that rapes were committed, that some victims became pregnant, that some rapists intended this result, and that some pregnant women were prevented from terminating their pregnancies. It is also necessary to show that these occurred on a large scale with a severe and demonstrable effect on births among Bosnian Muslims, and that the practices of rape and enforced pregnancy were intended to achieve these results. Otherwise, the Genocide Convention would not apply.

A team under the auspices of the UN War Crimes Commission conducted a more thorough study than the one done by the European Community's investigative commission. Four physicians visited ex-Yugoslavia in January 1993, the month following the EC investigation. A participant, Dr. Shana Swiss, discussed the findings:

> The team identified 119 pregnancies that resulted from rape from a small sample of six hospitals in Bosnia, Croatia, and Serbia. According to estimates established in medical studies, a single act of unprotected intercourse will result in pregnancy between 1% and 4% of the time. Based on the assumption that 1% of acts of unprotected intercourse result in pregnancy, the identification of 119 pregnancies, therefore, represents some 11,900 rapes. These numbers, however, must be interpreted carefully. Underreporting, along with the reluctance of many physicians to ask women seeking abortions or prenatal care whether they had been raped during the war, would lead to an underestimate of the number of women raped. On the other hand, multiple and repeated rapes of the same women were frequently reported and could lead to an overestimate of the number of women (as opposed to the number of incidents of rape) involved.[20]

Cautious as this study was, it left the question of the numbers unresolved. If pregnancy resulted 4 percent of the time, the 119 cases translate as 2,975 rapes. And if many of those women experienced multiple rapes, the number of rape victims would be smaller yet. One would also need some way to measure underreporting and some knowledge of what proportion of victims of the war those six hospitals treated to project how many women were raped during the Bosnian war up to the point the study was done and how many women became pregnant as a result.

The UN War Crimes Commission's Final Report summed up what it was able to discover about the prevalence of rape in the wars in Croatia and Bosnia:

> The reports contained in the Commission's database identify close to 800 victims by name or number. An additional 1,673 victims are referred to, but not named, in reports of victims who indicate that they have wit-

nessed or know of other similar victims. Additionally, there are some 500 reported cases which refer to an unspecified number of victims. . . . The reported cases identify some 600 alleged perpetrators by name. . . . About 80 percent of the reported cases specify that they occurred in settings where the victims were held in custody.

A significant finding by the commission was that the incidence of rape declined when the issue achieved international notoriety, starting about December 1992. "The majority of the rapes occurred from April [when the war in Bosnia began] to November 1992," the UN body reported. "[F]ewer occurred in the following five months." The commission saw this as an indication of command control. Five distinct patterns of rape emerged from the commission's analysis:

- "Gang atmosphere" rapes, in which small groups committed sexual assault "in conjunction with looting and intimidation of the target ethnic group."
- Rapes committed after an attack on a town or village. In many such cases, villagers would be rounded up and some women would be selected to be raped publicly in front of their neighbors.
- Detention camp rapes, in which women would be selected from the inmate population for rape by groups of guards or visiting soldiers.
- Detention for the purpose of rape. "In those camps, all of the women are raped quite frequently, often in front of other internees, and usually accompanied by beatings and torture. Some captors also state that they are trying to impregnate the women."
- "Detention of women in hotels or similar facilities for the sole purpose of sexually entertaining soldiers. . . . These women are reportedly more often killed than exchanged."[21]

What is evident from this analysis is that rape was rarely a solitary act. It usually was done before witnesses—other combatants or guards, other detainees, or other villagers. The rapists did not fear that they would be found out; they did what was tolerated, or expected of them, or what they were required to do. Had their commanders disapproved, or indicated that the practice would result in punishment, some rapes might nevertheless have taken place, but they would have been furtive acts. The public nature of the rapes was no doubt intended to exacerbate the pain and humiliation suffered by the victims and to terrorize other villagers and detainees who witnessed them. It also demonstrated that the rapists had no cause to fear the wrath of their commanders.

The Commission determined that rape "was deliberately and systematically employed as a tool of 'ethnic cleansing.' . . . This became obvious when the same patterns of behavior aimed at publicly humiliating the immediate victims of sexual violence and their families were reported throughout distant territories and over more than one year. None of that could have occurred spontaneously. When coincidences are so frequently reported, they cease to be that."[22] The number of rapes did not decline until they became an international cause célèbre and the Bosnian Serb leaders calculated that the costs to their side outweighed the benefits of using rape to expedite ethnic cleansing.

Most Bosnian women who were raped in detention camps and survived were ultimately turned over to the International Committee of the Red Cross, and in cooperation with UNHCR, transported to Croatia. Yet Croatia, which has strict laws on adoption, registered a negligible number of cases in which Bosnian women sought to give up their children. Organizations in Europe that offered to take the babies born as a result of rape, and families from Europe and the United States who traveled to Croatia seeking babies to adopt—as they had to Romania in 1990, after the fall of Ceauşescu, seeking children from that country's notorious orphanages—could not find babies to take. But there were some births as a consequence of rape. Among women who carried to term, it is possible that some kept the babies—despite what I was told at Kosevo Hospital about the rejection of their babies by these rape victims—or arranged for their families to keep them. And it is even possible that a few babies were secretly murdered at birth. All that can be said with any certainty is that the rapes did not produce a host of little Chetniks.

The crusade led by Catharine MacKinnon that equates pornography with rape as a violent assault on women has been under way in the United States for two decades. The tragedy of rape victims in Croatia and Bosnia provided her an opportunity she seized to extend her equation: Not only does pornography equal rape, but rape equals genocide. Hence, in this syllogism, pornography is genocide, which accounts for her demand that Serbian pornographers be dealt with as Nuremberg dealt with the anti-Semitic publisher Julius Streicher.

Despite objections to the way MacKinnon and some others exploited the rape issue to serve their own agendas, I believe feminist groups did far more good than harm. The clearest evidence is the decline in the frequency of rapes noted by the UN War Crimes Commission after the feminists helped to push the issue into the media spotlight. (It was not the only form of abuse that proved sensitive to media attention; following publication of Roy Gutman's accounts in *Newsday,* and the avalanche of press attention they inspired, the detention of civilians and violence against detainees also declined sharply.) Despite the controversy over numbers, no one disputes that a lot of rapes were committed. The nearly three thousand rapes tabulated by the UN War Crimes Commission is an enormous figure, even if it seems small by comparison with the figures cited by MacKinnon. Though rape is not genocide, it is a terrible crime, the more so because many victims were gang-raped or raped repeatedly over extended periods. Because the circumstances were deliberately intended to heighten the sense of degradation. Because their captors taunted them that they would give birth to little Chetniks. Because the prolonged detention of some victims, whatever their number, made it impossible for them to terminate pregnancies before giving birth. And because it contributed to the "ethnic cleansing" that was the goal of the military and political leaders who deliberately used rape as an instrument of warfare.

To some trying to promote accountability for the many great crimes in ex-Yugoslavia, the way certain feminists seized on the rape issue caused discomfort. Like Lawrence Eagleburger, Catharine MacKinnon did the right thing for the wrong reason. Nevertheless, MacKinnon and company made an important contribution as some of the most outspoken advocates for prosecution and punishment of the war criminals. If the tribunal succeeds, MacKinnon, like Eagleburger, will deserve part of the credit.

12

Incitement
to Mass
Murder

O<small>N</small> O<small>CTOBER</small> 1, 1946, Julius Streicher, one of the twenty-one top Nazi leaders tried before the International Military Tribunal at Nuremberg on charges of waging aggressive war and crimes against humanity, was sentenced to death by hanging. Fifteen days later, the sentence was carried out. Half a century later, Streicher's conviction is again coming under close scrutiny as prosecutions proceed for the crimes committed in ex-Yugoslavia and Rwanda.

By all accounts, Streicher was a loathsome character. The most rabid of anti-Semites, he was despised even by many fellow Nazis for his corruption, sadism, and sexual perversity. Rebecca West, who reported on Nuremberg for *The New Yorker,* memorably described him as "a dirty old man of the sort that gives trouble in parks." In 1940, just months after Germany's invasion of Poland launched World War II, Streicher's venality led to his dismissal as gauleiter of Franconia (a district that includes the city of Nuremberg, where he met his end) and his removal from all Nazi party posts. For most of the war, during the years when virtually all the crimes against humanity were carried out, he was not a government official. Yet thanks to the continued patronage he received from Adolf Hitler, Streicher maintained his post during the war years as editor of the vile weekly newspaper *Der Stürmer,* which he had founded in 1923, the year of Hitler's Beer Hall Putsch in Munich. In its pages, he continued to foment hatred of the Jews.

The charge of waging aggressive war could not be sustained in Streicher's case, the Nuremberg tribunal held. Its judgment stated the reasons:

> Streicher was a staunch Nazi and supporter of Hitler's main policies. There is no evidence to show that he was ever within Hitler's inner circle of advisers; nor during his career was he closely connected with the formulation of the policies which led to war. He was never present, for example, at any of the important conferences when Hitler explained his decisions to his leaders. Although he was a Gauleiter there is no evidence to prove that he had knowledge of these policies. In the opinion of the Tribunal, the evidence fails to establish his connection with the conspiracy or common plan to wage aggressive war as that conspiracy has been elsewhere defined in this Judgment.

Although the tribunal decided that its jurisdiction was limited to those crimes committed in connection with the war and did not reach back to the period before September 1, 1939, its judgment briefly reviewed Streicher's earlier career:

> For his 25 years of speaking, writing, and preaching hatred of the Jews, Streicher was widely known as "Jew-Baiter Number One." In his speeches and articles month after month, he infected the German mind with the virus of anti-Semitism and incited the German people to active persecution. Each issue of *Der Stürmer,* which reached a circulation of 600,000 in 1935, was filled with such articles, often lewd and disgusting.

The grounds for his actual conviction, however, were his published works while crimes against humanity were taking place, inciting those engaged in such crimes:

> With knowledge of the extermination of the Jews in the Occupied Eastern Territories, this defendant continued to write and publish his propaganda of death. . . . Streicher's incitement to murder and extermination at the time when Jews in the East were being killed under the

most horrible conditions clearly constitutes persecution on political and racial grounds in connection with War Crimes as defined by the Charter, and constitutes a Crime Against Humanity.

In retrospect, the fate of Julius Streicher raises a troubling question: Should even the most hateful messages—the kind he routinely produced and disseminated—be denied the protection for freedom of expression ordinarily accorded to writers, editors, and publishers by societies that respect human rights? The issue is germane for the ex-Yugoslavia and Rwanda tribunals, because in both instances the slaughter was fomented by news media. In Rwanda, in fact, genocide was explicitly incited and organized by radio.

Article 19, a London-based organization that combats censorship worldwide, published a study, *Forging War,* on the role the news media played in ex-Yugoslavia in provoking the wars in Croatia and Bosnia and the crimes that characterized those wars.[1] The report points out that in prior years, "The media in the Socialist Federative Republic of Yugoslavia (SFRY) were more abundant, varied and unconstrained than in any other Communist state." The state maintained legal and ideological controls over the media, but less heavy-handedly than in other Communist countries.

One reason for the relative diversity in the media was what probably would be called target marketing today: Most newspapers and magazines, as well as radio and television broadcasts, were organized to serve audiences in the several republics that constituted Yugoslavia. But when the federation diminished in significance during the latter half of the 1980s and the country fragmented along the lines of the republics, the leaders of those mini-states stepped up their pressure on the media to make them into propaganda instruments for their nationalist causes.

The process began in Serbia in 1987, with Slobodan Milosevic's assumption of power. He had won great popularity by exploiting Serb fears of Albanian domination of Kosovo—"Old Serbia," to Serbs—where the most important Serb historical sites and religious monuments are located. It was the Kosovo issue that enabled Milosevic to become leader of the League of Communists, the party organization. He wasted no time in taking control of the media. According to Article 19, "The League's media policy consisted of pressuring or forcing every significant organ of information and opinion to chorus the same litany of complaints and demands. The phrasing varied slightly, according to the source and the intended audience: sometimes the Albanians were characterized as anti-Yugoslav counterrevolutionaries, sometimes as Muslim rapists of nuns. The upshot was always the same: Kosovo must be regained for Serbia [since the adoption of Yugoslavia's 1974 Constitution, Kosovo had been an autonomous province] or, as Milosevic put it, Serbia will be united or it will not exist." Dusan Mitevic, deputy director of TV Belgrade, subsequently acknowledged that "We showed Milosevic's promise [to regain Kosovo] over and over again on the TV. And this is what launched him."[2]

Milosevic canceled the autonomy of Kosovo and also Vojvodina, which had a Serb majority but included in its population a large ethnic Hungarian minority, a smaller number of Slovaks, and many other nationalities. In the process, he claimed the seats these territories had held in the collective presidency governing Yugoslavia since the death of Tito in 1980. Given Serbia's close ties with Montenegro, the smallest republic in the federation, Milosevic effectively controlled four of eight places in the presidency. For the remaining republics of Slovenia, Croatia, Bosnia-Herzegovina, and Macedonia, continued federation meant domination by Serbia—and by a man who had demonstrated his capacity and taste for nationalist demagoguery. Again, his principal weapon was the media he controlled. As the authors of *Yugoslavia: Death of a Nation* point out, "Belgrade Television—state run and immensely powerful in shaping public opinion—was firmly in Milosevic's grip. It was the ideal tool for stirring up hatred against 'the enemies of the Serbian people'—first Kosovo's Albanians, then the Slovenes, the Croats . . ."[3] Any chance that the federation would survive was doomed: Milosevic's political power plays and his exploitation of the media, particularly television, had handed it a death warrant.

Under the circumstances, it was hardly surprising that the other republics began to see a new nationalism as their salvation. In Croatia, Franjo Tudjman rode his own brand of nationalism to the presidency in April 1990; two months later, Croatia declared its independence and secured immediate recognition from Germany. The Serbs responded by recalling the bad old days of World War II, when the Nazis' Croatian puppets called for its one-third policy (convert a third, expel a third, and kill a third of the Serbs). Meantime, the Croats did little to calm fraying Serb nerves. To the contrary, the new Croatian state's use of symbols associated with the Ustasha, such as

the *sahovnica,* a red-and-white checked shield, as the emblem on its
national flag, only made matters worse.

The headlines that followed in *Politika,* Serbia's leading newspa-
per—closely tied to Milosevic—established the tone:
"Attack on the Serb People"
"The Whole Serb People Is Attacked"
"We Are Not Fascists, We Are Ustase"
"All Means to Resist Terror of Ustasoid Government"
"Croatian Specials Speak Albanian"
"Genocide Mustn't Happen"[4]

For all of Croatia's insensitivity in its choice of symbols, the attempt to convince Serbs that the new state was about to reinvent the
Ustasha killers of World War II was manufactured out of whole cloth.
Yet it arguably started the Balkan wars of the 1990s by stirring up so
much nationalist fervor that the subsequent Serb attacks on Vukovar
and other civilian population centers in Croatia were almost a foregone conclusion.

Zvornik, population 81,000, sits on the Drina River in northeastern
Bosnia along the border with Serbia. When the war began in April
1992, it was the first town of any size to suffer "ethnic cleansing."
Before the war, 59 percent of its residents were Muslims; 38 percent
were Serbs. Zvornik was attacked by the Yugoslav Army (JNA) and
Serb paramilitaries, and most of the town was overrun on April 8,
1992.[5] The Serbs summarily executed many of Zvornik's citizens,
including Kjasif Smajlovic, correspondent for the Sarajevo newspaper *Oslobodenje.* As his fellow correspondent Zlatko Dizdarevic
subsequently reported, "Friends who buried Kjasif tell us he had
gone to the office to file his report on how the attackers began
their reign of terror. He was dragged out, feet first, and calmly
executed on the sidewalk."[6] Some residents of Zvornik held out
for another twenty days in Kula Grad, a medieval fortress. *Forging
War* discusses *Politika's* coverage of the assault on this town, in
which several thousand Muslims were butchered and the rest driven
away:

> *Politika* first mentions the town on 6 April: Serbs were packing and
> leaving, due to the "tensions in the Zvornik area." On 9 April, *Politika*
> reported "no peace," because Muslim extremists had attacked "the Serb
> municipality of Zvornik. . . ."

Next day, *Politika*'s front page bore the headline "Serb forces in control of Zvornik." On page 6, under "Zvornik liberated," was the news that "[all vital buildings in the town] have been taken and the customary cleansing of the town is under way." Instead of accepting the ultimatum to surrender, reports correspondent D. Pejak, the other side "fired on members of the Territorial Defence of the Serb municipality of Zvornik. . . . Green berets are, by tried and tested means, keeping defenseless people hostage." (The word used for defenseless people was *nejac*, a folklore archaism connoting epic travails under the Ottoman empire.) . . . On 21 April, *Politika* reported that "Muslim forces are still shooting at peace."

Then a brief item appeared on 26 April, "All quiet in Zvornik," an appraisal contradicted the next day when *Politika* ran a story under the headline: "The stronghold of Muslim extremists in Zvornik has fallen." Here, readers learned that Yugoslav and Serbian flags now flew from Kula Grad above Zvornik. "Relief [was felt] on both sides of the River Drina" (the border between Serbia and Bosnia). The extremists had rejected all the Territorial Defence's appeals to surrender; calls for peace were met with bullets. Prisoners revealed that "Alija's army" [referring to Alija Izetbegovic, president of Bosnia-Herzegovina] includes Bangladeshis and *siptars* [a derogatory term for Albanian Muslims], and that Bosnian Muslims from Sarajevo and Bihac had been in command.[7]

As *Forging War* comments, "So much for the fate of Zvornik. In the pages of Serbia's most prestigious daily, the seizure and genocidal devastation of this town never happened. After provocations and tensions, the Muslim extremist forces had lost fair and square; their dastardly plans to enslave the local Serbs were foiled. *Politika*'s reporting of Foca, Bijeljina, Visegrad and Prijedor (all attacked in a similar way) repeated the pattern."[8]

An eyewitness account of what actually took place in Zvornik has been provided by José María Mendiluce, the United Nations High Commissioner for Refugees chief in the former Yugoslavia at the time. Before the war in Bosnia, UNHCR's main office in the region was in Sarajevo, a location intended to reflect neutrality between Serbs and Croats, then the main antagonists. By chance, Mendiluce was driving from Belgrade back to his office in Sarajevo and passed through Zvornik as an "ethnic cleansing" operation by the White Eagles, the paramilitary group led by Vojislav Seselj, was under way. Mendiluce told journalist David Rieff: "I saw kids put under the treads of tanks, placed there by grown men, and then run over by other

grown men. . . . Everywhere, people were shooting. The fighters
were moving through the town, systematically killing all the Muslims
they could get their hands on. . . . These people had a coherent strat-
egy. The whole point was to inflict as much terror on the civilian
population as possible, to destroy as much property as possible, and
to target as much of the violence as possible against women and
kids."9

Though *Politika*'s coverage was pure fiction, it paled in comparison to the state broadcasting system, Radio Televizija Srbije (RTS),
which has enjoyed a monopoly in disseminating news and information in much of Serbia. Describing the language and tone that characterized RTS's radio and television broadcasts throughout the
Croatian and Bosnian wars, *Forging War* states:

> The emphasis in RTS coverage was on the defensive nature of Serb ac-
> tivity; the Serbs were "fighting for freedom," "defending" and "guard-
> ing," protecting their "native soil" from "the Muslims," who were waging
> a religious war, and wanted to force Serbs to belong to an Islamic state,
> and from "the Croats," who wanted to unite with Croatia, and whose
> anti-Serb fascism was already known. The RTS journalists' terms for
> their enemies were manifold . . . "evil-doers," "cut-throats," *"ustashe,"*
> "Islamic *ustashe,"* *"mujahedin,"* *"jihad* warriors," "commando terrorist
> groups" and "Muslim extremists."

In the period leading up to the wars in Croatia and Bosnia, RTS
broadcast bloodcurdling accounts of atrocities supposedly committed
against Serbs by Croats and Muslims. In some cases, photographs
from World War II that show the victims of Ustasha crimes were re-
cycled for these purposes. In other cases, footage used elsewhere in
ex-Yugoslavia to depict Croat or Bosnian victims was shown with
narration claiming they were Serbs. "Every night for five years,"
according to Warren Zimmermann, the last U.S. ambassador to a unified Yugoslavia, "everybody in Yugoslavia watched highly manipu-
lated pictures of the maimed and the murdered, the cleansed and the
condemned."10 Serb atrocities against others were usually ignored.
When the information got through anyway to Serbs with satellite
dishes, short-wave radios, or access to limited-circulation print
media, RTS claimed that the Croats and Bosnians had inflicted these
horrible crimes upon their own people to discredit Serbia. There was,
for example, the "bread line massacre" of May 27, 1992, when seventeen people were killed and many more injured by a mortar shell

in Sarajevo. RTS said in broadcasts that the Bosnians had shelled themselves, a version of the episode that also appeared in *Politika*. As *Forging War* points out, RTS "constructed a version of reality in which Serb forces never attacked Bosnia, never slaughtered scores of thousands of its people and displaced scores of thousands more, never besieged its cities and towns, and never laid waste to its villages."

The reality constructed on radio and television is one thing in a society where opposing views are regularly broadcast and the audience expects one commentator may be contradicted by the next. It is quite another in a country such as Yugoslavia, where official views were presented as facts and no contrary opinion or information was aired. Peter Maass of *The Washington Post* recounted an anecdote that underscores the impact such propaganda can have. Maass talked to a Serb woman, Vera, about what had happened in her village in Bosnia. Vera told him that "everything was peaceful because the Muslims had been rounded up immediately. I asked why. Vera said the Muslims were planning to arrest all the Serb men and put all the Serb women into 'harems.' This was ludicrous, and I asked her why she believed it: She responded with a line that was half question, half-statement: 'Why would the radio lie?' " The same woman told Maass that her relations with Muslims before the war had always been very good because "they were very nice people."[11]

Although RTS, *Politika,* and other press outlets in Serbia were in a nasty class of their own when it came to fomenting war and war crimes, the Tudjman government in Croatia was no slouch at using the media to stir up hatred. *Forging War:* "By the time Serbia and its proxies [that is, the Bosnian Serbs and the Serbian paramilitary forces] launched war in Bosnia in April 1992, the Croatian media were tightly controlled: 'unreliable' journalists and editors had been removed. When Croatian forces began their undisguised land-grab in Herzegovina and central Bosnia, and the 'ethnic cleansing' of Muslim areas in January 1993, the only truly independent medium with a nationwide audience was the *Slobodna Dalmacija* newspaper which was seized by the government a few weeks later."

Like its Serb counterparts, the controlled press in Croatia habitually used provocative terms such as *mujahedin* to label Bosnian forces, suggesting that they were Islamic fanatics. The Croatian media also invented atrocities that never took place. *Forging War* cited a report by the Croatian news agency, *Hrvatska Izvjestajna Novinsk Agencija* (HINA), in August 1993 that "Croat witnesses who escaped from Zenica [a Bosnian government–controlled city] report that 35 Croats were hanged on the square in front of the Catholic church, for refusing to wear the uniform of the Muslim army" and that Croats and Serbs in Zenica were being forced to adopt Turkish names and to pay large sums for new identity cards. As for Croatian television, HTV, *Forging War* took note of a thirteen-point decree issued on August 28, 1991, early in the war between Croatia and Serbia, by its news editor-in-chief and its programming editor-in-chief. Among their instructions to the staff:

- "Do not use the terms 'Chetniks' and 'extremists' but only 'Serb Terrorists.' "
- "Do not call the JNA [Yugoslav Army] anything except 'Serbo-Communist Army of Occupation.' "
- "Casualty figures of Guardsmen and police must always be accompanied with 'fell for Croatia's freedom,' 'gave their lives to defend the homeland,' 'heroes in defense of the homeland.' "
- "Do not conceal defeats at the front, but stress the tremendous forces employed by the enemy and his unscrupulousness, and always finish such reports with optimistic declarations and avowals ('but we shall bring back freedom to our Kijevo,' for example)."

When CNN and Sky Television broadcast reports in October 1993 of a massacre of Bosnian Muslim civilians by Croatian forces in the village of Stupni Do, HTV responded with a specially made propaganda film purporting to demonstrate that what actually took place was a fierce battle between opposing military forces and that Stupni Do was a Bosnian military base from which a Croatian village had been bombarded.

In any war, the armed forces exercise some control over the press, and it is expected that correspondents from a combatant country will be aligned with their own nation's military. During World War II, journalists covering the war even wore military uniforms. Britain's Field Marshal Bernard Montgomery described journalists as "an element of my staff," and his American counterpart, General Dwight D. Eisenhower, said "I have always considered as quasi–staff officers [the] correspondents accredited to my headquarters."[12] The Vietnam War probably ended forever, at least in countries with a more or less free press, such ties between the media and the military. Coverage of the war by a significant number of journalists was unlike the reporting on any previous conflict. Far from being propagandists for their own side, some American journalists made clear in their reporting that they questioned the rationale for the war and the manner in which it was fought, and they were highly skeptical of the official version of events. In effect, they helped to establish a new ethos among journalists: that at least in principle, the press should be independent even in times of war.

The fact that journalists in many countries now see their relationship to combatant forces in a different light has not put an end to military efforts to control the media. The Gulf War was an interesting case in point. On the Iraqi side, Baghdad required the media to publish and broadcast handouts from its military press office. On the American side, the military tried to shape press coverage through control of information about the war and access to the war zone. But the U.S. effort didn't work very well. Some media, including CNN, maintained coverage from the Iraqi side as the war was under way. Perhaps more important, many enterprising journalists managed to work around the restrictions imposed by the JIB (Joint Information Bureau) set up by the Pentagon in Saudi Arabia, reporting on the battlefield—and on the military's attempts to manipulate them.

Incitement of a war by the media is not unprecedented, even in countries with a free press. One of the most notorious examples is the role of William Randolph Hearst's *New York Journal* and its star reporter, Richard Harding Davis, in promoting the Spanish-American War in 1898. Hearst was motivated primarily by the desire to sell newspapers at a time when his paper was engaged in fierce competition with Joseph Pulitzer's *World*. The *Journal* took up the Cuban independence struggle and did everything possible to pump up interest and get the United States into the war, including the invention of Spanish atrocities. Hearst's campaign succeeded when the battleship *Maine* blew up in Havana harbor, perhaps by accident. His newspapers persuaded Americans that it was a Spanish plot, bringing about both the war and the circulation boost that he sought.

What differentiates the role of the press in ex-Yugoslavia from what we have come to expect in armed conflicts is that the media incited wars and wartime practices that were different. They were not fought principally for control of population and territory. Some combat of that sort took place, but what happened in Prijedor and Zvornik had nothing to do with conquest. The Serbs established their control in those areas right away. "Ethnic cleansing," which was the way most deaths occurred during the war, took place mainly in such communities that were not contested militarily. The purpose was to eliminate permanently from controlled territory a segment of the population, just as the Nazis attempted to eliminate permanently all Jews from countries occupied and subjugated by German troops. In ex-Yugoslavia, as we have seen, the Serbian and Croatian media legitimized genocide by inventing atrocities or claiming they were self-inflicted or by demonizing Bosnian Muslims. The media in Serbia and in Croatia incited crimes against humanity as they were taking place. In that respect, they were no different from Julius Streicher, who was hanged at Nuremberg. Streicher was more explicit in calling for extermination than were the editors of *Politika* or the managers of RTS, but the latter may have had more detailed knowledge of the actual commission of crimes against humanity, since their correspondents sometimes were on the scene when the battles were under way.

Telford Taylor, a prosecutor at the first Nuremberg trial, and subsequently the chief American prosecutor, has written that the conviction of Streicher "seemed to me legally defensible, but I cannot justify the Tribunal's failure to mention other facts, such as that from 1940 until the end of the war, Streicher was living on his farm in forced seclusion and his connection with *Der Stürmer* was his only 'outside' source of information, that the paper's circulation had dwindled to about 15,000 copies during most of the war, that he had no connection with Himmler or any contact with those in Poland or the Soviet Union who were perpetrating the atrocities, and that publication of a newspaper, however maddening and unconscionable it may be, should be touched with criminal accusations only with the greatest caution."[13]

In Taylor's view, these circumstances should have been considered in mitigation of Streicher's crime: While his conviction was appropriate, his death sentence was not. Although the Nuremberg tribunal held that its jurisdiction in judging crimes against humanity was restricted to the period following September 1, 1939, the death sentence apparently reflected the view of the judges that what was published in *Der Stürmer* in prior years played a decisive role in producing the Holocaust and that what Streicher published while the Holocaust was under way reflected his intent that the crimes he had incited should actually be committed.

Perhaps the clearest single case of genocide since the Holocaust was the slaughter in Rwanda from April to July 1994. Control of territory was never an issue in Rwanda; the only point of what took place was to exterminate the Tutsis. The best estimates of the death count—mainly Tutsis, but also large numbers of the Hutu intelligentsia—settle at about 800,000. Again, the media played a pivotal role. Radio Mille Collines (formally, Radio Television Libere des Mille Collines, RTLM) broadcast calls to government troops and pro-government militias to kill every last Tutsi, including children; Radio Rwanda was less explicit but conveyed the same message. Radio Mille Collines even outdid Streicher—and certainly the press in Serbia—in the specificity of its incitement of genocide: One broadcast reminded its listeners that "when you kill the rat do not let the pregnant one escape."[14]

The Rwandan genocide began when a plane carrying the presidents of Rwanda and neighboring Burundi was shot down, killing both men. By then, the incitement had already begun, as journalist Bill Berkeley reported:

> Long before the unexplained April 6 [1994] plane crash of President Juvenal Habyarimana, Radio Rwanda and a station owned by members of Habyarimana's inner circle, Radio Mille Collines, had been terrorizing the Hutus with warnings about the evil Tutsi-led RPF [Rwandan Patriotic Front, an insurgent group that achieved victory in July 1994, ending the genocide] and Hutu oppositionists, who were labeled "enemies" or "traitors" and who "deserved to die." Endless speeches, songs and slogans demonized the Tutsis. Hutus were warned that the Tutsis were coming to kill them, take their land, reclaim the dominant role they had enjoyed for centuries, before they were ousted in the bloody Hutu uprising that led to Rwanda's independence from Belgium in 1962.[15]

The level of incitement escalated after the plane crash. According to Africa scholar Gerard Prunier: "Within the next few hours the calls turned into hysterical appeals for ever greater quantities of blood. It was difficult to credit that normal people could broadcast such things as 'You have missed some of the enemies in this or that place. Some are still alive. You must go back there and finish them off' or 'The graves are not yet quite full. Who is going to do the good work and help us fill them completely?' "[16]

The U.S. Committee for Refugees, an organization that investigated the massacres in Rwanda, has described a case in which Polish priests hid twenty people on the grounds of their mission in the Rwandan capital, Kigali, and were bringing food to them. "According to Father Stanislas," the organization reported, "Radio RTLM, the extremist radio station run by members of President Habyarimana's political party, announced that the church was still harboring the *Inkotanyi* (supporters of the RPF). Four days later, on the afternoon of April 12, approximately 100 *Interahamwe* [youth militia members affiliated with the ruling party] entered the church grounds and demanded the keys to the chapel. The metal door to the chapel had been locked from the inside, and according to Father Stanislas, the priests did not have keys. The *Interahamwe* tried without success to shoot the lock and otherwise break down the door. Failing that, the mob broke the narrow windows, poured gasoline into the roughly 12' by 12' room, threw in grenades . . ."[17]

Article 19 has published the most thorough study of the media's role in Rwandan genocide, just as it did on the press's role in promoting war and ethnic cleansing in ex-Yugoslavia.[18] The authors of the Rwanda report argue that it is a mistake to hold RTLM entirely responsible for incitement, because doing so implies that genocide would not have taken place except for its hate-filled broadcasts. As they see it, this suggestion accepts the view that the genocide was a product of ancient and deep-seated enmities between Hutus and Tutsis that were let loose by the dissemination of hate propaganda. Rather, according to Article 19, the more important connection of RTLM to the genocide was precisely in such episodes as the one reported by the U.S. Committee for Refugees at the Polish missionary church in Kigali. RTLM identified the targets and their location to their killers. "The fundamental reality which cannot be stated too often is that genocide is not caused by mass media," the Article 19 study asserts. "All the evidence points to the fact that the Rwandan genocide was a highly planned affair. . . . The apparatus of militias, hit squads, arms caches and death lists was meticulously put in place in the months before April 1994."[19]

An important factor in Article 19's analysis is that there was a significant difference in the content of RTLM's broadcasts prior to April 6, 1994, and what it broadcast once the genocide was under way. Before the genocide, in Article 19's description, RTLM patterned itself on American talk radio, complete with audience participation. Its commentators helped to create a climate of fear of the Tutsi rebel Rwandan Patriotic Front and generated antagonism against the political opposition as "traitors," but the station did not broadcast explicit calls to do direct harm to Tutsis. A few days prior to the genocide, RTLM began to broadcast predictions of violence. It was only when the genocide started, however, that its truly venomous broadcasts began. Its calls for violence accompanied the genocide rather than preceded it. Accordingly, Article 19 concludes that "the radio station did not incite genocide so much as organize it."[20]

This argument is not entirely persuasive. In essence, Article 19 has defined incitement to violence as meaning the same thing as causing violence. Though Article 19's discussion of the difference in the content of the broadcasts prior to the genocide does help to demonstrate that RTLM's broadcasts were not the cause, the station deserves to be charged with incitement for egging the killers on once the genocide started. Moreover, the information compiled by Article 19 and others who have reported on Rwanda suggests that RTLM's broadcasts were a factor in the mass participation in the genocide. That is, the organizers of the genocide used RTLM to enlist a large part of the population in carrying out the slaughter. Article 19 is correct in arguing that RTLM helped to organize the genocide, but to point that out does not exculpate the station of the lesser charge of also inciting it as it was under way, if not in advance.

In this case, *incitement* of genocide and *organization* of genocide are so closely connected they cannot be separated. Indeed, Jean Bosco Barayaqwiza, a founder and one of the directors of RTLM, also was a leader of a Hutu political party, the Coalition pour la Défense de la République (CDR), that deployed its militia to massacre Tutsis. (Another RTLM director, Ferdinand Nahasima, was apprehended in Cameroon and, along with other leading organizers of the genocide, was sent to Arusha, Tanzania, seat of the Rwanda tribunal, in January 1997 for trial.) This, in effect, was a sickening turnkey enterprise: Barayaqwiza's militia carried out the genocide that his radio incited and organized.

Following defeat of the government forces and militias that carried out the genocide, RTLM was still in business, broadcasting from a new venue false accounts of massacres supposedly committed by the victorious Rwandan Patriotic Front. These phony reports, in turn, sent more than a million Hutus fleeing into Zaire, causing thousands of additional deaths from dysentery, cholera, and other diseases. In the refugee camps in Zaire, the broadcasters continued their deadly work, terrifying those who might have returned to their homes with new fabrications of RPF revenge massacres. In fact, there were revenge killings by RPF soldiers, but their extent was greatly exaggerated by the broadcasters.[21]

Readers who are familiar with my career may know that as the executive director of the American Civil Liberties Union in the 1970s, I defended freedom of speech for American Nazis seeking to hold a demonstration in the town of Skokie, Illinois. The case, one of many in which we upheld First Amendment rights for Nazis, fascists, the Ku Klux Klan, and other extremists, aroused particular attention because Skokie was home to a large number of Holocaust survivors. For a fifteen-month period during 1977 and 1978, the Skokie case was the subject of almost daily press coverage and inspired many magazine articles, a television docudrama, and several books, including one I wrote upholding the free speech side of the debate.[22]

How is it possible to insist that American Nazis should be accorded the rights to speak, publish, and demonstrate in favor of Nazi views in Skokie or elsewhere in the United States and at the same time suggest that those who incited crimes against humanity in Bosnia or in Rwanda should be brought to judgment? In fact, I believe that these positions, which may at first appear contradictory, are consistent.

The essence of the defense of the rights of the American Nazis at Skokie is that it took place in a context in which freedom of speech operated. The ACLU's efforts were aimed at assuring the widest possible latitude for expression. A central purpose was to block any attempt by government, or by citizens invoking the authority of government, to regulate the content of speech. Morally, the defense of freedom of speech for the Nazis at Skokie rested not only on the intrinsic value of freedom of expression and the belief that governments must not be entrusted with the power to control the dissemination of information or ideas, it also turned on the consequentialist premise that the best chance of preventing the message of the Nazis from being translated into reality was in making certain that freedom prevailed, even when that meant extending the benefits of freedom to the enemies of freedom.

In Serbia, Croatia, and Rwanda, in contrast, the governments controlled the media to make certain that most citizens would hear only what those governments wanted them to hear. Freedom of speech did not exist. In Rwanda, for example, Radio Mille Collines started broadcasting nine months prior to the genocide with a license that was denied to those who might offer different views. Its broadcasters had exclusive access to most listeners in the thousand hills for which the station was named. Also, as Gerard Prunier has pointed out, "it was effective. It knows how to use street slang, obscene jokes and good music to push its racist message. . . . Yet people went on listening to it with a kind of stupefied fascination, incredulous at the relaxed joking way in which it defied the most deeply cherished human values."[23] A few dissenting voices tried to make themselves heard, and protecting them to the greatest extent feasible was significant. But when a government monopolizes or virtually monopolizes control of expression and only allows propaganda to be heard that incites crimes against humanity and justifies those crimes, freedom of expression is not advanced by protecting its dissemination. The concept of freedom of speech requires freedom for a broad range of views—even Nazi views—provided that all other views, including those of anti-Nazis, may be expressed; it is not a license for a government to disseminate an official view to the exclusion of others. When that exclusive official view incites crimes against humanity, it does not warrant defense as freedom of expression. Also, when incitement is so closely intertwined with the actual commission of the crime that they cannot be separated, it does not warrant the protection accorded to freedom of speech. Such an intertwined connection between expression and criminality may occur in circumstances in which only one point of view may be heard. The connection is severed when many voices compete.

In the book I wrote about Skokie, I discussed the famous dictum by Supreme Court Justice Oliver Wendell Holmes, Jr., that "free speech would not protect a man in falsely shouting fire in a crowded theater and causing panic." It provides an analogy to the circumstances in Bosnia or Rwanda—indeed, in the case of the flight to Zaire provoked by RTLM, the analogy is painfully exact. I wrote in *Defending My Enemy*:

> The shout of fire in a crowded theater is the antithesis of free speech. Reason is not free to combat it. No free and open encounter is possible between truth and falsehood. The panic takes place too quickly. Only

one side can possibly be heard. The shout of fire takes place in circumstances where it creates what Justice Holmes called "a clear and present danger."

In Skokie, by contrast, free speech could operate. Many other points of view may be heard in addition to the views of the Nazis. Even if the Nazis should carry signs saying Jews should be put into ovens, there is no "clear and present danger" that anyone will act in accordance with this advice before reason has a chance to combat it. . . .

Moreover, because the residents of Skokie are so opposed to the Nazis, the circumstances that would create a "clear and present danger" are especially remote. If the Nazis marched in a neighborhood where they had large numbers of sympathizers, there would be a much greater likelihood of a "clear and present danger."

In circumstances where a lynching is possible, for example, free speech would not protect a Nazi who said to a crowd of followers, "There's a Jew. Let's get him." Even if the speaker refrained from participating in the attack, "the clear and present danger" that violence would immediately result would permit the criminal prosecution of the speaker.

The leading decision by the United States Supreme Court on these issues is a 1969 case, *Brandenburg v. Ohio,*[24] involving a Ku Klux Klan leader who told a dozen hooded Klan members, some of them carrying guns, that "if our President, our Congress, our Supreme Court continues to suppress the white, Caucasian race, it's possible that there might have to be some revengeance [sic] taken." The Supreme Court reversed Clarence Brandenburg's conviction and his sentence of one to ten years in prison, saying that "the constitutional guarantees of free speech and press do not permit a state to forbid or prosecute advocacy of the use of force or of law violation except where such advocacy is directed to inciting or producing imminent lawless action and is likely to produce such action." As the court recognized, imminence and likelihood, which depend on context, are crucial in determining when incitement is so closely linked to criminality that the two cannot be separated.

By controlling the media to prevent other voices from being heard, and by inciting crimes against humanity and genocide in circumstances that met the test of imminence and likelihood, governments in ex-Yugoslavia and Rwanda established contexts for use of their media propagandists as equivalents of the speaker inciting a lynch mob. The Genocide Convention of 1951, drafted by Raphael

Lemkin with full knowledge of the part played by Julius Streicher's *Der Stürmer,* states that one of the acts punishable as genocide is "direct and public incitement to commit genocide." This language was repeated by the UN Security Council in the statutes it promulgated for the ex-Yugoslavia and Rwanda tribunals. It allows the criminal prosecution of those government propagandists who directly incited the slaughter, because their culpability in circumstances where they had a monopoly or a virtual monopoly on communications was not less than that of those who sniped at children in Sarajevo or threw grenades into crowded churches in Rwanda.

13

Guilt

Shortly after the end of World War II, the German philosopher Karl Jaspers published a book, *Die Schuldfrage,* that appeared in English as *The Question of German Guilt.*[1] It was a subject that Jaspers could discuss without personal embarrassment. A steadfast opponent of the Nazis, he was stripped of his university professorship and his right to publish before the start of the war and eventually obtained permission in 1942 to emigrate to neutral Switzerland. But his wife, Gertrud, who was Jewish, was denied the right to leave, so Jaspers stayed too. She went into hiding and survived. He reportedly was scheduled to be sent to a concentration camp in 1945, but Germany collapsed and the end of the war came just in time to prevent his internment. He was probably the most distinguished anti-Nazi intellectual to survive the war in Germany.

In *Die Schuldfrage,* Jaspers identified four varieties of guilt: criminal, political, moral, and metaphysical.

"Criminal guilt," he wrote, consists of "acts capable of objective proof . . . [that] violate unequivocal laws." Such crimes can be dealt with in judicial proceedings by courts that determine the facts and adjudicate guilt or innocence in accordance with applicable law.

"Political guilt," according to Jaspers, involves the deeds of the state, for which each and every citizen must bear the consequences, because all of us share responsibility for the way we are governed. It follows that even those among us who did not approve of the actions of the state and, indeed, may have struggled without success to prevent those acts, nevertheless must bear the consequences of the acts of our leaders.

"Moral guilt," he said, means that "I, who cannot act otherwise than as an individual, am morally responsible for all my deeds, including the execution of political and military orders. It is never simply true that 'orders are orders.' . . . Every deed remains subject to moral judgment."

"Metaphysical guilt," Jaspers's final category, is based on a solidarity among men and women as human beings that makes all responsible for every wrong and every injustice in the world, especially for crimes committed in their presence or with their knowledge. "If I fail to do whatever I can to prevent them," Jaspers wrote, "I too am guilty. If I am present at the murder of others without risking my life to prevent it, I feel guilty in a way not adequately conceivable either legally, politically or morally. That I live after such a thing has happened weighs upon me as indelible guilt." Metaphysical guilt may be distinguished from moral guilt in Jaspers's definition of these in that it applies not only to one's deeds but to that which is not done.

Advocates of prosecuting those who committed crimes against humanity in ex-Yugoslavia have argued that the effect is to individualize guilt. What they have in mind, of course, is criminal guilt. Some of the strongest voices advocating this—all strong supporters of the tribunal—have come from inside the former Yugoslavia. They and others have maintained that in a territory where violent ethnic conflict has taken place three times in the twentieth century, it is crucial to break the cycle of the collective attribution of guilt. Serbs, as a people, did not commit mass murder, torture, and rape in Croatia and Bosnia; rather, particular Serbs, and also particular Croats and Muslims, committed particular crimes. If those directly responsible are tried and punished, the burden of blame will not be carried indiscriminately by members of an entire ethnic group. Culpability will not be passed down from generation to generation. Trials will single out the guilty, differentiating them from the innocent.

The concept of collective guilt, according to Dwight Macdonald, writing toward the end of World War II, when the debate over what to do with Nazi war criminals was just beginning, embodies a Hegelian, statist approach in which individuals lack will, thought, and conscience except as these are united in the "organic totality" of the state. This view, Macdonald argued, leads directly to the absolution, or self-absolution, of those who actually commit great crimes on the grounds that if all are guilty, no one is guilty. *They* did not commit rape, torture, or murder on their own and cannot be held individually responsible, since they were mere bit players in a historical drama. The absence of a sense of responsibility, of course, makes it far easier for them to commit such crimes. Macdonald cited the following dialogue between an American war correspondent and an official of a Nazi death camp to illustrate the manner in which collective guilt can be invoked by the criminal to free himself of any sense of responsibility for his own actions:

Q. Did you kill people in the camp? A. Yes.

Q. Did you poison them with gas? A. Yes.

Q. Did you bury them alive? A. It sometimes happened.

Q. Did you personally help to kill people? A. Absolutely not. I was only paymaster in the camp.

Q. What did you think of what was going on? A. It was bad at first, but we got used to it.

Q. Do you know the Russians will hang you? A. *(bursting into tears)* Why should they? What have I done?[2]

To advocates of individualizing guilt in courts of law, the offstage efforts to shelve Bosnian war crimes trials by the British Foreign Office in Prime Minister John Major's government, and by some UN officials eager for peace at any price, was shortsighted at best. If peace is to last, it will be because different ethnic groups are again able to live together or at least to live alongside one another, as they did for more than four decades following World War II before nationalist demagogues stirred them to conflict. Peaceful coexistence seems much less likely if those who were victimized see no one called to account for their suffering. In such circumstances, the victims or their ethnic kin may take revenge themselves, in the same way victims of an ordinary crime might respond if they see no effort by the state to prosecute and punish the criminal. Establishment of a system of lawful punishments signifies that the community at large considers a crime against one of its members to be a crime against all, and that the responsibility for redress lies with the community and not with the victim. On such grounds, prosecutions are styled "The People vs. John Doe" or "The State vs. John Doe." Each time the community carries out this responsibility, it reasserts the rule of law. Conversely, when the community of nations shies away from responsibility for bringing to justice the authors of crimes against humanity, it subverts the rule of law.

French literary and political essayist Alain Finkielkraut makes the point in the context of Nazi war crimes trials: "At Nuremberg, the world judged history, instead of submitting to its verdict or seeking the truth in its unfolding. Defining the human race by its *diversity* and no longer by its *forward march,* realizing that it is not Man who inhabits the earth but men [and women] in their infinite plurality, the judges spoke in the name of all international society because, as they thought, it was society as a whole that had suffered an irreparable wrong."[3] The very phrase "crimes against humanity" connotes that it is not only a particular group that has been injured but the entire human race. Accordingly, all have a responsibility to see that justice is done. A prosecution before an international tribunal is "Humanity vs. Radovan Karadzic" or "The World vs. Radovan Karadzic." Where the world shirks its responsibility to judge crimes against humanity and where lawful punishments for irreparable wrongs are not available, a lawless response is a possible or even probable consequence.

The resentments that Serbs harbored against Croats for the unpunished crimes of the Ustasha state during World War II was a major factor in the catastrophic developments in ex-Yugoslavia more than four decades later. Justice provides closure, its absence not only leaves wounds open, but its very denial rubs salt in them. Accordingly, partisans of prosecutions argue, peace without justice is a recipe for further conflict. In the fast-forward world in which we live, it is unlikely that another four or five decades would elapse before the next war.

But even those who have called for trials to individualize responsibility for war crimes struggle with a critical question: Can the line between guilt and innocence be drawn sharply and clearly? If one guard at a detention camp raped, and another only patrolled the perimeter, and a third drove the truck that brought detainees to the camp, are not all as culpable as the paymaster in Dwight Macdonald's story? The rapist could not commit his crimes if the others had not done their part. What about the person who agreed to make a farm storage building or a sports hall available as a detention center, or the town clerk who identified the ethnicity of those detained, or the neighbor who pointed out their hiding places? What is their guilt?

Indeed, under generally accepted principles of criminal law, many people could be prosecuted in such situations. If they acted with intent to commit a crime—that is, they possessed what the law refers to as *mens rea*—and committed an overt act in furtherance of a conspiracy to murder, rape, detain a civilian unlawfully, or engage in some other crime, guilt could be established.

Necessarily, of course, the overwhelming majority of those who conspired to commit crimes against humanity (by definition, crimes on a great scale) or knowingly aided in their commission cannot be prosecuted. It is inconceivable that the international community would marshal the resources or that the states where they reside would demonstrate the will to bring to account such a large number of criminals. If only on practical grounds, prosecutions must be limited largely to those whose guilt is greatest—that is, those with the highest level of responsibility for the most egregious crimes. Prosecutions must focus on political leaders and military commanders who gave the orders or who demonstrated by their conduct that widespread abuses were desired or would be tolerated, as well as on those down the line who were not just guards at the perimeter of a camp such as Omarska but who directly murdered. The fact that others who abetted the commission of great crimes will go free makes them innocent only in the formal sense that they have not been proven guilty in a court of law.

If it's difficult to cast a net wide enough to capture all the criminals who participated in "ethnic cleansing" in the former Yugoslavia, imagine the much greater challenge in coming to grips with the genocide in Rwanda. When the long list of twentieth-century horrors is compiled, Rwanda will deserve a special place. In certain respects, what happened there in less than three months, in 1994, is as horrifying as the Nazi Holocaust that has seemed the embodiment of the most extreme evil that humans could devise.

There was madness by definition in both, but the methods used in Rwanda and Nazi Germany were much different. The Nazis bureaucratized genocide, deliberately circumscribing the number of

Germans who directly killed Jews and the others chosen for elimination. Until the late stages of the war, when the process was accelerated in an attempt to complete the task and the Wehrmacht became an instrument for the commission of genocide, the mass murderers (that is, those who deliberately killed noncombatants) were relatively few in number. They included three thousand members of the *Einsatzgruppen* (four mobile killing units that followed in the wake of the German military to kill civilians who had come under German control, assisted in this task by auxiliary police units of Estonians, Latvians, Lithuanians, and Ukrainians);[4] members of the SS, who administered the death camps; those who planned and directed their activities; and some Ukrainians and others who were employed by the Nazis to do much of the dirtiest work at certain camps. Moreover, by using such devices as poison gas and crematoria, the Nazis sought to sanitize the killing process. We already have seen that a great many more Germans took part directly in practices that contributed to the Holocaust, such as the enforcement of race laws, deportations, and forced labor. Yet much about the way the Final Solution was carried out indicated an intent to insulate most of the perpetrators of genocide, including the actual killers, and particularly the Germans among them, from the goriest and foulest work.

In a 1996 book that attracted much attention and stirred wide controversy, Daniel Joseph Goldhagen argued that a murderous anti-Semitism was deeply rooted and pervasive in German society, that Germans generally were "willing executioners" of the Jews, and that direct participation in the Holocaust was more widespread than had been recognized previously.[5] Goldhagen insists the list of direct participants in Nazi genocide must include at least 19,000 members of 38 police battalions *(Ordnungspolizei)* that he argues were "as integral to the commission of the Holocaust as the *Einsatzgruppen*";[6] and 25,000 members of three SS brigades that, "under Himmler's direct command, slaughtered Jews in the Soviet Union from 1941 to 1943." In addition, by taking into account rotations in service, Goldhagen estimates that the actual number of men who served in the *Einsatzgruppen* at various times was over 6,000. The total "number [of Germans] who became perpetrators of the Holocaust," he says, "was certainly over one hundred thousand." He adds that "it would not be surprising if the number turned out to be five hundred thousand or more."[7]

This is not the place to enter the debate over Goldhagen's evidence and the conclusions he has drawn from it. Rather, it is possible to accept his figure of 100,000 direct perpetrators—although perhaps not his unsupported suggestion of five times that number—as a measure of how many fellow human beings were required to murder 6 million Jews in the manner in which they were slaughtered during World War II. Even given the careful planning that went into the organization of the Holocaust, the availability of efficient bureaucratic machinery, and the intent to limit the number of Germans directly engaged in murder, one can readily imagine that the self-assigned task of the Nazis required 100,000 killers. They may well have carried out their duties as willingly as Goldhagen argues. Similarly, he may be right in contending that many other Germans were ready to step into their shoes and to perform the same deeds. But Goldhagen's findings do not fundamentally alter the picture of the Holocaust painted by Raul Hilberg, the foremost historian of the destruction of the European Jews, in his 1992 book:

> The process of destruction was based on three premises. The first was an insistence not to exempt any segment of Jewry from the application of anti-Jewish measures. No Jew was to be overlooked in the dragnet. . . . Second, the complex relationships between Jews and non-Jews were to be severed with least harm to individual Germans and to the economy as a whole. . . . Third, the killings had to be conducted in a manner that would limit psychological repercussions in the ranks of the perpetrators, prevent unrest among the victims, and preclude anxiety or protest in the non-Jewish population. To this end, relatively large numbers of indigenous collaborators were employed in shooting operations in Eastern Europe, and an elaborate system of deportations was organized to transport Jews in sealed trains from western and central European areas to secluded camps, equipped with gas chambers, in occupied Polish territory.[8]

The first of these premises—that no Jew should escape—meant that the number of perpetrators had to be adequate to the task. The second and third premises, however, required that the number be limited and information on their activities be restricted.

Methodologically, what took place in Rwanda in 1994 was the antithesis of the extermination of the Jews. Like what happened in Nazi-occupied Europe, the genocide in Rwanda was premeditated and deliberate. But there the resemblance ended. Far from concealing information, the Hutu organizers of the Rwandan genocide broadcast it explicitly on the radio and enlisted as many of their fellow Hutus as possible in the killing. The openness with which the slaughter took place indicated confidence that no external force would intervene and that the organizers would be secure against reprisals. On this conclusion, they were on solid ground. The war in Bosnia had been under way for more than two years, and little had been done to stop it. Although the tribunal for ex-Yugoslavia had been established, the Security Council had not yet designated a chief prosecutor. No indictments had been issued, and hardly anyone anticipated that those responsible for "ethnic cleansing" would face a day of reckoning. If the international community was so slow when it came to slaughter in the center of Europe, why would it move more swiftly to stop genocide in the center of Africa? The prospect of international prosecution of crimes committed in Rwanda was unimaginable, so there was no reason for the organizers of the genocide to mask their actions. Enlisting the Hutu population in the broadest way possible to carry out massacres also had its rationale: If all are guilty, no one is guilty.

Gerard Prunier has pointed out that "the main agents of the genocide were the ordinary peasants themselves. This is a terrible statement to make, but it is unfortunately borne out by the majority of the survivors' stories. The degree of compulsion on them varied greatly from place to place, but in some areas, the government version of a spontaneous movement of the population to 'kill the enemy Tutsi' is true."[9] Many of those who took part in the killing subsequently told journalists who sought them out in the refugee camps in Zaire that they were ordered or coerced to do what they did. Whether this testimony is credible is difficult to say. Since many thousands of Tutsis were chased down in hiding places, however, it seems evident that their killers could have evaded taking part in murder had they chosen to do so. Often, several people took part in the killing of a single victim, hacking the person to death with machetes. Accordingly, if the number of those killed really was roughly 800,000, there may have been as many who actually killed. For a tiny country with a total population of about 8 million (fewer than half of them adults), the number of probable killers is even more mind-boggling than the number who died.

The Hutu and Tutsi populations were thoroughly intermingled before the genocide. Therefore, every surviving Rwandan of school age or older must have known several of those who were killed and also knew well some of the killers. Since the overwhelming majority of the survivors are Hutus, the killers probably included close relatives, if the survivors were not themselves killers. They did not use methods of killing that might have put some distance between the murderers and the murdered. Most victims were hacked to death, and many of those who survived suffered appalling injuries from machete blows. The killing did not take place at special sites established for the purposes of putting people to death and disposing of the remains. It took place throughout the country, in virtually every village and in almost every urban neighborhood.

Mahmood Mamdani, a Ugandan who is one of Africa's leading social scientists, traveled around Rwanda a year after the genocide in an attempt to understand what took place and why it happened. In the village of Ntarama, about 90 minutes from the capital by car, he encountered a survivor, a man named Callixte, who described the events there:

> On the 7th of April [the day after the genocide began], in the morning, they started burning houses over there and moving towards here. Only a few were killed. The burning pushed us to this place [a church]. Our group decided to run to this place. We thought this was God's house, no one would attack us here. On the 7th, 8th, up to the 10th, we were fighting them. We were using stones, they had pangas [machetes], spears, hammers, grenades. On the 10th, their numbers were increased. On the 14th, we were being pushed inside the church. The church was attacked on the 14th and the 15th. The actual killing was on the 15th.
>
> On the 15th, they brought Presidential Guards. They were supporting *Interahamwe* [militias], brought in from neighboring communes. I was not in the group here. Here, there were women, children, and old men. The men had formed defense units outside. I was outside. Most men died fighting. When our defense was broken through, they came and killed everyone here. After that, they started hunting for those hiding in the hills. I and others ran to the swamp.

Mamdani asked Callixte about the composition of the population of his *secteur.* Callixte told him:

> In my *secteur,* Bahutu were two-thirds, Batutsi one third. *[Ba* is the prefix used to denote a group; *Mu,* as in Muhutu or Mututsi, refers to a sin-

gle individual.] There were about 5,000 in our *secteur*. Of the 3,500 Bahutu, all the men participated. It was like an order, except there were prominent leaders who would command. The rest followed.

Mamdani asked what happened in cases of intermarriage. Callixte explained that Hutus rarely allowed their daughters to marry Tutsis because the latter were poor, and it was dangerous. On the other hand, about one-third of the daughters of Tutsis were married to Hutus because the union would improve their prospects. But as Callixte pointed out, intermarriage did not save them:

> Batutsi women married to Bahutu were killed. I know only one who survived. The administration forced Bahutu men to kill their Batutsi wives before they got to kill anyone else—to prove they were true *Interahamwe*. One man tried to refuse. He was told that he must choose between the wife and himself. He then chose to save his own life. Another Muhutu man rebuked him for having killed his Mututsi wife. He was also killed. Kallisa—the man who was forced to kill his wife—is in jail. After killing his wife, he became a convert. He began to distribute grenades all around.

Prunier reports that Hutu teachers killed their Tutsi pupils, and one unnamed relief worker was quoted in press accounts as saying that mothers with babies strapped to their backs killed other mothers with babies strapped to their backs. It is such images, unlike any that emerged from the Holocaust, that suggest as ghastly a killing field as anything the world has known.[10]

Despite the number of participants in the genocide in Rwanda, what took place there in a very short space of time—incredibly, three weeks in April 1994 for the great majority of the killing—was not a Hobbesian war of all against all. It was highly organized, centrally directed slaughter. According to the U.S. Committee for Refugees, an organization that has long monitored developments in Rwanda and investigated the massacres: "Political killings and massive slaughters against members of Rwanda's Tutsi ethnic minority were carried out by army units, civilian police, and mobs or militia organized by the government. These killings took place at police—and militia—manned roadside checkpoints where ethnicity-specific, state-issued identity cards were used to identify minority group members. Large scale massacres took place at public buildings (churches, stadiums,

hotels) to which the Tutsi had fled in hopes of finding safety and protection."[11] Prunier says "the killers were controlled and directed in
their task by the civil servants in the central government, *prefets,
bourgmestres,* and local councilors, both in the capital and in the interior." He contends that "the efficiency of the massacres bore witness to the quality of Rwandese local administration. . . . This fact will
of course cause immense problems for any future government where
almost the entire local civil service should be charged with crimes
against humanity."[12]

More than 120,000 alleged participants in the Rwandan massacres
were jailed in the country after the Rwandan Patriotic Front achieved
power. Many of the leaders who planned and organized the genocide fled abroad, but most of those indicted by the International
Criminal Tribunal for Rwanda were apprehended where they took
refuge. They could not obtain protection against prosecution in their
own country, because they were defeated by a rebel force principally
made up of Tutsis from Uganda who were the children of Rwandan
refugees from previous massacres. At this writing, Belgium,
Cameroon, Zambia, and Kenya have already turned accused leading
organizers of the genocide over to the tribunal in Tanzania. Other
countries of refuge, perhaps even France, which has obstructed the
work of both tribunals, also may be driven by international public
opinion to turn over those alleged leaders of the genocide they are
harboring.

Although it has been easier to gain custody of the authors of
monstrous crimes in Rwanda than their counterparts from ex-Yugoslavia, large numbers cannot be prosecuted. The international tribunal has the resources to try no more than a few dozen and has
made it clear from the outset that it would concentrate only on those
with the highest level of responsibility. Even if the Rwandan government wanted to deal with the great majority of those who killed directly, it would be impossible. Few of the accused murderers in
custody can be brought before local courts because the courts, like
virtually every other institution, were left nonfunctional by the genocide and the aftermath of mass flight. After some leaders are tried and
convicted, the scores of thousands of foot soldiers jailed for their alleged roles in the genocide will have to be released—without ever
coming to trial. This is not justice, but it is not easy to propose alter-
natives.

•   •   •

Given the small number of criminals who actually may be tried for crimes in ex-Yugoslavia and Rwanda, is it possible to prevent the victims and their ethnic kin from ascribing collective guilt to members of the ethnic group of their persecutors? Will it suffice to prosecute only political leaders, military commanders, and a few others who committed barbarous crimes? The victims and their familes know all too well that a great many others also contributed to their suffering through criminal acts. Often they know their identities. Indeed, if ordinary Rwandan Hutus or Bosnian Serbs were "willing executioners," in the phrase Goldhagen uses to describe ordinary Germans during the Nazi Holocaust, is the guilt of the followers any less than that of their leaders? If ethnic groups wind up living together again, victims would be likely to see people on the street whom they know to be murderers. How is it possible that a handful of trials could establish individual criminal guilt and break the cycle of collective attribution?

Some have even questioned whether the concept of criminal guilt is adequate as a way of thinking about such barbarous crimes. Hannah Arendt, a student of Karl Jaspers in the 1920s who subsequently kept up a correspondence with him interrupted only by World War II, wrote on August 17, 1946, after reading the manuscript for *Die Schuldfrage,* to express her concern:

> Your definition of Nazi policy as a crime ("criminal guilt") strikes me as questionable. The Nazi crimes, it seems to me, explode the limits of the law; and that is precisely what constitutes their monstrousness. For these crimes, no punishment is severe enough. It may well be essential to hang Goering [her letter was written while the first Nuremberg trial was under way], but it is totally inadequate. That is, this guilt, in contrast to all criminal guilt, oversteps and shatters any and all legal systems. . . . [T]he Germans are burdened now with thousands or tens of thousands or hundreds of thousands of people who cannot be adequately punished within the legal system.[13]

Jaspers was not persuaded. Responding on October 19, 1946, in words that seem to have had a lasting impact on Arendt's own thinking and have been indelibly associated with her since the publication of *Eichmann in Jerusalem*[14] seventeen years later, Jaspers wrote:

> You say that what the Nazis did cannot be comprehended as a "crime"—I'm not altogether comfortable with your view, because a guilt that goes beyond all criminal guilt inevitably takes on a streak of "great-

ness"—of satanic greatness—which is, for me, as inappropriate for the
Nazis as all the talk about the "demonic" element in Hitler and so forth.
It seems to me that we have to see these things in their total banality,
in their prosaic triviality, because that's what truly characterizes them.
Bacteria can cause epidemics that wipe out nations, but they remain
merely bacteria.[15]

The analogy to bacteria, though powerful, elides the point that
the guilt of some criminals is greater than that of others. Many took
part in crimes, and a lot were willing executioners, but some planned
and directed. Their guilt is greater because they made it possible for
others to act criminally. That they were leaders does not excuse those
who were followers, but the constant companion of leadership must
be heightened responsibility. Moreover, if their planning and direct-
ing involved criminality on a large scale, they are more culpable still.

Criminal trials even of a few archcriminals, followed by convictions and appropriate punishment, serve two principal purposes.
They constitute an acknowledgment, through proceedings with the
requisite gravitas, of the suffering inflicted on the victims. International prosecution and punishment are particularly significant—an
unambiguous statement that the whole world has joined in the condemnation of those criminals. Punishment by an international body
seems especially fitting when criminality reaches the level of crimes
against humanity or genocide. The other purpose served by trials is
to demonstrate that the most fundamental rules that make a civilized
society possible may not be flouted with impunity and that even the
highest leaders cannot be shielded.

Some proponents of the tribunals have focused on the significance of prosecutions as a deterrent—specifically, to new crimes in
ex-Yugoslavia or Rwanda, and generally, to crimes in other countries
that might be prone to ethnic armed conflict. The extent to which
punishment is a deterrent to ordinary crime is much debated, but it
is widely recognized that the certainty that it will follow a crime, and
the swiftness with which it will occur, are at least as significant as the
severity. It probably is the same with crimes against humanity. No international tribunal was convened for nearly half a century after
Nuremberg and Tokyo, so there is little prospect that those committing great crimes in other places, such as Chechnya or Liberia, will
come to believe anytime soon that punishment is imminent. Accordingly, the significance of what the tribunals achieve for ex-Yugoslavia

and Rwanda in deterring additional crimes against humanity may not
be great. The contributions of the two ad hoc tribunals will have to
be measured by what they do for the victims, what they do to advance the principle that international rules against barbarism matter,
and what they can contribute to creating a sense of closure—necessary, perhaps, if Croats, Serbs, and Muslims in ex-Yugoslavia and
Hutus and Tutsis in Rwanda are ever to live together again.

Like criminal guilt, moral guilt and metaphysical guilt are individual,
according to Karl Jaspers. Only political guilt is collective, in his view.
Discussing this, he wrote:

> The restriction of the Nuremberg trial to criminals serves to exonerate
> the German people. Not, however, so as to free them of all guilt—on
> the contrary. The nature of our real guilt only appears the more clearly.
>
> We were German nationals at the time when the crimes were com-
> mitted by the regime which called itself German, which claimed to be
> Germany and seemed to have the right to do so, since the power of the
> state was in its hands and until 1943 it found no dangerous opposition.
>
> The destruction of any decent, truthful German policy must have its
> roots also in modes of conduct of the majority of the German popula-
> tion. A people answers for its polity.
>
> Every German is made to share the blame for the crimes commit-
> ted in the name of the Reich. We are collectively liable. The question is
> in what sense each of us must feel co-responsible. . . . Yes—inasmuch
> as we let such a regime rise among us. No—insofar as many of us in
> our deepest hearts opposed all this evil. . . .
>
> One might think of cases of non-political persons who live aloof of
> all politics, like monks, hermits, scholars, artists—if really quite non-
> political, those might possibly be excused from all guilt.
>
> Yet they, too, are included among the politically liable, because
> they, too, live by the order of the state. There is no such aloofness in
> modern states.

There is less aloofness today, or a widespread recognition that
there is less of a right to aloofness, than when Jaspers wrote. Although his book appeared in the immediate aftermath of the Nazi
state, what happened under its rule had not yet imprinted itself on
our collective consciousness; that would take decades. Indeed, there
was a time, particularly in the first fifteen years following World War
II—prior to the capture of Adolf Eichmann in Argentina and his trial

in Jerusalem—when many worried that the Holocaust would be largely forgotten. Instead, as the years have passed, knowledge of what the Nazis did has grown. There are more and more memorials to the victims, and more and more Holocaust museums, all attracting huge numbers of visitors. The Holocaust has achieved a special place in popular culture, making possible a film like *Schindler's List* or a book like Goldhagen's. The resulting awareness has helped to make it virtually impossible that someone today could write, as Jaspers did, about wholly nonpolitical "monks, hermits, scholars, artists" who "might be excused from all guilt." The contemporary counterparts of those Jaspers had in mind could not be so oblivious of political developments in our time, if only because of heightened knowledge of what happened in Jaspers's time. We would not excuse them for their ignorance of or indifference to contemporary crimes against humanity.

Although Jaspers held that moral guilt and metaphysical guilt are individual, the line separating them from the collective in his description may seem so faint as to disappear. Discussing moral guilt, he acknowledged that everyone in Germany, or almost everyone, engaged in outward compliance with the Nazis. There was no alternative. The Hitler salute had to be given to maintain one's existence. It was not a meaningless ritual. Each time someone gave the salute, the authority of the state was reinforced. Through such routine displays of loyalty, or of subservience to Nazism, everyone acquired a moral burden. This burden did not confer moral guilt, according to Jaspers. "Impotence excuses; no moral law demands a spectacular death," he wrote. "Plato already deemed it a matter of course to go into hiding in desperate times of calamity, and to survive." Yet Jaspers also appeared to contradict this view, pointing out that "passivity knows itself morally guilty of every failure, every neglect to act whenever possible, to shield the imperiled, to relieve wrong. . . . Blindness for the misfortune of others, lack of imagination of the heart, inner indifference toward the witnessed evil—that is moral guilt."

A similar ambivalence infuses Jaspers's discussion of metaphysical guilt. On the one hand, he argued that "Germany under the Nazis was a prison. . . . To hold the inmates of a prison collectively responsible for outrages committed by the prison staff is clearly unjust." Yet he also acknowledged that "we survivors . . . did not go into the streets when our Jewish friends were led away; we did not scream until we too were destroyed. We preferred to stay alive, on the feeble, if logical, ground that our death could not have helped anyone. We are guilty of being alive. We know before God which deeply humiliates us." As Tacitus wrote of the murder of Galba nearly two millennia earlier, "A shocking crime was committed on the unscrupulous initiative of a few individuals, with the blessing of more, and amid the passive acquiescence of all."[16]

Today Germans, like many non-Germans, accept the idea that they should feel some form of collective guilt for the crimes of the Nazis. We expect to see memorials to Holocaust victims in Berlin. This was not always the case. Before the Nuremberg trials, as the war was drawing to a close and Hitler's forces were retreating, American war correspondent Martha Gellhorn wrote about her visit to a town in territory that had fallen to the Allies:

> No one is a Nazi. No one ever was. There may have been some Nazis in the next village, and as a matter of fact, that town about twenty kilometers away was a veritable hotbed of Nazidom. To tell you the truth, confidentially, there were a lot of Communists here. We were always known as very Red. Oh, the Jews? Well, there weren't really many Jews in this neighborhood. Two, maybe six. They were taken away. I hid a Jew for six weeks, I hid a Jew for eight weeks. (I hid a Jew, he hid a Jew, all God's chillun' hid Jews.) We have nothing against the Jews; we always got on well with them. . . . We have had enough of this government. Ah, how we have suffered. The bombs. We lived in the cellars for weeks. We refused to be driven across the Rhine when the SS came to evacuate us. Why should we go? We welcome the Americans. We do not fear them; we have no reason to fear. We have done nothing wrong; we are not Nazis.[17]

The sheer magnitude of Nazi criminality, documented at Nuremberg and other war crimes trials and in huge volumes of painstaking research, has played a major role in the widespread acceptance of guilt today. Another factor also may play a part: Proportionately, the crimes committed *against* Germans were not commensurate with those committed by the Nazis. The firebombing of Hamburg and Dresden, the destruction of Berlin, and the rapes of German women by Russian troops were great crimes, but even they pale in comparison to the Holocaust.[18] Moreover, the actual targets of extermination programs by the Nazis never had a chance to avenge themselves against their persecutors. Under the circumstances, it is very difficult for Germans to assuage their guilt by focusing on their victimization.

The image of Willy Brandt sinking to his knees and begging forgiveness—even though he himself fought against the Nazis and could hardly be held guilty for their crimes—is emblematic of what the world has come to expect from righteous Germans. Although Germans collectively do not bear criminal or moral guilt, we welcome their assumption of collective moral and political responsibility.

Few Japanese, on the other hand, appear to feel any sense of collective guilt or responsibility for their countrymen's crimes during World War II. Japanese forces murdered millions of noncombatants, raped tens of thousands of women, forced hundreds of thousands to become their sexual servants, enslaved great numbers of Koreans and Chinese, conducted painful and lethal medical experiments on thousands of Chinese, and subjected prisoners of war to the most appalling cruelty. But as horrible as it was, their record did not include the ultimate crime committed in another part of the world: genocide. The fact that the Holocaust took place at the same time has had the effect, at least in the West, of overshadowing Japanese criminality. But as we have seen earlier, the main reason for the relative absence of guilt among Japanese comes down to two words: Hiroshima and Nagasaki. In the eyes of many Japanese, perhaps even a significant majority, the two atomic bombs made their country as much victim as victimizer.

This absence of guilt or collective moral responsibility causes a periodic stir in countries that fought against Japan or suffered its occupation, and Japanese cabinet officers have been forced to resign when intemperate remarks offend U.S. public opinion. Even greater scandals have erupted, however, when it is suggested that Americans should feel a sense of guilt for their country's wartime attacks on the Japanese. The Smithsonian's National Air and Space Museum in Washington, for example, was scheduled to open an exhibit in May 1995 displaying the *Enola Gay*, the plane that dropped the atomic bomb on Hiroshima. As originally planned, a sign identifying the plane was to have included the following statement: "Some have argued that the United States would never have dropped the bomb on the Germans because Americans were more reluctant to bomb 'white people' than Asians." The statement was certainly accurate enough: Some *have* made the argument, which, though not subject to proof and perhaps unpersuasive, is not frivolous. But predictably, the suggestion of a racist element to the nuclear attacks created a furor. An even bigger controversy had to do with the exhibit's sharp reduction in the estimated number of casualties the United States would have suffered in an invasion of Japan. This made it seem that the use of nuclear weapons was not required, and it also appeared to justify an emphasis in the exhibit on Japanese suffering. Members of Congress called for the dismissal of the museum's curator, Martin O. Harwitt, and eventually most of the exhibit was eliminated. Harwitt resigned in May 1995. Just as Hiroshima has seemed to Japanese to absolve them of guilt for the crimes committed by Japanese forces, it is inconceivable to many Americans—who recall that the Japanese started the war by treacherously bombing Pearl Harbor—that they should feel guilt for anything done to the Japanese.[19]

Despite much effort by their leaders to hide or distort the facts, it is probably difficult for many Serbs to avoid an awareness of what was done in their name. They know, for example, that their country was subjected to international economic sanctions for an extended period and that this reflected international condemnation. Advocates of sanctions consider global censure to be the main justification for such measures, which rarely inflict direct economic harm on the leaders principally responsible for the actions that inspire them. What sanctions do achieve is public consciousness within the target countries that the policies and actions of their leaders are condemned by other nations and, if sanctions are universally applied, by the entire world community. International economic sanctions and a sports boycott of South Africa had this effect, and it helped end apartheid.

The impact of trials on a public sense of guilt is more difficult to foretell. In Rwanda, for instance, the unprecedented nature of the slaughter makes it impossible even to speculate about the impact on the national psyche of trials of those who organized the genocide. The manner in which that genocide was carried out suggests that those who planned and incited it were intent on instilling mass hatred, reflecting their understanding of a phenomenon described by Tacitus: It is human nature to hate those whom you have injured.[20] By engaging so large a portion of the population in the slaughter of the Tutsis and members of the Hutu intelligentsia, Hutu organizers of the genocide made hundreds of thousands of ordinary Hutus bloody their hands. In so doing, they deepened hatred of the victims and spread the guilt. On similar grounds, some street gangs demand that initiates prove themselves by some violent act against a rival group, and corrupt police insist that new recruits must take their share of bribes and booty.

There also were practices in the wars in Croatia and Bosnia in which tens of thousands were enlisted to help carry out ethnic cleansing. Not only did a lot of citizens take part in roundups, detentions, and abuses of detainees, but a great many more villagers and townspeople lent a hand by seizing the property and occupying the homes of those who were slaughtered or driven away. In justifying their actions to themselves, it is only natural that they should hate the victims, portraying those they hurt as the embodiment of evil: *Mujahedin,* Islamic fanatics, Ustasha, Chetniks, and on and on.

The participation of great numbers in wrongdoing raises the question: Does trying and punishing a handful of top criminals effectively individualize criminal guilt? If the leaders in ex-Yugoslavia and Rwanda deliberately implicated thousands of others in their crimes, a relatively few trials of high-ranking people still may be an appropriate response. Those criminals not prosecuted for lack of resources will know that their leaders were judged and that, by definition, their own conduct has been condemned. Criminal prosecution and conviction of those who commanded and incited will help the thousands—or tens of thousands—of others to confront their own political, moral, and metaphysical guilt.

14

Putting Criminals in the Dock

RADOVAN KARADZIC AND General Ratko Mladic were indicted for the full range of abuses committed by Bosnian Serbs under their leadership. Two other strongmen of the Balkans, Slobodan Milosevic of Serbia and Franjo Tudjman of Croatia, have not been indicted for anything, despite ample evidence of crimes committed under their leadership, if not at their specific command. Given this apparent anomaly, what are the standards used to determine when to indict political leaders and military commanders for crimes carried out by their subordinates? The question, like many having to do with war crimes, is a matter of much historical debate. An important case in point involved a Japanese general tried at the end of World War II.

On February 6, 1946, General Douglas MacArthur affirmed the death sentence imposed on General Tomayuki Yamashita by a United States military commission that tried him for atrocities committed by Japanese forces in the Philippines. The trial was exhaustive, with 286 witnesses testifying—many providing accounts of murder, rape, and other crimes. The commission also examined a small mountain of documentary evidence: affidavits, captured papers, diaries compiled by Japanese troops, and other items. In MacArthur's memorable words:

> Rarely has so cruel and wanton a record been spread to the public gaze. Revolting as this may be in itself, it pales before the sinister and far-reaching implication thereby attached to the profession of arms. The soldier, be he friend or foe, is charged with the protection of the weak and unarmed. It is the very essence and reason for his being.
>
> When he violates this sacred trust he not only profanes his entire culture but threatens the very fabric of international society. The traditions of fighting men are long and honorable, based upon the noblest of human traits—sacrifice.
>
> This officer, of proven field merit and entrusted with a high command including authority adequate to his responsibility, has failed this irrevocable standard; has failed his duty to his troops, to his country, to his enemy, and to mankind; he has failed utterly his soldier faith.

Yamashita appealed his conviction to the United States Supreme Court, arguing that he had not committed the crimes for which he was found responsible or ordered that they be committed.[1] Writing for the court in rejecting the appeal, Chief Justice Harlan Fiske Stone stated: "[T]his overlooks the fact that the gist of the charge is an unlawful breach of duty by an army commander [Yamashita] to control the extensive and widespread atrocities specified. . . . It is evident that the conduct of military operations by troops whose excesses are unrestrained by the order or efforts of their commander would almost certainly result in violations. . . . Hence the law of war presupposes that its violation is to be avoided through the control of the operations of war by commanders who are to some extent responsible for their subordinates."

Justices Wiley B. Rutledge and Frank Murphy dissented because, as the latter wrote: "Nowhere was it alleged that [Yamashita] personally committed any of the atrocities, or that he ordered their commission, *or that he had any knowledge of the commission thereof by members of his command*" (italics added). Murphy pointed out that the situation in the Philippines was confused at the time Japanese troops committed the atrocities for which Yamashita was convicted, and that it had been the purpose of the victorious American forces to disrupt Yamashita's communications with the troops under his command. "Nothing in all history or in international law, at least as far as I am aware, justifies such a charge against a fallen commander of a defeated force," Murphy wrote. "To use the very inefficiency and disorganization created by the victorious forces as the primary basis for condemning officers of the defeated armies bears no resemblance to justice or to military reality." On February 23, 1946, two weeks after General MacArthur affirmed the sentence, General Yamashita was hanged.

The opposing views in the Yamashita case represent two main schools of thought about command responsibility. General MacArthur, Chief Justice Stone, and the military commission that convicted Yamashita considered it dereliction of duty for a commander not to control the behavior of his troops. This embodies a "should have known" or "must have known" approach. Indeed, the commission said that "the evidence of crimes was so extensive and widespread, both as to time and area, that they must have been willfully permitted by the Accused, or secretly ordered by the Accused. . . . It is absurd to consider a commander a murderer or rapist because one of his soldiers commits a murder or rape. Nonetheless, where murder and rape and vicious, revengeful actions are widespread offenses, and there is no effective attempt by a commander to discover and control the criminal acts, such a commander may be held responsible, even criminally liable." The fact that the high court refused Yamashita's appeal suggests that in U.S. jurisprudence, the "should have known" or "must have known" approach to command responsibility is the law of the land. (The exoneration of Captain Medina for the massacre at My Lai and the failure to prosecute higher-ranking officers, as described in Chapter 6, are of course impossible to reconcile with Justice Stone's opinion for the Supreme Court in the Yamashita case.)

Justice Murphy's dissent embodies the other main approach — that is, prosecutors must prove a commander knew about the commission of widespread crimes by his troops before his failure to take action against such conduct makes him criminally liable. (Even by Murphy's standard, Captain Medina probably could have been convicted.) Although Murphy's view did not save General Yamashita, his argument won the day in international law. Article 86 of Protocol 1 of 1977 Additional to the Geneva Conventions of 1949, regarding the duty of the parties to an international armed conflict to act against grave breaches, provides that "if they knew, or had information which should have enabled them to conclude in the circumstances at the time" that such crimes were taking place, they were required to "take all feasible measures within their power to prevent or repress" their commission.

Michael Walzer, in *Just and Unjust Wars,* has questioned this standard:

> [H]olding officers automatically responsible for massive violations of the rules of war forces them to do everything they can to avoid such violations, without forcing us to specify what they ought to do. But there are two problems with this. First of all, we don't really want commanders to do everything they can, for that requirement, taken literally, would leave them little time to do anything else. . . . [W]e must expect them to devote a great deal of time and attention to the discipline and control of the men with guns they have turned loose in the world. But still not all their time and attention, not all the resources at their command.
>
> The second argument against strict liability in criminal cases is a more familiar one. Even doing "everything" is not the same as doing it successfully. All we can require is serious efforts of specific sorts; we cannot require success, since the conditions of warfare are such that success is not always possible. And the impossibility of success is necessarily an excuse—given serious effort, an entirely satisfactory excuse for failure.[2]

At Nuremberg, the issue loomed large, dealt with in the prosecution summation in the High Command case:

> Somewhere, there is unmitigated responsibility for these atrocities. Is it to be borne by the troops? Is it to be borne primarily by the hundreds of subordinates who played a minor role in this pattern of crime? We think it is clear that is not where the deepest responsibility lies. Men in the mass, particularly when organized and disciplined in armies, must be expected to yield to prestige and authority, the power of example. . . . Mitigation should be reserved for those upon whom superior orders are pressed down, and who lack the means to influence general standards of behavior. It is not, we submit, available to the commander who participates in bringing the criminal pressures to bear, and whose responsibility it is to insure the preservation of honorable military traditions.[3]

In the aftermath of Nuremberg and Tokyo, where Japanese cruelty to prisoners of war was a major focus, the authors of the Third Geneva Convention of 1949 made it clear that high-level officials, including civilian leaders, are responsible for the treatment of prisoners. They provided in Article 12 that "prisoners of war are in the hands of the enemy Power, but not of the individuals or military units who have captured them. Irrespective of the individual responsibilities that may exist, the Detaining Power is responsible for the treatment given them."

The statute adopted by the Security Council for the operations of the tribunal for ex-Yugoslavia, following the standard of Protocol 1 and of Justice Murphy's dissent in the Yamashita case, provides that commanders are culpable if they knew about crimes that were being committed by their forces and did not do what they could to stop them. "The fact that any of the acts referred to in Articles 2 to 5 of the present statute [specifying the crimes over which the tribunal has jurisdiction] was committed by a subordinate," it states, "does not relieve his superior of criminal responsibility if he knew or had reason to know that the subordinate was about to commit such acts or had done so and the superior failed to take the necessary and reasonable measures to prevent such acts or to punish the perpetrators thereof." Though such a provision is more restrictive than the rule upheld by the majority in *Yamashita*, it is not a serious obstacle to the prosecution of commanders in ex-Yugoslavia.

The use of the word *reasonable* responds to the concern raised by Walzer that commanders cannot devote all their time and attention to controlling the acts of their men in an effort to prevent abuses. A standard of reasonableness is implicit in the requirement of Protocol 1 that the commander should take all "feasible" measures to prevent and repress abuses; the adjective *reasonable* in the statute of the tribunal makes it explicit. The same word also deals with Walzer's other point—that what is reasonable is not what is guaranteed to be successful. A commander appearing before the tribunal on charges that his troops committed abuses should prevail, even if he cannot show that his actions ended all abuses, so long as he can demonstrate that the measures he took met the standard of "necessary and reasonable" required by the statute, what Walzer calls a "serious effort." This is not too much to ask of any commander.

It would be surprising in ex-Yugoslavia, given the extent and systematic character of abuses, if commanders who are indicted and brought to trial even attempt a defense along these lines. There is little possibility for them to claim they did not know of abuses or lacked information on them. Rarely, if ever, have war crimes been documented and reported so widely and in such detail as they were

taking place. The wars in Croatia and Bosnia were covered extensively by the news media. Whether or not they read or listened to
press accounts, the political leaders and military commanders were
confronted constantly by journalists, who sought their comments on
the abuses attributed to their forces. Other sources of information
were reports compiled during the fighting by nongovernmental
human rights groups, the United Nations Special Rapporteur on
Human Rights, Tadeusz Mazowiecki, and the United Nations War
Crimes Commission, led by Cherif Bassiouni. These reports were
published, reported in the press, and when feasible, submitted directly to the leaders of the warring parties.

Yet another source of information was the United Nations Protection Forces in Bosnia and Croatia. UNPROFOR soldiers often
seemed helpless in the field, but they frequently challenged commanders about the actions taken by their troops, helping to ensure
that the commanders knew of atrocities.[4] Similarly, the representatives of the United Nations High Commissioner for Refugees, which
was the primary agency delivering humanitarian assistance, and various nongovernmental relief groups constantly complained to military and political leaders about such abuses as attacks on medical
facilities and prevention of access to civilian detainees. These complaints were also embodied in several UN Security Council resolutions made known to the parties to the conflict by UN officials on the
scene.

Foreign governments supplied information as well. Many complained directly to political leaders about abuses by their troops. On
occasion, they compiled detailed accounts of abuses that they presented directly to those leaders. These reports also were submitted to
the UN War Crimes Commission and subsequently to the UN war
crimes tribunal and can be used by the prosecution to show that leaders did not take all feasible measures within their power to prevent
or repress these grave breaches of the laws of war.

The International Committee of the Red Cross provided some of
the most detailed—but confidential—information to military commanders and political leaders on grave breaches of the Geneva
Conventions and Protocols. One of the organization's specialties is
visiting detainees, who provide statements about beatings, torture,
or rape they suffered and about abuses of others they witnessed.
ICRC workers discuss these accounts with officials up the chain of
command and put the information in writing in an effort to curb

such abuses. As the organization itself has noted, "ICRC delegates are in constant touch with all the parties to any given conflict in the course of their activities (visits to prisoners, protection and assistance for the civilian populations affected). They protest directly to the competent authorities against any persecution they have observed, bringing to their attention any practices that are inadmissible under international humanitarian law so that they may put an end to them."[5]

In January 1993, I went to ICRC headquarters in Geneva to talk to top officials of the organization about the war in Bosnia. I asked whether the ICRC was reporting grave breaches to political and military leaders and, as I expected, was told that of course this was being done. But when I pointed out that those leaders were getting information that would help to demonstrate their culpability for grave breaches if they did not take action, ICRC officials became alarmed. Their concern: If they were summoned to testify at a war crimes tribunal, it would compromise their ability in the future to obtain the confidential access that is essential to their work.

A year and a half later, however, the ICRC warned that despite the general rule that it would "not divulge publicly what its delegates hear or see in the performance of their duties, especially when visiting places of detention," there could be exceptions: "The authorities should not . . . count on a conspiratorial silence by the institution in the event of grave, repeated violations and when these authorities, having been advised of an infringement, fail to take appropriate remedial action. In some cases the ICRC may renounce its confidentiality, in accordance with guidelines it has set itself and made public."

Those guidelines provide that the ICRC reserves the right to make public statements concerning violations of international humanitarian law if the following conditions are fulfilled:

- The violations are major and repeated.
- The steps taken confidentially have not succeeded in putting an end to the violations.
- Such publicity is in the interest of the persons or populations affected or threatened.
- The ICRC delegates have witnessed the violations with their own eyes, or the existence and extent of those breaches have been established by reliable and verifiable sources.

The ICRC said it had "issued many appeals to belligerent parties and public declarations, for example, in the context of conflicts in the former Yugoslavia." It also has acknowledged the possibility that the tribunal would request the organization, or its staff, to furnish evidence, but it has not said how it would respond.[6]

The question of disclosure is a difficult and painful one for the ICRC. On the one hand, it considers its policy of confidentiality crucial in gaining access to places from which all other institutions—governmental, intergovernmental, and nongovernmental alike—are barred, enabling it to furnish assistance to victims that no one else can provide. On the other hand, its leaders are well aware that the most controversial chapter in its history was the ICRC's failure to disclose publicly during World War II what it knew about the destruction of the European Jews. An indication of its angst came in 1988, when it published a book by an Israeli legal scholar and historian—himself a survivor of Auschwitz—that is sharply critical of the ICRC's failure to do more to save the Jews of Hungary from the Holocaust. The book appeared with a letter from the director general of the ICRC reproduced opposite its title page stating that the organization "remains unconvinced on quite a number of points" but "respects your academic freedom and has decided to authorize the publication" of the book by the ICRC itself.[7]

In all likelihood, the prosecution will not try to compel ICRC delegates to testify before the ex-Yugoslavia tribunal, especially since there should be more than enough testimony from other sources. It seems unlikely that leaders such as Radovan Karadzic and Ratko Mladic could defend themselves as General Yamashita did by claiming that they did not know about the massacres, torture, rape, summary executions at detention camps, and indiscriminate bombardment of civilian population centers by their forces. In some cases, such as the prosecution of Mladic for Srebrenica, there may be testimony that they directly participated in or ordered these crimes. Whether or not such testimony is available, however, they knew that these crimes were being committed, and it should be possible to prove their knowledge because they were given information in so many ways.

The leaders and commanders who received information about abuses may claim, of course, that they did not believe the journalists, human rights investigators, UN military officials, relief agencies, and governments that informed them. In that event, they also should have to demonstrate why they dismissed those reports. Did they conduct their own investigations? If so, how were the investigations undertaken, and by whom? What witnesses were interviewed? Were alleged victims such as camp inmates asked to testify? Were conditions arranged so that they could testify without fear of reprisal? Were doctors asked to examine alleged torture or rape victims? Were alleged mass grave sites exhumed to examine corpses? If those accused of responsibility for massacres say they gave orders to end abuses, where are those orders? How, when, and where were they disseminated? What measures were taken to enforce them? Were disciplinary measures taken? Against whom?

The UN War Crimes Commission for the former Yugoslavia considered the question of command responsibility in circumstances in which it could not be shown that political or military leaders had directly ordered abuses. Its final report provides a guide to dealing with such cases:

> It is the view of the Commission that the mental element necessary when the commander has not given the offending order is a) actual knowledge, b) such serious personal dereliction on the part of the commander as to constitute wilful and wanton disregard of the possible consequences, or c) an imputation of constructive knowledge, that despite pleas to the contrary, the commander under the facts and circumstances of the particular case, must have known of the offenses charged and acquiesced therein. To determine whether or not a commander must have known about the acts of his subordinates, one might consider a number of indices, including:
>
> a) The number of illegal acts.
> b) The type of illegal acts.
> c) The scope of illegal acts.
> d) The time during which illegal acts occurred.
> e) The number and type of troops involved.
> f) The logistics involved, if any.
> g) The geographical location of the acts.
> h) The widespread occurrence of the acts.
> i) The tactical tempo of operations.
> j) The *modus operandi* of similar illegal acts.
> k) The officers and staff involved.
> l) The location of the commander at the time [8]

This is a far cry from the "must have known" approach embraced by Chief Justice Stone in *Yamashita*. Stone based his opinion on General Yamashita's post of command. The commission, on the other hand, focused on whether the circumstances made it possible for a commander to exercise fully his command authority.

Leaders who knew about crimes could attempt to escape responsibility by denying they exercised authority over the troops that committed particular abuses. Radovan Karadzic has hinted publicly that this would be his own line of defense by describing the first several months of the Bosnian war—the period in which the greatest number of detention camp abuses and some of the bloodiest "ethnic cleansing" took place—as a chaotic period. Assuming it could not show that Karadzic directly ordered the commission of crimes, the prosecution still could counter such a defense by presenting evidence of a clear pattern of abuses, demonstrating planning and coordination. Moreover, it could demonstrate the persistence of certain abuses throughout the conflict, such as the indiscriminate bombardment of Sarajevo and other civilian population centers, and the repetition of the most extreme practices that characterized the genocidal crimes at Srebrenica in the final months of the war.

In the purportedly chaotic early period of the Bosnian war, many observers noted a clear pattern of operations by the Serbs. First, regular Yugoslav Army forces attacked a community, employing the heavy weaponry they controlled. After resistance collapsed under the assault, control passed to paramilitary leaders. At times, regular army troops donned the insignia of the paramilitary groups during this period, joining the looting, raping, and killing. In addition, the paramilitary units conveyed captured civilians to detention camps often administered by locals associated with them. The subdued town or village was then administered by armed civilians from the area. Former police who were Serbs often played a leading part in the administration. At times, regular army troops, once again changing their insignia, were left behind to assist in such duties.

This pattern, in which authority shifted, complicates the process of identifying the ground-level commanders responsible for abuses at various periods. Unfortunately, immunity or the prospect of a reduced sentence for lower-ranking criminals in exchange for testimony against superiors—a tool widely used in the United States— will not be possible very often in the cases before the ex-Yugoslavia tribunal. The use of this technique requires custody of the potential defendants, which is the most difficult problem facing the prosecution. As a result, prosecutors must count heavily on testimony from victims and other witnesses to abuses. Local commanders also may be identified by information gathered from those who reported publicly on abuses or interceded with commanders on behalf of international agencies. In a few cases, there may be testimony from combatants who eventually had moral qualms about the way their side conducted itself. It was, for example, the testimony of a former guard at the Susica detention camp that was crucial in the tribunal's choice of Dragan Nikolic as the first to be indicted. Of course, some governments—especially the United States and the Netherlands, which had the responsibility within NATO for monitoring the Yugoslav armed forces—possess surveillance data gathered by electronic means, but the standard reluctance of governments to reveal information that discloses "intelligence sources and methods" sharply limits the availability of such evidence to the prosecution.

The difficulties in establishing local command responsibility do not apply to the prosecution of the leaders who exercised control over large amounts of territory. They negotiated with UNPROFOR, relief agencies, other governments, and UN and European Union mediators. They purported to speak for their forces and demonstrated their control over them in countless ways—by opening and closing airports, blocking and unblocking relief convoys, seizing and relinquishing heavy weapons, taking and releasing hostages, and negotiating prisoner exchanges. Furthermore, the statute adopted by the UN Security Council is explicit in providing that the highest ranks of all, and the civilian titles held by people like Karadzic, Milosevic, and Tudjman, are not barriers to prosecutions. It states that "the official position of any accused person, whether as Head of State or Government or as a responsible Government official, shall not relieve such person of criminal responsibility nor mitigate punishment." Virtually identical language appeared in the charter for the Nuremberg tribunal.

Since the statute for the tribunal was drafted to make it clear that heads of state were subject to prosecution, why have Milosevic and Tudjman escaped indictment? Without being privy to confidential information in the possession of the prosecutor, we can only speculate. In all likelihood, the tribunal lacks direct evidence that Milosevic and Tudjman exercised control over the forces that engaged in abuses. It is also possible that indictments of either Milosevic or Tudjman, or both, have been handed down secretly or will take place at a later date, when more evidence against them has been assembled.

They certainly did not lack knowledge. All the press reports and inquires, remonstrations by UN agencies and foreign governments, Security Council resolutions, and reports by human rights investigators that were provided to Karadzic and Mladic also were given or were available to the leaders of Serbia and Croatia. Presenting evidence of their knowledge should not pose great difficulties for the prosecution.

If Milosevic is ultimately indicted, prosecutors may decide that the charges against him should be limited to matters showing direct involvement by the Yugoslav People's Army. That would make for an impressive bill of particulars—the indiscriminate bombardment of the Croatian city of Vukovar in 1991, the summary execution of patients of the Vukovar hospital, and early episodes of "ethnic cleansing" in Bosnian towns such as Zvornik. Prosecutors also might charge him with responsibility for the crimes of the Serbian paramilitary groups led by "Arkan" and Seselj, and for a broad array of crimes committed by the Bosnian Serbs over a sustained period. Although many suspect that he exercised control over the forces that committed those crimes, the tribunal's prosecutors probably have found it difficult to produce hard evidence that would stand up in court. They would need testimony from those who dealt with Milosevic directly or documents that demonstrate his control or surveillance data, such as telephone conversations recorded by the United States or another government.

An indictment of Tudjman might be similarly limited to matters in which regular Croatian armed forces were involved. Their destruction of the homes of Serbs they pushed out of the Krajina in 1995 could form the basis of such an indictment. It could be more difficult, but nevertheless possible, to demonstrate Tudjman's control over the Bosnian Croat forces that committed a great number of crimes in the war in Bosnia, such as the shelling of the Muslim section of Mostar; or his control over the Croatian paramilitary groups that murdered elderly Serbs who refused or were unable to join the mass exodus when Croatian troops invaded the Krajina.

If the evidence needed to indict Milosevic and Tudjman for major crimes exists and is available to prosecutors, they should be indicted as quickly as possible. If they have been indicted secretly, this fact should be made public. The way to fulfill the purposes for which the tribunal was created is by bringing prosecutions against those with the highest level of responsibility for the most serious crimes and by making it known that this is being done. But if the evidence isn't there, prosecutions just for the sake of indicting nasty heads of state would do a disservice to the cause of international criminal justice. It is one thing to believe they exercise control; it is another to prove it.

What about the subordinates who claim they were just following orders? What is their culpability and how should they be judged?

The Security Council's statute for the tribunal is unambiguous: "The fact that an accused person acted pursuant to an order of a Government or of a superior shall not relieve him of criminal responsibility." This language also derives almost verbatim from the charter of the Nuremberg tribunal. At Nuremberg, even such high-ranking Nazis as Joachim von Ribbentrop, Germany's foreign minister, defended themselves on the ground that they were following orders. The tribunal rejected such a defense, stating that "Hitler could not make aggressive war by himself. He had to have the cooperation of statesmen, military leaders, diplomats and businessmen. When they, with knowledge of his aims, gave him their cooperation, they made themselves parties to the plan he had initiated. They are not to be deemed innocent because Hitler made use of them, if they knew what they were doing. That they were assigned to their tasks by a dictator does not absolve them from responsibility for their acts. The relation of leader and follower does not preclude responsibility here any more than it does in the comparable tyranny of organized domestic crime."

In ordinary circumstances, soldiers must obey the orders of superiors. Yet under international law, and under the domestic laws of most countries, this does not excuse a soldier who receives an order that is patently illegal, such as a command to kill a captured prisoner or to commit torture or rape. A soldier has not only the right but the duty to disobey such orders. If he carries out an order that the entire civilized community deems illegal, he is held to be individually responsible. This principle was asserted by British common law courts as far back as the seventeenth century in a famous decision, *Axtell's Case*.[9] It concerned an officer tried for treason for his part in the murder of King Charles I. He defended himself on the grounds that he was carrying out the orders of his commander, whom he was required to obey. The court was not persuaded. "Where the command is traitorous, there the obedience to that command is also traitorous," the court held. The judges added that "even a common soldier must have known that it was an act of treason to participate in the execution of one's king." Similarly, a common soldier, or even a civilian member of a paramilitary gang, knows it is a crime to rape and torture, or to line up captive combatants and noncombatants and execute them. As the chief of the Argentine Army, General Martín Balza, stated in 1995 when he apologized to the nation for the crimes committed by the military during the dirty war two decades earlier: "No one is obliged to carry out an immoral order or one at odds with the law and military regulations. Whoever does so commits a criminal act, deserving of the penalty its seriousness merits. Without euphemisms I clearly declare: Whoever violates the National Constitution is committing a crime, whoever gives immoral orders is committing a crime, whoever executes immoral orders is committing a crime, whoever employs unjust means to achieve an end he considers just is committing a crime."[10]

Are there no exceptions? One is circumstances of duress. If a soldier can demonstrate that the penalty he faced for disobeying an unlawful order would be severe, and not merely dismissal from his post, he may exculpate himself. The burden is on the soldier to show that he was coerced.

Commenting on these questions, Michael Walzer has written:

> It is a feature of criminal responsibility that it can be distributed without being divided. We can, that is, blame more than one person for a particular act without splitting up the blame we assign. When soldiers are shot trying to surrender, the men who do the actual shooting are fully responsible for what they do, unless we recognize particular extenuating circumstances; at the same time, the officer who tolerates and encourages the murders is also fully responsible, if it lay within his power to prevent them. . . . The case looks very different, however, when combatants are actually ordered to take no prisoners or to kill the ones they take or to turn their guns on enemy civilians. . . . In such a case, we are likely to divide as well as distribute responsibility: We regard soldiers under orders as men whose acts are not entirely their own and whose liability for what they do is somewhat diminished.[11]

This may be a legitimate defense in particular cases in Rwanda, where many Hutus claim that their lives would have been in danger if they refused to take part in the genocide. What happened there in the systematic and comprehensive effort to make as many Hutus as possible take part in the killing is without known parallel. But otherwise, Walzer is off the mark. Although it clearly is different if orders were given, absent duress it is dangerous to suggest that responsibility or liability is diminished. The overriding importance of the principle that each combatant is responsible for his own acts is apparent.

How, then, should we take into account the difference that is created by orders? In fact, judicial practice has addressed this issue and solved it in what appears to be a satisfactory manner. It is customary in prosecutions of military men to consider superior orders in determining punishment. The tribunal established by the Security Council is no exception. Its statutes provide that compliance with the order of a superior "may be considered in mitigation of punishment if the International Tribunal determines that justice so requires." Here, too, the statutes for the tribunals for ex-Yugoslavia and Rwanda track the language of the charter for the Nuremberg tribunal.

The most difficult questions arise when it is not obvious to a combatant whether the duties he has been ordered to perform constitute a war crime. On the one hand, it is his duty to obey orders; on the other, he also has a duty not to attack noncombatants or commit other offenses that would violate the laws of war. For example, if his commander orders him to shoot at a group of people, identifying them as the enemy, and the soldier believes that they actually are unarmed civilians or combatants who have been disarmed and taken prisoner, what is he to do? This was not the case when the hospital patients at Vukovar or the Muslim men and boys of Srebrenica were massacred: They were clearly *hors de combat*. But it could be the case when a commander ordered mortar fire against a besieged town or village.

Although it is difficult to devise regulations that will deal with all such cases, the United States Army's *Rules of Land Warfare* provide valuable guidance. They state:

> The fact that the law of war has been violated pursuant to an order of a superior authority, whether military or civil, does not deprive the act in question of its character of a war crime, nor does it constitute a defense in the trial of an accused individual, unless he did not know and could not reasonably have been expected to know that the act ordered was unlawful. In all cases where the order is held out to constitute a defense to an allegation of war crime, the fact that the individual was acting pursuant to orders may be considered in mitigation of punishment.
>
> In considering the question whether a superior order constitutes a valid defense, the court shall take into consideration the fact that obe-

dience to lawful military orders is the duty of every member of the
armed forces; that the latter cannot be expected, in conditions of war
discipline, to weigh scrupulously the legal merits of the orders received;
that certain rules of warfare may be controversial; or that an act otherwise amounting to a war crime may be done in obedience to orders
conceived as a measure of reprisal. At the same time it must be borne
in mind that members of the armed forces are bound to obey lawful orders.[12]

In essence, this suggests that what is required to prove that a
combatant was culpable for a war crime in circumstances in which
he was following orders is *mens rea* (guilty intent). He probably
would escape conviction in a close case where, unsure of the situation, he deferred to the authority of his commander. On the other
hand, where the violation of the laws of war is clear, the defense that
the combatant was following orders is irrelevant to the question of
guilt or innocence and matters only in the question of punishment.

One case that came before the tribunal for ex-Yugoslavia raised
these issues dramatically. Drazan Erdemovic was of Bosnian Croat
origin, but he served in General Mladic's Bosnian Serb army. After
the war, he moved to Belgrade, where in March 1996 he and another
man told foreign journalists of their involvement in the massacre at
Srebrenica. This led to their arrest by Serb authorities, but as a result
of forceful intervention by the United States, they were released and
transferred to The Hague.

At a tribunal hearing, Erdemovic said that he had been a member
of a firing squad and had taken part in the execution of about twelve
hundred Muslim men on July 16, 1995, in a field about forty miles
north of Srebrenica. He told the court that he had tried to resist participation in the firing squad but had been told by his platoon leader
that he should "line up" with the men about to be killed if he felt that
way. He also testified that the Bosnian Serb commanders were so intent on implicating all witnesses to the executions that they required
each of the bus drivers who had brought the Muslims to that spot to
kill a prisoner. Erdemovic bolstered his claim that he acted under
duress by testifying that some weeks after the massacre, he and two
friends who opposed the killings were attacked and injured by another soldier who boasted of his part in the massacre.

The tribunal's decision in the Erdemovic case was based on its
evaluation of the credibility of his testimony and its judgment of

whether the circumstances he described constituted such duress that he had no reasonable alternative other than to take part in the executions. The fact that he came forward to tell his story and did not wait until he was identified and brought to book before claiming duress counted in his favor.

Although the tribunal determined that Erdemovic was not subjected to duress to the point where he warranted exculpation, it ruled that mitigation of his punishment was warranted. Accordingly, he was sentenced to ten years in prison for his part in the massacre at Srebrenica. On appeal, his sentence was reduced to five years.

The fact that victims and other witnesses could recognize those who carried out crimes—remember, they frequently came from the same communities—obviously made the task of identifying potential defendants much easier. Reports compiled by human rights organizations and the UN War Crimes Commission name hundreds and hundreds of those who allegedly committed rape, torture, and murder in the detention camps because the witnesses who provided testimony were able to name them. Alleged perpetrators sometimes include the commanders at the scene of the crime. The availability of such testimony, along with the information that can be obtained from agencies that interceded with higher-level commanders in an effort to stop abuses, means that it is possible for the tribunal for ex-Yugoslavia to identify many of those who ordered crimes or knew of them and failed to take the requisite measures to prevent and suppress them.

Perhaps the most important objection to the tribunal for ex-Yugoslavia was that it would not be possible to apprehend the defendants. Writing in *The New York Times* as the Security Council considered the issue, Professor Herman Schwartz, of the Washington College of Law at American University, argued that "the effort to hold such trials is almost certain to fail—instead of advancing the international rules of law, it is likely to set [them] back. . . . Serbia, the principal offender, is unlikely to turn them [accused war criminals] over, despite the obligation to do so."[13] Schwartz distinguished the wars in Croatia and Bosnia from previous conflicts that resulted in trials. "The Nuremberg trials were possible only because we had won World War II and had physical control of the accused," he wrote. "Argentina's trials in 1984–86 of senior military officers for human rights abuses were possible because they were internal trials conducted by a new regime.

Any Serbians or Croatians likely to be accused would be victors in the Balkan war. They would be anything but under our control."

Based on the numbers, Schwartz's analysis seems partially accurate: Five years after its establishment, the tribunal had about two dozen defendants in custody, although some eighty had been indicted publicly and an unknown additional number had been indicted secretly. (At the same point, the Rwanda tribunal had custody of the majority of the defendants it had indicted, including Colonel Theoneste Bagasora, the Rwandan counterpart of General Mladic, who was apprehended in Cameroon and, after a delay of several months, was handed over for trial in January 1997.) The highest-ranking defendant at the Hague court was Dario Kordic, who had been vice president of the Bosnian Croatian "state" of Herceg-Bosna and was charged with "ethnic cleansing" in Central Bosnia. Simo Drljaca, a top Bosnian Serb defendant who was accused of leading ethnic cleansing in Northwest Bosnia, died resisting arrest by NATO troops. Because NATO commanders are demonstrating increasing resolve, it seems probable that a good many more defendants will be apprehended.

But even if additional defendants are not taken into custody and brought before the tribunal, indicting them could mean their eventual arrest and trial before another court. And the indictments themselves serve an important function: Those indicted are no longer free to travel beyond the borders of their own country. To do so would be to invite arrest and trial. In the case of the Bosnian Serb leaders, even travel in the part of Bosnia their forces controlled is restricted, given fears that international troops in the area might take them into custody, and even the few arrests by NATO at this writing must make other defendants fear for their safety even in their own homes. The fact that some defendants have turned themselves in, and others who were brazenly visible in the first year and a half after Dayton have more recently dropped out of sight, is evidence of this. The Dayton agreement also barred those who were indicted from holding public office. Accordingly, Radovan Karadzic was forced to step aside as a candidate for office and, ostensibly, as his political party's leader in an effort to demonstrate compliance. Subsequently, General Mladic was stripped of his command by the Bosnian Serb political leadership.

Unfortunately, Karadzic's formal withdrawal effectively undercut mounting international pressure to have NATO troops in Bosnia arrest him and transfer him to The Hague. The agent of this sad turn of affairs, which dealt the Dayton agreement a serious blow, turned out to be Richard Holbrooke, the very man who negotiated Dayton in the first place.

Under Dayton, elections were to be held in Bosnia by September 14, 1996, provided that the Organization for Security and Cooperation in Europe (OSCE) certified at least two months in advance that the conditions were in place for free and fair elections. As the July 14 deadline for certification approached, the conditions clearly were not in place. Refugees and displaced persons—a large part of the potential electorate—had not been registered, and few refugees had returned to the communities from which they had been "ethnically cleansed." Freedom of movement by the different ethnically aligned forces was minimal to nonexistent. Independent media that would allow candidates for office to get their message to the electorate did not reach most of the country. And most symbolically important of all, Radovan Karadzic had not stepped aside as a candidate for office, as required by Dayton.

But the Clinton administration was determined that the elections take place on schedule, and it mounted heavy pressure on the OSCE to certify. Following the completion of the Dayton negotiations, in December 1995, President Clinton had sent 20,000 American troops to Bosnia as part of a NATO force of 60,000 but had promised the Congress and the American public that the troops would be out of Bosnia in a year—home by Christmas 1996. Running for reelection, Clinton did not want to give his opponents ammunition by reneging on the Bosnia pledge—at least not before November. It was evident, however, that the troops would have to stay long enough to ensure that the elections proceeded smoothly and peacefully and to allow the installation in office of those who won. If the date for elections were delayed, the withdrawal of troops also would have to be delayed.

One obvious way to end Karadzic's participation in the elections was for NATO troops to arrest him and send him to The Hague. But NATO would not act unless American troops participated. The European members of NATO resented America's failure to deploy ground troops as part of UNPROFOR, leaving the task primarily to Britain and France. Because they provided by far the largest number of troops to UNPROFOR, their troops had suffered the most casualties. They were not about to engage in a firefight with Karadzic's bodyguards while the Americans stayed out of harm's way.

Here, too, election-year considerations were determinative. Early in Clinton's presidency, eighteen American soldiers died in Mogadishu in a botched effort to arrest General Mohamed Farah Aidid, one of the Somali warlords. Clinton had successfully deflected the blame to the United Nations. If Americans were killed trying to arrest Karadzic, the press certainly would remind voters of the administration's responsibilities in the Mogadishu affair—and that, in turn, might pose a clear and present danger to the president's campaign for a second term. Clinton's dilemma was not without some irony: In 1992, American inaction on Bosnia was dicated mostly by President Bush's reelection concerns.

Holbrooke, who had resigned from the State Department after Dayton to enter private business, was summoned back to solve the Clinton administration's problem. Before he reentered the scene, however, Karadzic agreed to step aside as a candidate, keeping his post as Serbian Democratic Party (SDS) leader. That satisfied no one. Under Communism, the party leadership post was more powerful than that of president. Who, after all, remembers who was president of the Soviet Union while Stalin was general secretary of the Communist Party? Karadzic had given up a title but not power.

The indictment against Karadzic made it impossible for Holbrooke to negotiate directly with the Bosnian Serb leader, so the American diplomat turned again to the man who had negotiated at Dayton in Karadzic's stead. And once again, Slobodan Milosevic was only too happy to oblige. It served Milosevic's interests for Western officials to turn to him to accomplish their purposes in Bosnia—especially when what they sought was exactly what he wanted.

Milosevic did not want NATO forces to capture Karadzic and take him to The Hague. That would have endangered Milosevic himself, since Karadzic's defense would have tried to shift the blame to the Serbian leader. Karadzic had dealt directly with Milosevic during the first two and a half years of the war in Bosnia, and the Bosnian Serb boss could have told the tribunal what role Milosevic had played in the crimes of that period. And that could have provided crucial evidence for an indictment. At the time of Holbrooke's renewed intervention, Karadzic's aides were telling an investigator for the tribunal, who was negotiating with them in a vain effort to get the Bosnian Serb leader to turn himself in, that Milosevic would never let Karadzic get to The Hague alive.

But while Milosevic did not want Karadzic to go to The Hague, he did want him out of politics. The two had become political enemies, and Milosevic was supporting a group that opposed Karadzic's party in the forthcoming elections. It plainly was in Milosevic's interest to pass Holbrooke's message on: Clinton was actively considering Karadzic's arrest if the Bosnian Serb leader did not bow out of politics completely. Karadzic could not have been unaware of this mix of Bosnian and American politics, so the threat seemed credible. And it worked: Karadzic announced that he was giving up his party post as well as his campaign for office, and that he was renouncing politics. Holbrooke had accomplished his mission.

Slobodan Milosevic had still another reason for helping Holbrooke: The Serb leader also wanted the elections to go forward by September 14, 1996. Under the Dayton agreement, economic sanctions could be reimposed on the Federal Republic of Yugoslavia only up to the point that elections were held in Bosnia. If the elections were delayed, the high representative (former Swedish prime minister Carl Bildt) charged with implementing the civilian side of Dayton would have more time to declare that the FRY had not complied with its pledges. Failure to turn over to The Hague regular army officers such as Lieutenant Colonel Sljivancanin, who was indicted for the massacre of patients at the Vukovar hospital, violated Milosevic's commitments at Dayton. If Bildt said Yugoslavia was in violation, economic sanctions would be reimposed automatically, and it would take an affirmative vote of the Security Council to end them. Milosevic wanted to eliminate that threat as soon as possible, which made him eager for elections in Bosnia.

If sanctions are worrisome for real and potential defendants, indictments are to be feared because they will not disappear. Even if the tribunal were dissolved, the principle of universal jurisdiction would permit another international court or the court of another country to bring defendants to trial. The indictments greatly increase the likelihood that this will happen. Yet another possibility is that their own state will undergo political changes and put them on trial, as South Korea did to its former leaders sixteen years after the Kwangju massacre. There is no statute of limitations for war crimes, crimes against humanity, or genocide. A trial could take place twenty or thirty or forty years later. More than seven thousand accused Nazis, for example, have been tried in Germany between the 1950s and today. Adolf Eichmann was arrested in Argentina and tried in Israel in 1960, and Klaus Barbie, another notorious Nazi, was tried four decades after his crimes. In July 1995, an eighty-four-year-old man, Szymon Serafinowicz, was arrested in England and charged with complicity in Nazi crimes committed in his homeland of Belarus fifty-three years earlier. The prosecution against Serafinowicz had to be dropped in January 1997 because he was then suffering from dementia due to Alzheimer's, but the arrest made the point. In Italy, a trial for Nazi war crimes was completed in 1998 with the conviction of the defendant; and in France, the trial of a Vichy official, Maurice Papon, for crimes against humanity during World War II, led to his conviction in 1998.

In cases where an indictment has been brought by an international tribunal, the prospect of a long-delayed trial in another country under the principle of universal jurisdiction is not far-fetched. Indeed, those indicted by the tribunal for the former Yugoslavia will be particularly susceptible to actual trial because evidence gathered in The Hague will be preserved and available to prosecutors elsewhere long after the tribunal winds up its own work. Indictments are swords suspended over the necks of defendants. The criminals may evade trial for a time, but eventually those swords could fall, because the governments of the world have an ongoing *legal* obligation to find and bring to trial those charged with great crimes by an international tribunal.

It is possible, of course, that some of those indicted for war crimes in Bosnia and Croatia will live out their lives without being apprehended. The international community might lack the resolve to enforce its own decisions. Or states harboring the accused may continue to protect them against extradition and arrest. But the tribunal's Rules of Procedure and Evidence[14] anticipate refusal by the parties to turn over defendants, and they deal with the problem in an innovative way designed to increase pressure on recalcitrant governments and further stigmatize the indictees if all else fails. It is a procedure that avoids the violation of due process inherent in trials in absentia, which are also prohibited by the Security Council's statute for the tribunal.

Under a rule proposed by the tribunal's first president, Antonio Cassese, the prosecutor lays out his case in open court against a defendant who evades trial so that the judges may determine whether the evidence provides reasonable ground for confirmation of the indictment. In what is known as a Rule 61 proceeding, evidence of murder, rape, and other great crimes is fully disclosed and the probative character of that evidence is assessed. However, the judges do not determine whether guilt has been proved. Such proof, the rule recognizes, is not possible unless the accused is present in court and has had a full opportunity to defend himself. If the defendant ultimately shows up for trial, the evidence must be presented again so that objections can be made, witnesses for the prosecution can be cross-examined, and the defense case can be presented. To ensure that the case is considered *de novo,* judges who preside at a Rule 61 proceeding cannot serve as trial judges for the same defendants. In short, a Rule 61 proceeding is no substitute for having a defendant in the dock, but its consequences—identification as a war criminal and the lifelong threat of trial—cannot be lightly dismissed.

At every stage of the push to establish the tribunal, partisans were conscious that its failure could severely set back the effort to hold accountable those responsible for great crimes. That fear has proved unfounded. What is surprising is not how little the tribunal has traveled but how far it has gone, even if governments of good conscience still have further to go to fulfill its mandate.

15

Epilogue: Toward a Permanent International Criminal Court

Aₗₜₕₒᵤgₕ ₐᵢᵥₑ yₑₐᵣₛ have elapsed at this writing since the United Nations Security Council resolution establishing the tribunal for ex-Yugoslavia, and more than three years have passed since adoption of a resolution creating the tribunal for Rwanda, the scorecard on their accomplishments is far from complete. The Rwanda tribunal has obtained custody of the majority of those believed to be the principal organizers of the 1994 genocide, and the number of defendants apprehended by the ex-Yugoslavia tribunal is now respectable, even though the most notorious remain conspicuous by their absence. Still, neither tribunal has completed a significant number of trials.

Some of the major powers that voted for establishment of the tribunals share the blame for their failure to make more headway. It is France, after all, whose troops in Bosnia patrol the zone where Radovan Karadzic has taken shelter—and France that has provided a safe haven for defendants indicted by the Rwanda tribunal. But the slow pace also reflects bureaucratic shortcomings in the tribunals themselves of a sort all too characteristic of bodies estab-

252

lished by the United Nations. At one point, for example, the UN insisted on collecting a tax from governments and nongovernmental bodies that seconded personnel to work for the tribunals. The United States and some others refused to pay the tax, thus costing the tribunals many talented staff members they urgently needed.

As a result, even some dedicated partisans of the two tribunals have experienced deep frustrations at times over the operations of these bodies on which so much depends if the cause of international justice is to prosper.

For all the difficulties, however, it is possible that the tribunals will bring about a sea change in international human rights protection. Up to now, that protection has consisted principally in the promulgation of standards by the United Nations and various regional intergovernmental bodies and the documentation of violations by the media and by an ever larger and more sophisticated number of nongovernmental human rights organizations. Supplementing these efforts from time to time have been truth commissions, purges of officials who committed abuses, and infrequently, criminal prosecutions. But the odds against bringing human rights abusers to justice remain astonishingly high. Indeed, the absence of effective means of sanctioning abuses reveals a tragic anomaly of the post–World War II era. On the one hand, the nations of the world, all but universally, have committed themselves to a series of detailed covenants in which they have pledged to one another and to the larger international community that they will respect human rights. On the other hand, far more extensive and terrible violations of human rights have occurred than during any other period except World War II itself.

The establishment of the tribunals and the consequences of their operations could galvanize dramatic change in two ways. First, the tribunals in effect are helping to rewrite international law. As discussed, these changes permit international prosecution of those committing crimes in the internal armed conflicts so pervasive in our era, and they enhance the prospect that domestic courts in many countries will invoke universal jurisdiction to try, prosecute, and punish those responsible for such crimes no matter where they were committed. Up to now, only a handful of such prosecutions have been instituted in a small number of countries, but as awareness of the shift in international law spreads, and as human rights groups press for such prosecutions, the number may well increase significantly.

The second way that the tribunals are bringing about fundamental changes is by focusing international attention on the need to establish a permanent international criminal court. In fact, it's now likely that such a court will be created by the year 2000. What remains to be decided is how effective that court will be in ending impunity for war criminals and their kind.

The idea of an international court to prosecute war crimes was broached at the Versailles Peace Conference in 1919, following World War I. A provision for the establishment of a temporary body was incorporated in the agreement reached there as a way to try Kaiser Wilhelm for Germany's role in starting the war. A commission was created, and eventually it drew up a list of 895 alleged war criminals to be tried before such a court. In addition, the commission proposed to prosecute officials of Germany's wartime ally, Turkey, for "crimes against the laws of humanity" for the genocide against the Armenians that took place in 1915 as a sideshow to the war. But neither recommendation was pursued: The victorious Allies were not eager to humiliate Germany further and had grown concerned about Turkey's political stability. As a result, the proposal for an international criminal court came to naught. In 1923, the Treaty of Lausanne formally concluded World War I between Turkey and its wartime opponents and, in the process, provided the perpetrators of the Armenian genocide with an amnesty.

A proposal to establish a permanent international criminal court arose following World War II. It seemed a natural outgrowth of the tribunals at Nuremberg and Tokyo, and one of those espousing it then was the principal American judge at Nuremberg, former U.S. attorney general Francis Biddle. The proposal made no significant headway at the time, however, because the major powers were preoccupied with the developing Cold War and could not agree on anything that would vest an international body with such authority. The idea died a little-noticed death in the deliberations of the International Law Commission (ILC), a UN body.

Fast-forward to 1989 and a proposal from Trinidad and Tobago to the UN General Assembly to establish a court to prosecute international drug trafficking. Once again, it was referred to the International Law Commission, where, no doubt, it would have died again had the propitious sweep of history not intervened. The Cold War

ended in 1989, and the wars in ex-Yugoslavia began not long thereafter. Accordingly, on November 25, 1992, with atrocities in Bosnia
dominating news broadcasts and headlines worldwide, the UN General Assembly adopted a resolution calling on the ILC to draft an actual statute for a permanent international criminal court.

The ILC submitted its proposal for a court to the General Assembly two years later. By then, the genocide in Rwanda had also
taken place, and the ad hoc tribunal for ex-Yugoslavia had been established and was in the process of handing down its first indictment, and the Security Council was launching a second tribunal, for
Rwanda. Still, many member states of the UN were fearful of a permanent court, and some supporters of the idea were dissatisfied
with the statute drafted by the ILC. Accordingly, on December 9,
1994, the General Assembly adopted a resolution creating an Ad
Hoc Committee to "review the major substantive and administrative
issues arising out of the statute drafted by the International Law
Commission" and "to consider arrangements for the convening of
an international conference of plenipotentiaries [that is, representatives of governments who could sign a treaty establishing a court]."
No such conference was called. But meetings of the Ad Hoc Committee clarified some of the issues involved in the creation of a
court and led to the establishment by the UN in 1996 of yet another
body, a Preparatory Committee, that held a series of meetings to
thrash out issues involving the jurisdiction and operations of the
court. The process culminates at a UN-sponsored Diplomatic Conference in Rome in June/July 1998, at which a treaty on the establishment of a court is being negotiated and submitted to the
signatory states for ratification. Assuming that a sufficient number of
states act during the balance of 1998 and in 1999, the court could
begin its operation in the first year of the new millennium.

A permanent international criminal court will have certain characteristics, on which a consensus has emerged. Among other things,
it will be created by an international treaty at a meeting sponsored
by the United Nations rather than by a resolution of the UN General
Assembly or the Security Council. As such, though it will be a body
associated with the UN, it will not be subject to UN procedures and
rules in the same manner and to the same degree that the ad hoc tribunals for ex-Yugoslavia and Rwanda were. As a consequence, it
could have a better chance than those bodies to operate effectively
and efficiently.

Although the current effort to establish the ICC began with Trinidad and Tobago's proposal for a court to deal with international drug trafficking, at least at the outset, that will not be part of its jurisdiction. It is widely accepted that the ICC should begin with a jurisdiction that is limited to what are being referred to as the "core" crimes: war crimes, crimes against humanity, and genocide. Over time, however, its jurisdiction may well be broadened. Germany and Italy favor inclusion of the crime of waging aggressive war—the most disputed component of the jurisdiction of the Nuremberg and Tokyo tribunals. Some Caribbean nations, in addition to Trinidad and Tobago, want prosecutions for international drug trafficking brought before the ICC. And still other governments propose that the court be authorized to try cases of international terrorism, such as the accusations against the Libyans named by the United States and Britain as the culprits in the bombing of Pan Am 103, the jet that crashed at Lockerbie, Scotland.

Dealing with such questions is far from a simple matter. It would require the governments that signed and ratified the treaty establishing the ICC also to agree upon an international criminal code that would spell out the elements of those crimes. That could take an extended period, which is why the ICC will begin with the core crimes where—aside from the urgency of dealing with them—a well-developed body of existing international law has simplified the task of securing an agreement.

Rape and other crimes of aggression against women are specifically cited in the provisions of the treaty establishing the ICC that deal with war crimes and crimes against humanity—a lasting consequence of concern about such offenses that emerged during the war in Bosnia. The treaty also includes a provision for "complementarity"—that is, the ICC will not be a substitute for national prosecutions. National governments will remain under an obligation under the Geneva Conventions and other international agreements to seek out and prosecute in their domestic courts those committing war crimes and other gross abuses of human rights, and the ICC will have no basis for interfering with their sovereignty as long as they honor those obligations. Except in the case of genocide, where it has been proposed that the ICC should have "inherent" jurisdiction, the ICC will complement the operations of national justice systems by prosecuting only those offenses where justice is "ineffective or unavailable" in national courts. If Serbia, for example, were to prosecute Lieutenant Colonel Sljivancanin in good faith for the massacre at the Vukovar hospital, or hand him over for prosecution by Croatia, the ICC would defer to the national court. If a prosecution in a national court is grossly deficient ("ineffective"), however, or simply does not take place ("unavailable"), the ICC could assume jurisdiction.

Finally, there is agreement that the ICC must be a model of due process protection for the defendants brought before it. Trials in absentia will not be permitted; defendants will have the right to know the charges and the evidence against them; they will have a right to the effective assistance of counsel, and if need be, counsel will be assigned; they will be able to confront their accusers and to cross-examine them; they will be able to present witnesses in their own behalf; and they will have the right to a public trial before impartial judges and to an appeal. In short, as in the ad hoc tribunals for ex-Yugoslavia and Rwanda, the protections provided by the ICC to defendants will resemble those that are available in American jurisprudence. But the ICC will probably model itself on the civil-law systems of continental Europe in not allowing the plea bargaining that is such a prominent feature of American judicial practice.

The most contentious issues in the drafting of the treaty establishing the ICC have involved the independence of the court and what is referred to as the "trigger mechanism" for launching prosecutions. Governments intent on nullifying the court's capacity to embarrass them or convict their officials—again, France most significantly—have argued that the consent of the states where an alleged crime took place, where the victims lived, or where the accused perpetrators are located should be required before an investigation begins. This is opposed by a large group of countries that are strong supporters of the ICC.

The permanent members of the United Nations Security Council, however, have espoused another proposal that could be almost as damaging to the court. The proposal initially supported by all five members—the United States, Britain, France, Russia, and China—would bar the ICC from investigating crimes in any conflict in which the Security Council has exercised its peacekeeping authority under the UN Charter unless the Security Council authorizes the ICC to become involved. The impact of this proposal on the ICC would be devastating, because the Security Council invokes its peacekeeping authority in a great many conflicts. Moreover, the formula is one that would permit any one of the five permanent members to veto a prosecution before the ICC.

Had such a rule been in effect during past conflicts, the United States would have been able on its own to keep the ICC away from cases concerning the Vietnam War or those involving the activities of a close ally such as Israel in Lebanon or Gaza. France could have kept the ICC out of Rwanda. Russia could have barred the ICC from considering Serbian crimes in Bosnia or Iraqi crimes in Kuwait or Kurdistan. China could have stopped the ICC from prosecuting the Khmer Rouge, and the British could have prevented the ICC from dealing with crimes committed by Nigeria during the Biafran war. Only cases involving countries that lack a patron among the permanent members of the Security Council could not be blocked. In addition, of course, the permanent members could ensure the impunity of their own nationals. The obvious effect would be to undermine the court's prestige from the outset, diminishing greatly the impact of its work even on cases that it is able to consider.

Fortunately, Singapore proposed a way to resolve the issue that provides due deference to the role of the Security Council in peacekeeping and that substantially preserves the independence of the ICC. Under the Singapore proposal, the ICC would refrain from investigating a case only when the Security Council acts affirmatively and advises it to stay clear. Such a rule would permit no single country to veto ICC involvement; only a majority vote of the Security Council could block a prosecution. Of course, there is still the possibility that the Security Council as a whole would choose political expediency over justice, but Canada proposed an amendment to Singapore's proposal that would take a long extra step in assuring the independence and evenhandedness of the ICC: A directive from the Security Council would expire automatically after twelve months unless it is renewed unanimously. This would permit deferral of a prosecution for a period while a delicate negotiation is under way but would ensure that political considerations could not permanently constrain the work of a body that can only fulfill its potential if it gains acceptance worldwide for doing justice impartially.

As I write, the Labor government of British prime minister Tony Blair (and of his foreign secretary, Robin Cook, a strong supporter of the ad hoc tribunals for ex-Yugoslavia and Rwanda) has broken ranks with its Tory predecessor and the other permanent members of the Security Council to endorse the Singapore proposal. That has forced the United States to reconsider its position. The Clinton administration, particularly through the words of Secretary of State Madeleine Albright, has expressed strong support for the ICC and is not eager to become known internationally as a spoiler—especially after its embarrassing performance with respect to the 1997 Landmines Treaty, which it refused to sign. At the same time, however, the administration is mindful that its capacity to deliver U.S. Senate ratification of a treaty creating the ICC will be much reduced if it is not able to assert that it has ensured America's unilateral capacity to block any prosecution of American soldiers before an international court. The prospect that a future Lieutenant William Calley or a Captain Ernest Medina might come before judges from all parts of the globe sitting in The Hague is a rallying cry for opponents of the ICC and could result in a humiliating setback for the administration.

The ad hoc tribunal for ex-Yugoslavia was a significant advance over the tribunals at Nuremberg and Tokyo, because it had a mandate to prosecute and punish malefactors from all sides in the wars in Croatia and Bosnia and has carried out its charge. Accordingly, unlike its predecessors, it is not susceptible to accusations of victor's justice. The ICC would continue the trend by having a mandate to deal with those who commit crimes within its jurisdiction whether they are from small states in Central Europe or Central Africa or from the richest and most powerful nations on earth. The United States could avoid subjecting its soldiers to trial before the ICC by ensuring that they do not commit war crimes, crimes against humanity, or genocide—or it could head off an ICC prosecution by bringing accused war criminals to trial before its own courts, as it did with Lieutenant Calley. But the United States cannot secure establishment of an effective international criminal court while carving out an exception that would insulate Americans from any possibility of being tried by such a court.

U.S. backing for an effective ICC is crucial, both because of America's stature and significance internationally and because it provides the best possibility of obtaining support by the other permanent members of the Security Council. If that support is forthcoming, and an international criminal court with appropriate independence is created, it will truly be possible to say that a new era in international human rights protection has begun. If it is not forthcoming at the outset, it might nevertheless be provided subsequently. For the first time in human history, those committing war crimes, crimes against humanity, or the ultimate crime, genocide, would have to reckon seriously with the possibility that they would be brought before the international bar to face truth, be held accountable, and serve justice.

Notes

Part One: Dealing with War Crimes Before Bosnia

Chapter 1: Vukovar: Where It Began

1. This scene was also witnessed by a French journalist, Jean Hatzfeld of *Liberation,* who wrote "The Fall of Vukovar" in *Granta,* no. 47, spring 1994. According to Hatzfeld, who was severely injured by gunfire in Bosnia in June 1992, "[i]t was obvious what was about to happen" to the wounded evacuated from the hospital basement. "These prisoners would not reappear until the discovery of mass graves."

2. See Human Rights Watch, "War Crimes in Bosnia-Hercegovina," August 1992, pp. 76–79.

3. See Christopher Joyce and Eric Stover, *Witnesses from the Grave* (Boston: Little Brown, 1991).

4. In December 1997, Milutinovic was declared president of Serbia after a disputed election. He succeeded Milosevic, who had shifted to the federal presidency of Yugoslavia, and, through their close alliance, cemented the latter's control of the country.

Chapter 2: The Laws of War
    1. Herodotus, *The Histories* 7:136.
    2. Phillip Knightley, *The First Casualty* (New York: Harcourt Brace Jovanovic, 1975).
    3. Cecil Woodham-Smith, *Florence Nightingale* (London: Constable, 1950), p. 133.
    4. Knightley, *The First Casualty,* p. 28.

Chapter 3: The United Nations
    1. Louis Henkin, cited in Henry J. Steiner and Philip Alston, *International Human Rights in Context* (Oxford: Clarendon Press, 1996), p. 123.
    2. The commission currently is made up of representatives of fifty-three member states. Countries serve on the commission by designation of the UN's Economic and Social Council. An acceptable human rights record is not a prerequisite for membership on the commission. In 1996, the members included China and Cuba; in 1994, Iran, Sudan, and Syria. The only criterion is that seats on the commission should be distributed in accordance with each geographical region's share of UN membership.
    3. Detailed complaints against the Khmer Rouge were submitted to the UN Human Rights Commission by the American, British, Canadian, and Norwegian governments, as well as by Amnesty International; accordingly, the failure to take a stronger stand was not due to a shortage of information.
    4. The UN's Center for Human Rights, in Geneva, has a staff of about 120. Though the high commissioner outranks any official at the center, the commissioner did not have the authority to direct the work of its staff until a reorganization in 1997.
    5. A private organization, the United Nations Association–USA, has proposed that the high commissioner should issue an annual human rights report on all the member states of the UN, along the lines of the U.S. State Department's annual *Country Reports.* Unfortunately, it is an impractical proposal, as the high commissioner lacks information resources in the field and would have to depend on the information-gathering capacity of other bodies. More important, the member states of the UN would not put up with frank assessments of their human rights practices by a UN official. See United Nations Association of the USA, "Inalienable Rights, Fundamental Freedoms: A UN Agenda for Advancing Human Rights in the World Community," 1996, pp. 30–31.
    6. The report is reprinted in *The United Nations and El Salvador 1990–1995,* The United Nations Blue Book Series (New York: United Nations, 1995), pp. 290–414.
    7. January 27, 1982.
    8. A definitive account by Mark Danner appeared in *The New Yorker* in

1993 and was subsequently published by Vintage Books, *The Massacre at El Mozote,* in 1994.

9. Douglas Farah, "Talk Show Helps Knit El Salvador," *The Washington Post,* January 17, 1997.

Chapter 4: The Battle for Truth

1. In 1954, five years before Castro came to power in Cuba, the United States sponsored a coup that overthrew the government of President Jacobo Arbenz Guzmán in Guatemala. The Eisenhower administration had worried that Arbenz was leading Guatemala toward Communism. The U.S. role in the coup made it particularly important for the Guatemalan armed forces to deny responsibility for assassinations of leftists. Guatemala's pioneering role in disappearances more than a decade later was a consequence. See Michael McClintock, *The American Connection,* vol. 1, *State Terror and Popular Resistance in El Salvador,* and vol. 2, *State Terror and Popular Resistance in Guatemala* (London: Zed Books, 1985), for a history of the development of counterinsurgency in Latin America.

2. Horacio Verbitsky, *The Flight: Confessions of an Argentine Dirty Warrior* (New York: The New Press, 1996).

3. Jacobo Timerman, *Prisoner Without a Name, Cell Without a Number* (New York: Knopf, 1981).

4. Argentina's invasion of the Falklands/Malvinas produced a falling-out between Kirkpatrick and Alexander Haig. Kirkpatrick sought support for the Argentines, who had done such favors for the United States as organizing and training former Nicaraguan national guardsmen and launching them in Honduras as the contras. On the other hand, Haig, after a bootless effort to mediate between Argentina and the British, argued strenuously for support for America's NATO ally, Britain (previously, Haig had served as NATO's military commander). Haig prevailed in securing U.S. backing for the British, but not long thereafter, he lost his job as secretary of state. Kirkpatrick's hostility reportedly played a part in his downfall.

5. An English-language version was published by Farrar, Straus & Giroux in the United States in 1986 as *Nunca Mas: The Report of the Argentine National Commission on the Disappeared.*

6. Quoted in Verbitsky, *The Flight,* p. 149.

7. One case was exempted from an amnesty law decreed by Pinochet in 1978: the killing of Chile's former defense minister, Orlando Letelier, and an American colleague, Ronni Karpen Moffitt, in a car bombing in Washington, D.C., in 1976. In deference to American outrage over political assassinations carried out in the United States, the possibility of prosecuting those responsible had to be left open. A federal grand jury in Washington indicted top Chilean intelligence officials, including the chief of the secret

police, General Héctor Contreras, and another top officer, General Pedro Espinoza Valdés, for the crime. After the issuance of the Truth and Reconciliation Commission report, they were prosecuted in Chile for the Letelier-Moffitt murders, and at this writing, Espinoza is serving a prison sentence for that crime. Contreras at first took refuge in a navy hospital, claiming to be too ill to be taken to prison. After a long stand-off, however, the civilian government of Chile prevailed and took Contreras off to begin serving his prison sentence.

8. Quoted in *The New York Times* from a Reuters dispatch, August 22, 1996.

9. Quoted in *The New York Times,* August 23, 1996.

10. New York: Grove Press, 1986.

11. Tiedmann's essay, "Japan Sheds Dictatorship," appears in *From Dictatorship to Democracy,* edited by John H. Herz (Westport, Conn.: Greenwood Press, 1982).

12. "The Ghosts of Ishii," *Newsweek,* October 3, 1994.

13. Ian Buruma, *The Wages of Guilt* (New York: Farrar, Straus & Giroux, 1994), p. 114.

14. John W. Dower, *War Without Mercy: Race and Power in the Pacific War* (New York: Pantheon, 1986), pp. 40–41.

15. Buruma, *The Wages of Guilt,* pp. 175–76.

16. Subsequent mistreatment of African Americans and of Indians are beyond the scope of this book.

17. Later on, Warren, who became a great champion of civil liberties as chief justice of the United States, was deeply ashamed of his wartime role. "There was nothing that Chief Justice Warren regretted more poignantly," according to a biographer, Jack Harrison Pollack, in *Earl Warren: The Judge Who Changed America* (Englewood Cliffs, N.J.: Prentice-Hall, 1979).

Chapter 5: Purges and Criminal Regimes

1. For further information, see Lawrence Weschler's essays "The Trials of Jan Kavan" and "From Kafka to Dreyfus" in the October 19, 1992, and November 2, 1992, issues of *The New Yorker.*

2. Address, March 22, 1991. Reprinted in *Uncaptive Minds,* summer 1991.

3. The dialogue between Michnik and Havel was published in *Gazeta Wyborcza* on November 30, 1991. English-language excerpts appeared in the *Journal of Democracy,* January 1993.

4. "Kavindication," *The New Yorker,* February 12, 1996.

5. Klaus Kinkel, "Wiedervereinigung and Strafrecht," *Juristen Zeitung,* vol. 47, no. 10 (May 22, 1992), p. 487. Quoted in A. James McAdams, "The Honecker Trial: The East German Past and the German Future," Kellogg Institute, Notre Dame University, January 1996, pp. 5–6.

6. Interview in the Polish weekly *Wprost*, translated in *Uncaptive Minds*, summer 1992.

7. See Todd Gitlin, "I Did Not Imagine That I Lived in Truth," *The New York Times Book Review*, April 4, 1993.

8. Hannah Arendt, *Essays in Understanding, 1930–1954* (New York: Harcourt Brace, 1994), p. 257.

9. John H. Herz, *From Dictatorship to Democracy* (Westport, Conn.: Greenwood Press, 1982), pp. 23–24.

10. Ibid., p. 27.

11. Ingo Müller, *Hitler's Justice: The Courts of the Third Reich* (Cambridge, Mass.: Harvard University Press, 1991).

12. Ibid., p. 196.

13. Ibid., p. 274.

14. "Zur Aufarbeitung des SED Unrechts," *Aus Politik und Zeitgeschichte*, no. 4 (January 22, 1993), p. 3. Quoted in A. James McAdams, "The Honecker Trial," p. 3.

15. See *The Haunted Land: Facing Europe's Ghosts After Communism* (New York: Random House, 1995) for a discussion of lustration and other efforts to deal with the repression of the past in the Czech Republic, Slovakia, Germany, and Poland. An earlier work, *Children of Cain: Violence and the Violent in Latin America* (New York: Morrow, 1991), dealt with political repression in another part of the world.

Chapter 6: Doing Justice Abroad and at Home

1. Amnesty International, *Torture in Greece: The First Torturers' Trial 1975*, 1977. Excerpts reprinted in the United States Institute for Peace, *Transitional Justice: How Emerging Democracies Reckon with Former Regimes*, vol. 2, 1995, p. 268.

2. Quoted in Mark J. Osiel, "Ever Again: Legal Remembrance of Administrative Massacre," *University of Pennsylvania Law Review*, December 1995, p. 472. The quote is from *Radical Evil on Trial*, a forthcoming book of Niño's essays.

3. The story of Uruguay's struggle over accountability is well told in Lawrence Weschler's book *A Miracle, A Universe: Settling Accounts with Torturers* (New York: Pantheon, 1990).

4. Aryeh Neier, "What Should Be Done About the Guilty?," *The New York Review of Books*, February 1, 1990.

5. Juan E. Méndez, "Accountability for Past Abuses," Kellogg Institute, University of Notre Dame, May 3, 1996.

6. The complete text of Zalaquett's paper appears in *State Crimes: Punishment or Pardon*, Aspen Institute, 1989.

7. H.L.A. Hart, *Punishment and Responsibility: Essays in the Philosophy of Law* (New York: Oxford University Press, 1968), pp. 234–35.

8. Edward Behr, *Kiss the Hand You Cannot Bite: The Rise and Fall of the Ceauşescus* (New York: Villard, 1991), pp. 128–29.

9. See Human Rights Watch/Africa, "Ethiopia: Reckoning Under the Law," December 1994, for background information on the preparation of the prosecutions.

10. Telford Taylor, *Nuremberg and Vietnam: An American Tragedy* (New York: A New York Times Book, 1970), pp. 128–29.

Chapter 7: The Trouble with Amnesty

1. Letter from President Sanguinetti to Amnesty International, March 31, 1987. Reprinted in Neil J. Kritz, *Transitional Justice: How Emerging Democracies Reckon with Former Regimes*, vol. 3 (United States Institute for Peace, 1995), p. 600.

2. National courts have issued conflicting decisions on these questions. The Constitutional Court of Hungary held that crimes committed at the time of the 1956 revolution are subject to punishment despite a statute of limitations in domestic law, because there is no statute of limitations in the Geneva Conventions. On the other hand, another respected court, the Constitutional Court of South Africa, declined to invalidate that country's amnesty law because of the conflict with international law.

3. Judgment, Inter-American Court of Human Rights, series C, no. 4 (1988).

4. Francis Bacon, *A New Abridgement of the Law*.

5. Quoted in Anthony Lewis, "Revenge or Reconciliation," *The New York Times,* April 10, 1990.

6. *The Azanian People's Organization v. The President of the People of South Africa,* Case CCT 17/96, decided on July 25, 1996, J. Didcott concurring.

Part II: Bosnia, Rwanda, and the Search for Justice

Chapter 8: Calling for a Tribunal: The Right Deed for the Wrong Reason?

1. T. S. Eliot, *Murder in the Cathedral* (London: Faber & Faber, 1935).

2. Noel Malcolm, *Bosnia: A Short History* (London: Macmillan Papermac, 1994), p. 188.

3. These reports, and others of a similar nature, are cited in Richard West, *Tito and the Rise and Fall of Yugoslavia* (London: Sinclair-Stevenson, 1994). See the chapter called "Ustasha Terror," pp. 77–102.

4. Ibid., pp. 88–90.

5. This episode was recalled in a book published in Sarajevo in 1990 edited by Vladimir Dedijev and Antun Miletic, *Genocide an Muslim Anima*

1941–1945. An appendix identifies by name some 3,525 Muslims who were the purported victims.

6. See the October 4, 1994, issue of *Pecat,* a weekly magazine published in Zagreb.

7. Robert J. Donia and John V. A. Fine, Jr., *Bosnia and Hercegovina: A Tradition Betrayed* (New York: Columbia University Press, 1994), p. 81.

8. Ibid., pp. 38–39.

9. An important memoir detailing the direct interventions in the wars in Croatia and Bosnia was published by Veljko Kadijevic, who served as minister of defense of Yugoslavia and chief of staff of its armed forces, the JNA, from May 15, 1988, to January 6, 1992, when he resigned for reasons of ill health. According to Kadijevic, summing up the achievements of the JNA:

> In Croatia, together with the Serb nation, it liberated the Serbian Krajina and forced Croatia to accept the Vance peace plan; in Bosnia-Hercegovina, first the JNA and later the army of the Republic of Srpska, which the JNA put on its feet, helped to liberate Serb territory, protect the Serb nation and create the favorable military preconditions for achieving the interests and rights of the Serb nation. . . . The JNA provided the basis for the formation of three armies: the Army of the Federal Republic of Yugoslavia, the Army of the Republic of Srpska and the Army of the Republic of Serbian Krajina. Considering the given domestic and international circumstances, it was done in a most organized way. This was a very important task. The JNA leadership made it a priority. [Veljko Kadijevic, *My View of the Break-Up* (Belgrade: 1993).]

Two years later, another memoir was published in Belgrade by another insider, Borislav Jovic, who had served as president of Yugoslavia until just prior to the wars in 1991 with the breakaway republics of Slovenia and Croatia. Jovic also described the role of the Yugoslav Army, under the leadership of Slobodan Milosevic, in establishing the Bosnian Serb Army. Borislav Jovic, *The Last Days of the Socialist Federation of the Republic of Yugoslavia* (Belgrade: 1995).

10. Raphael Lemkin, *Axis Rule in Occupied Europe* (Washington, D.C.: Carnegie Endowment for International Peace, 1944).

11. John Burns, "A Killer's Tale—A Special Report; A Serbian Fighter's Path of Brutality," *The New York Times,* November 27, 1992, p. A 1.

12. More than three years later, Herak was reported to have changed his story, saying that though he had witnessed many murders by Serb forces, his testimony confessing his own commission of murder and rape was false and had been coerced. Press accounts of Herak's change of story reflected skepticism of the charge of coercion. "Dozens of journalists made pilgrimages to the regional jail in Sarajevo to hear his grisly accounts," *The New York Times* reported. "At least some of those interviews were out of earshot of Bosnian guards." Kit R. Roane, "Symbol of Inhumanity in Bosnia Now Says 'Not Me' " (January 31, 1996).

13. *The Wall Street Journal,* July 13, 1995.

Chapter 9: The Return of the Concentration Camp

1. Many of Gutman's dispatches were reproduced in *Witness to Genocide* (New York: Macmillan/A Lisa Drew Book, 1993).

2. Ed Vulliamy, *Seasons in Hell* (New York: St. Martin's Press, 1994), p. 97.

3. See Peter Maass, *Love Thy Neighbor: A Story of War* (New York: Knopf, 1996).

4. August 13, 1992.

5. Michael Ignatieff, *Blood and Belonging: Journeys into the New Nationalism* (New York: Farrar, Straus & Giroux, 1994), pp. 33–34.

6. Chris Hedges, "Bosnian Mine Thought to Hold Mass Graves," *The New York Times,* January 11, 1996.

7. Final Report of the Commission of Experts Established Pursuant to Security Council Resolution 780 (1982), May 24, 1994, para. 171.

8. September 25, 1992.

9. August 1 and 2, 1994.

10. *The Prosecutor v. Dusko Tadic,* Appeals Chamber, International Tribunal for the Former Yugoslavia, October 2, 1995, p. 38.

11. Ibid., p. 39.

12. *The Spectator,* May 22, 1993.

13. David Owen's book, published about the time of the Dayton peace agreement, is at pains to suggest Bosnian government responsibility for abuses. An example, by no means the most pernicious that could be cited, is his discussion of the shooting down of an Italian plane bringing relief supplies to Sarajevo in September 1992. Owen writes that the plane was

> shot down over an area controlled by forces of the Bosnian Croat army (HVO). The territory contained some Bosnian government (mainly Muslim) forces, but the UN felt it most unlikely to have had any Bosnian Serb forces. Suspicion fell on the Croats, but what surprised me was that the senior people in the UNHCR who controlled the flights and UNPROFOR's senior officers all refused to rule out the possibility that the very people who would gain most from the relief supplies, the Muslims, might be responsible for shooting down the plane. Up until then I had no idea that their past conduct had given any grounds for any such suspicion. It was later thought that the Italian aircraft had been shot down by a Stinger hand-held ground-to-air missile which had been used to considerable effect against Soviet forces in Afghanistan. No party was identified as being responsible.

The unsupported suggestion that a Stinger missile was used and the reference to Afghanistan implies that the guilty parties may have been *mujahedin,* a term often used by the Bosnian Serbs to label Bosnian Muslims. Yet there is not an iota of evidence that Bosnian government forces ever had Stingers, much less in September 1992, when they lacked all but the most rudimentary weapons with which to defend themselves. David Owen, *Balkan Odyssey* (New York: Harcourt Brace, 1995), p. 41.

14. September 1, 1997. The story was subsequently published in *The New York Times* on September 5, 1997.

15. Rebecca West, *Black Lamb and Grey Falcon* (London: Penguin, 1982), p. 288.

16. The European Union has taken responsibility for humanitarian assistance in Mostar and at this writing has invested $200 million to help rebuild the city, though a far greater sum will be required before the city's bridges are rebuilt and before the east bank achieves the appearance of normalcy. Despite a peace agreement since early 1994 between the Bosnian Croats and the Bosnian government, the city remains divided. The Muslim section on the east bank of the Neretva River was devastated by the shelling by Croat forces, and for two years the survivors struggled to survive in shell-blasted homes without water, electricity, or gas. The west bank, inhabited by Croats, was virtually unscathed, and its residents had all utilities and the comforts that one expects in a European city.

17. See Human Rights Watch, *War Crimes in Bosnia-Hercegovina*, vol. 2 (April 1993), pp. 355–66.

18. The number cited in a UN Security Council report of December 22, 1995.

19. Aristotle, *Nichomachean Ethics*, book 5.

20. See Deborah E. Lipstadt, *Beyond Belief: The American Press and the Coming of the Holocaust 1933–45* (New York: Free Press/Macmillan, 1986).

21. Raul Hilberg, *The Destruction of the European Jews* (New York: Harper Colophon, 1979), p. 577. First edition was 1961.

22. Primo Levi, *Survival in Auschwitz* (New York: Collier Macmillan, 1961).

23. Ibid., pp. 578–80.

24. See, for example, Rezak Hukanovic, "The Evil at Omarska," *The New Republic*, February 12, 1996.

25. Ed Vulliamy, "Middle Managers of Genocide," *The Nation*, June 10, 1996.

26. Hilberg, *The Destruction of the European Jews*, p. 658.

Chapter 10: Sarajevo and Siege Warfare

1. May 27, 1992.

2. The UN War Crimes Commission reported that "on the days where a total shelling count was documented [by UN Protection Forces], Sarajevo was hit by an average of 329 shell impacts per day. The range of shelling activity on these days varied from a low of two impacts on both 17 and 18

May 1993 to a high of 3,777 impacts on 22 July 1993." *Final Report,* para. 188, May 24, 1994.

3. Michael Walzer's *Just and Unjust Wars* was published by Basic Books (New York, 1977) and is now available in a paperback edition from the same publisher (now in Washington).

4. June 6, 1992.

5. 333 House of Commons Debates (March 23, 1938). Cited in *The Prosecutor v. Dusko Tadic,* Decision on the Defence Motion for Interlocutory Appeal on Jurisdiction, Appeals Chamber, International Criminal Tribunal for the Former Yugoslavia, October 2, 1995, p. 55.

6. 337 House of Commons Debate (June 21, 1938). Cited in *The Prosecutor v. Dusko Tadic,* p. 56.

7. *League of Nations, O.J. Spec. Supp. 183,* at 135–36 (1938). Cited in *The Prosecutor v. Dusko Tadic,* p. 56.

8. See Stephen A. Garrett, *Ethics and Airpower in World War II: The British Bombing of German Cities* (New York: St. Martin's Press, 1993), p. 11.

9. Paul Fussell, *Wartime: Understanding and Behavior in the Second World War* (New York: Oxford University Press, 1989), p. 16.

10. See Human Rights Watch/Middle East, "Needless Deaths in the Gulf War," New York, 1991.

11. Christopher Simpson has cited a communication from the U.S. Army Air Force's headquarters in Algiers in 1943 opposing threats by the U.S. government to put German war criminals on trial for fear that the Nazis would retaliate by trying American airmen shot down during bombing raids. This indicates awareness that the Allied practice of indiscriminate bombing was susceptible to prosecution and punishment as a war crime. See *The Splendid Blond Beast* (New York: Grove Press, 1993), p. 346.

12. George H. Aldrich, "Some Reflections on the Origins of the 1977 Geneva Protocols," in Christophe Swinarski, *Studies and Essays on International Humanitarian Law and Red Cross Principles in Honour of Jean Pictet,* ICRC (Dordrecht, Netherlands: Martinus Nijhoff, 1984), p. 132.

13. December 26, 1992.

14. Final Report of the Commission of Experts Established Pursuant to Security Council Resolution 780 (1992), transmitted May 24, 1994, by Secretary General Boutros Boutros-Ghali to the President of the Security Council, paras. 205–9.

Chapter 11: Rape

1. "Three Who Planned Rape and Murder," April 19, 1993. Reprinted in Roy Gutman's book, *A Witness to Genocide* (New York: Macmillan/A Lisa Drew Book, 1993), pp. 157–67.

2. Final Report of the Commission of Experts Established Pursuant to Se-

curity Council Resolution 780 (1992), transmitted on May 24, 1994, by Secretary General Boutros Boutros-Ghali to the Security Council, para. 247.

3. January 9, 1993.

4. January 13, 1993.

5. April 7, 1993.

6. *Filartiga v. Pena-Irala,* 630 F. 2d, 876 (2d Cir. 1980).

7. See Laura Flanders, "C. MacKinnon in the City of Freud," *The Nation,* August 9/16, 1993, p. 176.

8. July/August 1993.

9. Catharine A. MacKinnon, "Turning Rape into Pornography: Postmodern Genocide," *Ms.,* July/August 1993, pp. 24–30.

10. See, for example, "Rape and Soldiers' Morale," *The New York Times,* December 7, 1992.

11. International Committee of the Red Cross, *Commentary on the Geneva Conventions of 12 August 1949: Geneva Convention Relative to the Protection of Civilian Persons in Time of War* (1958), p. 598.

12. Control Council Law No. 10.

13. International Tribunal for the Prosecution of Persons Responsible for Serious Violations of International Humanitarian Law in the Territory of the Former Yugoslavia since 1991, "Rules of Procedure and Evidence," adopted on February 11, 1994, as amended May 5, 1994, The Hague.

14. Amendment of January 1995.

15. See Theodor Meron, *Henry's Wars and Shakespeare's Laws* (Clarendon: Oxford University Press, 1993).

16. Hugo Grotius, *The Law of War and Peace* (1625), book 3, chap. 19.

17. In 1993, the Carnegie Endowment reissued the report with a new introduction by George Kennan.

18. Beverly Allen, *Rape Warfare: The Hidden Genocide in Bosnia-Herzegovina and Croatia* (Minneapolis: University of Minnesota Press, 1996), p. 100.

19. M. Cherif Bassiouni and Peter Manikas, *The Law of the International Criminal Tribunal for the Former Yugoslavia* (Irvington-on-Hudson, N.Y.: Transnational Publishers, 1996), p. 587.

20. Shana Swiss and Ivan E. Gitler, "Rape as a Crime of War," *Journal of the American Medical Association,* August 4, 1993, p. 613.

21. Final Report of the Commission, paras. 236–49.

22. M. Cherif Bassiouni and Marcia McCormick, "Sexual Violence: An Invisible Weapon in the Former Yugoslavia," International Human Rights Law Institute, De Paul University College of Law, 1996, p. 15.

Chapter 12: Incitement to Mass Murder

1. Article 19, *Forging War: The Media in Serbia, Croatia and Bosnia-Hercegovina,* written by Mark Thompson, London, May 1994.

2. Quoted in Laura Silber and Allan Little, *Yugoslavia: Death of a Nation* (New York: TV Books, 1996), p. 39.

3. Ibid., p. 120.

4. Ibid., p. 72.

5. A detailed account of the events at Zvornik has been compiled by an Austrian organization, the Ludwig Boltzmann Institute of Human Rights, which studied some nine hundred refugees in Austria from the Zvornik region. Its "Report on 'Ethnic Cleansing Operations' in the Northeast Bosnian City of Zvornik from April Through June 1992," based on more than five hundred interviews, was published on April 6, 1994, in Vienna.

6. Zlatko Dizdarevic, *Sarajevo: A War Journal* (Fromm International, 1993), p. 3.

7. *Forging War,* pp. 81–82.

8. Ibid., pp. 82–83.

9. David Rieff, *Slaughterhouse: Bosnia and the Failure of the West* (New York: Simon & Schuster, 1995), pp. 200–201.

10. Warren Zimmermann, *Origins of a Catastrophe* (New York: Times Books, 1996), p. 122.

11. Peter Maass, "Suddenly They Are Killers," *The Washington Post,* May 12, 1996.

12. Cited in Phillip Knightley, *The First Casualty* (New York: Harcourt Brace Jovanovic, 1975), pp. 305, 315.

13. Ibid., p. 590.

14. Cited in Robert Block, "The Tragedy of Rwanda," *The New York Review of Books,* October 20, 1994, p. 7.

15. Bill Berkeley, "Sounds of Violence," *The New Republic,* August 22 and 29, 1994.

16. Gerard Prunier, *The Rwanda Crisis: History of a Genocide* (New York: Columbia University Press, 1995), p. 224.

17. U.S. Committee for Refugees, "Genocide in Rwanda: Documentation of Two Massacres During April 1994," November 1994, p. 7.

18. *Broadcasting Genocide: Censorship, Propaganda and State Sponsored Violence in Rwanda 1990–1994,* October 1996.

19. Ibid., p. 166.

20. Ibid.

21. More than two years later, in 1997, the RPF-backed forces of Laurent Kabila in Zaire (now Congo) overthrew the long-term Mobutu dictatorship. Along the way, they massacred Hutu refugees in an apparent effort to prevent their formation of a military force that could have challenged the RPF

in Rwanda and resumed the slaughter of Tutsis, and perhaps also in revenge for the 1994 genocide.

22. Aryeh Neier, *Defending My Enemy: American Nazis, the Skokie Case, and the Risks of Freedom* (New York: Dutton, 1979).

23. Prunier, *The Rwanda Crisis,* p. 189.

24. 305 US 444 (1969).

Chapter 13: Guilt

1. Karl Jaspers, *The Question of German Guilt* (New York: Dial Press, 1948).

2. "The Responsibility of Peoples," *Politics,* March 1945. Reprinted in Dwight Macdonald, *Memoirs of a Revolutionist* (New York: Farrar, Straus & Cudahy, 1957), p. 60.

3. Alain Finkielkraut, *Remembering in Vain: The Klaus Barbie Trial and Crimes Against Humanity* (New York: Columbia University Press, 1992), p. 35.

4. Raul Hilberg, *The Destruction of the European Jews* (New York: Harper Colophon, 1979), p. 189.

5. Daniel Joseph Goldhagen, *Hitler's Willing Executioners: Ordinary Germans and the Holocaust* (New York: Knopf, 1996).

6. Ibid., p. 181.

7. Ibid., p. 167.

8. Raul Hilberg, *Perpetrators Victims Bystanders* (New York: Harper Perennial, 1993), pp. 20–21.

9. Gerard Prunier, *The Rwanda Crisis: History of a Genocide* (New York: Columbia University Press, 1995), p. 247.

10. Mahmood Mamdani, "Understand the Rwandan Massacre," *New Left Review,* London, no. 216, 1996, pp. 18–19.

11. U.S. Committee for Refugees, "Genocide in Rwanda: Documentation of Two Massacres in April 1994," November 1994, p. 2.

12. Prunier, *The Rwanda Crisis,* p. 244.

13. Hannah Arendt and Karl Jaspers, *Correspondence, 1926–1969,* edited by Lotte Kohler and Hans Saner (New York: Harcourt Brace Jovanovich, 1992), p. 54.

14. Hannah Arendt, *Eichmann in Jerusalem: A Report on the Banality of Evil* (New York: Viking, 1963).

15. Arendt and Jaspers, *Correspondence,* p. 62.

16. Tacitus, *The Histories,* book 1.

17. Martha Gellhorn, *The Face of War* (London: Granta Books, 1993), p. 176.

18. Writing of the indiscriminate bombardments of German cities by the Allies, Hannah Arendt pointed out: "These tactics resulted in a victory for the Nazis, as the allies abandoned the distinction between Germans and

Nazis." In "Organized Guilt and Universal Responsibility," *Jewish Frontier,* 1945, reprinted in Larry May and Stacey Hoffman, *Collective Responsibility: Five Decades of Debate in Theoretical and Applied Ethics* (Savage, Md.: Rowman & Littlefield, 1991), p. 274.

19. See Philip Nobile, *Judgment at the Smithsonian: The Bombing of Hiroshima and Nagasaki* (New York: Marlowe & Company, 1995), for the complete text of the Smithsonian's banned exhibit and a discussion of the controversy about the exhibit.

20. Tacitus, *The Agricola.*

Chapter 14: Putting Criminals in the Dock
1. *In re Yamashita,* 327 U.S. 1.

2. Michael Walzer, *Just and Unjust Wars* (New York: Basic Books, 1977), p. 321.

3. *United States v. von Leeb,* vol. 11, Trials of War Criminals 374. Cited in Telford Taylor, *Nuremberg and Vietnam* (Chicago: Quadrangle Books, 1970), pp. 170–71.

4. See Cedric Thornberry, "Saving the War Crimes Tribunal," *Foreign Policy,* vol. 104, fall 1996. The author was head of civil affairs and deputy head of misson for UNPROFOR from 1992 to 1994.

5. Maria Teresa Dutli and Cristina Pellandini, "The International Committee of the Red Cross and the Implementation of a System to Repress Breaches of International Humanitarian Law," *International Review of the Red Cross,* vol. 300, May–June 1994, p. 246.

6. Ibid., pp. 246–48.

7. Arieh Ben-Tov, *Facing the Holocaust in Budapest: The International Committee of the Red Cross and the Jews in Hungary,* 1943–1945, Henry Dunant Institute, Geneva (Dordrecht, Netherlands: Martinus Nijhoff Publishers, 1984).

8. Final Report of the Commission of Experts Established Pursuant to Security Council Resolution 780 (1992), transmitted on May 24, 1994, by Secretary General Boutros Boutros-Ghali to the UN Security Council, para. 58.

9. 84 Eng. Rep. 1060 (1660).

10. Quoted in Horacio Verbitsky, *The Flight: Confessions of an Argentine Dirty Warrior* (The New Press, 1996), p. 149.

11. Walzer, *Just and Unjust Wars,* p. 309.

12. FM27-10, para. 509.

13. April 10, 1993.

14. Adopted on February 11, 1994, and amended on May 5, 1994.

INDEX